Getting Employed,
Staying Employed

Getting Employed, Staying Employed

Job Development and Training for Persons with Severe Handicaps

edited by

Caven S. Mcloughlin, Ph.D.
College of Education
Kent State University
Kent, Ohio

J. Bradley Garner, M.S. (Ed.)
Medina City Schools
Medina, Ohio

and

Michael J. Callahan, M.Ed.
Marc Gold & Associates
Syracuse, New York

·P·A·U·L·H·
BROOKES
PUBLISHING CO.

Baltimore · London

Paul H. Brookes Publishing Co.
Post Office Box 10624
Baltimore, Maryland 21285-0624

Typeset by Brushwood Graphics Inc., Baltimore, Maryland.
Manufactured in the United States of America by
The Maple Press Company, York, Pennsylvania.

Library of Congress Cataloging-in-Publication Data
Mcloughlin, Caven S.
  Getting employed, staying employed.

  Bibliography: p.
  Includes index.
  1. Vocational rehabilitation.   2. Handicapped—Employment.   3. Handi-
capped—Training of.   4. Handicapped—Vocational guidance.   I.   Garner,
J. Bradley, 1949–   II.   Callahan, Michael J.   III.   Title.
HD7255.M395   1987   650.1'4'0240816   87-13185
ISBN 0-933716-70-2

Contents

Foreword: The Legacy of Marc Gold   *by Robert Perske* vi

Preface xiv

Section I   Structures versus Outcomes

Chapter   1   Sheltered Work Environments: A Dinosaur in
               Our Midst?   3

Chapter   2   Work: A Means or an End?   7

Chapter   3   The Elusive Concept of Employability 17

Chapter   4   Structures versus Outcomes: Service Models for
               Training and Employment 23

Section II   Job Development

Chapter   5   Approaches to Planning 33

Chapter   6   Practical Prospecting 47

Chapter   7   Getting the Appointment 57

Chapter   8   Cutting a Deal: The Initial Meeting 67

Chapter   9   Sealing the Deal with Follow-Up Negotiations 79

Chapter 10   Quality Considerations in Integrated Employment Sites 95

Section III   Employment Training

Chapter 11   Employee Profiles, Matching, and Selection 111

Chapter 12   Job Analysis 123

Chapter 13   Training and Assessment: The Acquisition of Job Skills 137

Chapter 14   Increasing Production Rate 155

Chapter 15   Final Considerations in Developing a Successful Worker 163

References 176

Appendices 181

Index 237

Foreword
The Legacy of Marc Gold

The Ambassador Hotel, Los Angeles, February 24, 1976. People used to talk glowingly about the times they attended jazz happenings here in the grand ballroom of this internationally famous hotel, where they were carried away by some of the world's greatest music. Something about the setting, the acoustics, and the excitement of making history really made jazz take off in this spacious hall. And entering the ballroom, even years later, one can't help listening, wondering if maybe—just maybe—the old lavish walls still do vibrate from the sounds and rhythms of Ella Fitzgerald, Count Basie, Benny Goodman, Duke Ellington, and Louis Armstrong.

This day—February 24th—and the two that followed would also make history, except that the conference leader (significantly, a former jazz musician) was there for another reason beside that of making music. All those who attended still recall this happening and continue to tell others about it. And there's no doubt about it, what happened there eventually led to the writing of this multifaceted, leading-edge book.

On this day, everyone waited anxiously for things to begin like concertgoers had done many times before. This time, however it was 9 A.M. and onto the stage came a small, 37-year-old athletic-looking man with long, coal-black hair tied in a ponytail. He wore blue jeans over slender hips, and an orange, open-collared polo shirt stretched over his weightlifter's chest and biceps. Moving center stage, he positioned himself on a stool and leaned toward his audience exactly as Lenny Bruce used to do. But, unlike Lenny, his forward-positioned face, with the black mustache and eyebrows, the intense dark eyes—and his soft, warm voice—communicated kindness and dignity to every person in the audience. Also unlike Bruce, he refused to use one word of profanity. Periodically he used sexual material as humorous illustrations, but it was always done with such respect that even a grandmother could laugh unabashedly—then suddenly catch a powerful point. But most important, little did the leader or the audience dream that the 1976 Ambassador Hotel sessions, would someday prove to be so significant. Yet, all those who attended still recall this momentous weekend, for it would mark a turning point in the valuing of people with disabilities as workers in regular industries.

The man on the stool was Dr. Marc Gold, the most unlikely doctor I ever saw. It was his task to lead a conference called "Try Another Way" (a conference on training people who are difficult to train), sponsored by the California State Department of Rehabilitation, the California State Department of Health and Community Services, the California Association for the Retarded, and the California Association of Rehabilitation Facilities.

For three full days this man, using his skill as an entertainer and facts from his applied research at the University of Illinois, kept his audience hungry for example after example, of how rehabilitation workers had shamefully underestimated the value, the dignities, and the skills of people with disabilities. He refused to define disabilities in terms of intelligence quotients and adaptive behavior tests. Instead, he defined the degree of disability by the amount of *training power* it took to teach a skill. "The time has come to *train* people," he said, "not constantly test them, then walk away, leaving them with just a bunch of awful numbers."

Gold showed how the more competent a person becomes, the more society will tolerate his or her deviancies, and he drove the idea home with humorous examples ("Take President Nixon. That guy had more competencies and deviancies than all of us in the room. But, too bad. His deviancies finally eased things out of balance . . . Now take our current President [Ford]. That poor guy hovers close to zero on both sides" [laughter]). With anecdote after anecdote, Dr. Gold, in jeans and ponytail, perched on that stool and convincingly and skillfully explained his competency/deviance hypothesis.

But Gold was not just a theorist; he was a practical man, too. In session after session that weekend, he showed his audience how to increase competence in any person, no matter how severe his or her disabilities, by meticulously *analyzing a task*: breaking it down into its smallest steps, then slowly and patiently—and lovingly—teaching it in smaller chunks. In one session, he challenged the audience to list the number of steps it takes to fold an ordinary sheet of paper into quarters. (By folding a paper on my lap and writing up the components, I broke the task down to 17 steps. Some who really got down to detail listed as many as 30!)

Gold's most convincing demonstration came when a young man with obvious severe spasticity and mental retardation (the kind of person professionals usually passed off quickly as "not feasible for employment" was slowly helped to the stage. The young man, whom Gold had just met a few minutes earlier, sat down at a table in front of a 15-compartment tray containing the sorted parts of a Bendix 70 bicycle brake. Gold positioned himself in a chair to the left of the man and slightly behind him. Then with little talking, Marc reached forward, took an axle from the first compartment, and step-by-step added parts from each of the other bins until he held a fully assembled bicycle brake. With a confident "Lookie there" he sent the brake assembly spinning around the axle.

Round two. With Gold's hands over the man's hands, all eyes focusing on the bicycle parts, they assembled a brake together.

Round three. The man was gently encouraged to assemble a brake himself. Then Gold's hands were less involved, and when a part was fitted on the axle wrong, Gold quietly said, "Try another way." The man did so, and the process continued until the assembly was complete.

Round four. The young man successfully put a brake together himself, spun in on the axle, and broke into a broad grin.

Some people reacted as if they had been watching a holy man at work. But when I mentioned this to a close colleague, he answered, "C'mon, Marc's no saint. He can be one cocksure, exasperating pain in the_____. He can make enemies, no doubt about that. It's just that he's a good scholar, has a great heart, and when it comes to people with disabilities, he refuses to accept limits other people set on them. He feels there's always got to be (a pause and a smile) another way."

The turnout exceeded 300. When the presentations ended, he received a standing ovation. This impressive reception, coupled with the fact that Marc had been quartered in the Ambassador's plush Presidential Suite, so overwhelmed him that he invited crowds up to his suite to celebrate with him between workshops. At one gala, he walked out on the balcony overlooking the swimming pool, cupped his hands over his mouth and shouted as loud as he could, "It's a long way from East L.A.!"

Marc saw the Ambassador Hotel experience as a culmination of events, like the ending of a good book with all parts coming together in a climax. He talked about what it was like to be a Jewish kid growing up in the Hispanic barrio of East Los Angeles, and how he dreamed of someday playing his saxophone on the stage of the Ambassador. He spoke of working with his father in the neighborhood's small bicycle and key shop on Whittier Boulevard for as far back as he could remember. He admitted freely that Morey Gold's gentle teaching of his son about assembling bicycle brakes became the core of his highly sophisticated research. He talked about "just fooling around" in high school or going off by himself and playing his beloved saxophone. While at Los Angeles Junior College as a music major, he became an accomplished jazz musician, playing in bands throughout the West Coast. "Then one day," he said, "I was asked to teach music to some 'mongoloid people'—that's what the guy called them—at the old Adams Center. I said I would. And I did. Three weeks later, I dropped out of music and went into special education."

From that day in 1956, Gold's was an unusual professional odyssey with many movements away from standard practice. And yet he always returned with fresh discoveries for his colleagues to ponder.

Marc first worked in the Los Angeles city school system "teaching students labeled retarded." Here he discovered that his students, although having severe disabilities, had more potential than others realized. He felt his students deserved the chance to live their lives like anyone else. And most important, *he felt that each one could learn—he just had to figure out how to teach them* (Callahan, 1986).

As Marc's interests and accomplishments increased, he went on to pursue a doctorate in experimental child psychology and special education at the University of Illinois, then stayed on as a research professor at the university's Institute of Child Behavior and Development. Marc's research focus was applying information from stimulus control research to the vocational training of persons labeled moderately and severely retarded (Gold, 1980).

His research netted him an invitation to present a paper at the prestigious Gatlinburg Conference, in Tennessee, where from 100 to 150 researchers gather each year to listen, argue, and hammer out their positions (Gold, 1980, p. 61). His paper, "Research on the Vocational Habilitation of the Retarded: The Present, the Future," received high enough ratings to be published in the *International Review of Research in Mental Retardation* (1973). The publication of this paper in the *Review* gave him great joy. And yet he confessed that his paper rated only a *B* when he submitted it as a doctoral student (Gold, 1980, p. 62).

By the time many professionals had begun to tout the "interdisciplinary team approach to training" as the greatest therapeutic method on earth, Marc, the good jazzman, moved off alone, looked at this belief from another angle, then came back and attacked it. His argument was that when the various disciplines gather around the same table to discuss a certain person, they are lousy communicators: they talk too many different professional languages (Gold, 1980, p. 15).

Marc challenged the way colleges prepared trainers, arguing for more inservice than preservice training ("They go from high school into college, out of college into teaching positions, never having experienced what it is to work in anything more than a candy shop or their uncle's delicatessen." (Gold, 1980, p. 22).

Additionally, the standard professional practice of giving a person a "mental age" had caused Marc great concern. He came to see the persons with whom he worked as being so much more than that. "When someone is labeled mentally retarded and diagnosed as performing at the mental level of a five-year-old," he said, "the tendency is to expect him to perform like a five-year-old. We must change that expectancy." (Gold, 1980, p. 106).

Since Marc hadn't been raised in a suburb where most people played the tunes of fairly compatible cultures, he became extremely sensitive when a service system pulled what he called *"progressive status quoism"*: helping people forward with one hand and holding them back with the other because of disability or race. "When a Puerto Rican is not able to get into the carpenter's union, we say he needs more education instead of doing something about the carpenter's union that will not admit him. A Puerto Rican can have a Ph.D. in wood and still not be admitted" (Gold, 1980, p. 107).

In the early 1970s, Marc met Irene Frieze, a social psychologist, an attribution theorist, on a plane flying out of Champaign, Illinois. Their conversations led to later discussions and Marc's subsequent discovery of E.P. Hollander's theory of idiosyncrasy-credits, that is, showing how one's acceptance in society depends on three factors: competence, comformity, and deviance (1958, 1960). To Marc's happy surprise, Hollander's theory supported his own belief beautifully. Hollander's point of view was that deviance refers to an individual's eccentricities, which are negatively evaluated because they fail to reward the surrounding society. Conversely, perceived competencies and conformity provide rewards that make the person attractive to society. One's acceptance is based on the credit balance between rewards and non-rewards. That hypothesis was all Marc needed. He sharpened the theory until it became a key to his own training program: "The more competence an individual has, the more deviance will be tolerated in that person by others" (Gold, 1975).

In 1974, he made a frontal attack on the generally accepted professional definition of mental retardation. He argued that the standard definition generalized too much, and that it was derived from test numbers that froze a person into a terrible, permanent classification. The definition ignored a person's areas of normal capability, failed to measure a person's real potential, and denied the fact that development in a person is a lifelong process. Gold also pointed out that the standard definition tended to be psychological and medical in nature, while his own definition tended to be sociological. Then Gold offered his own definition: "Mental retardation refers to a level of functioning which requires from society significantly above average training procedures and superior assets in adaptive behavior on the part of society, manifested throughout the life of both society and the individual" (Gold, 1980, p. 148). One would think this definition would be enough. Not for this man. He even tried to get it across with—believe it or not—a poem:

An End to the Concept of Mental Retardation:
Oh, What a Beautiful Mourning

If you could only know me for who I am
    Instead of for who I am not,
There would be so much more to see
    'cause there's so much more that I've got.

So long as you see me as mentally retarded,
    Which supposedly means something, I guess,
There is nothing that you or I could ever do
    To make me a human success.

Someday you'll know that tests aren't built
    To let me stand next to you.
By the way you test me, all they can do
    Is make me look bad through and through.

And someday soon I'll get my chance,
    When some of you finally adapt.
You'll be delighted to know that though I'm MR,
    I'm not at all handicapped (Gold, 1980, p. 144).

A member of the committee responsible for revising the *Manual on Terminology and Classification in Mental Retardation* discussed the definition with Marc and a copy was submitted. Later the man wrote to Marc: "Thanks for sending the definition, which was considered by the Terminology and Classification Committee and was most helpful. Look forward to talking to you in the near future about this (Gold, 1980, p. 146)." Marc hoped that his sociological definition might indeed be used as an adjunct to the psychologically and medically oriented standard definition. The committee member never wrote again. The 1977 edition of the manual came out without one word in the definition being changed from the 1973 edition (Gold, 1980, p. 146).

Judging from the way Marc brought fresh ideas to the field, one could expect clashes with the "old guard," and early in his career such clashes occurred. The entertainer-educator was to develop a healthier approach after a particular confrontation that took place in Wisconsin: "During the conference I was asked in front of the audience to critique some of the things about the conference. My reaction was so negative and insensitive that [two colleagues], who were and still are my friends, took me aside and basically said that I was a total jerk and that I had blown it completely. After reflecting on their comments and the way I had handled myself, I made appropriate apologies and privately resolved not to act that way again. To the best of my knowledge, I have kept that commitment to myself and have tried to retain the ability to be critical in a way that preserves people's dignity, including my own" (Gold, 1980, p. 21).

A few years before the Ambassador experience, this man who moved around like a bombastic butterfly trying to change everything that irritated him, slowly began to take all of his experiences and data, and moved back to step-by-step work in his own cocoon. As he did, he worked less and less in institutions and more in the community (Gold, 1980, p. 103); he gave up "fooling around with variables [in research]" (Gold, 1980, p. 123) in order to come up with the most practical, "hands-on" program of task analysis he could develop. And "Try Another Way" was born, a system containing three basic components for guiding trainer interactions: a *framework* for organizing the information to be trained, *strategies* for informing and motivating the trainer, and a *value base* (Callahan, 1986). To Marc, values served as the most important driving force; he found the following six values to be crucial:

1. People should be trained to do marketable tasks ("not dumb stuff nobody'll ever use," he used to say in training sessions).
2. People learn best when the trainer values their human worth and capabilities.
3. All people can demonstrate competence if the training meets their needs.
4. If a person is not learning, the trainer has failed to teach appropriately.
5. Testing in its present state will only limit people.
6. Labeling is unfair and counterproductive (Gold, 1980, p. 3).

And so, Marc began traveling throughout the United States and Canada delivering his 3-day workshops with the bicycle brake demonstration as the centerpiece. At the same time, he invested long periods as a trainer and consultant in sheltered workshops where, eventually, some of the most unlikely people learned to operate complex machinery (e.g., power saws, grinding jigs, metal stamping presses, massive paper cutters, hot plastic molders, and high-speed sewing machines), to assemble electronic circuit boards, and to perform countless other manufacturing and testing functions. Then came an invitation from officials in California, his native state, to lead a super Try Another Way workshop at the Ambassador. "This invitation," he said, "really has me running scared. After all, what if I flop with my own people, or what if nobody comes?" But even then Marc contemplated an alternative: "If we don't have a good turnout, there's going to be a lot of poor kids from East L.A. staying at the Ambassador for at least one night in their life."

One attendee of the Ambassador workshop, Dr. William Bronston, the California Medical Director of Developmental Disability Services, was so impressed that he returned to his home in Sacramento and talked about Gold to California State Director of Rehabilitation Ed Roberts (an interesting man in his own right who had once been diagnosed as "not feasible for employment" by the agency he later directed). Roberts suggested hiring Marc to conduct Try Another Way training workshops throughout California (Callahan, 1986). Seeing the task as more than a one-man job, Marc organized a company, Marc Gold & Associates to help conduct the workshops. Charles Galloway, a colleague from before the Gatlinburg Conference, was brought in as director of the California Project.

In the next 2 years, Galloway and seven handpicked MG&A employees—all under the close supervision of Marc—presented the Try Another Way program to 4,300 agency people. They trained 109 agency workers to develop 856 task analyses: every step was written for publication. These 109 agency personnel worked with 1,888 different persons having disabilities. Better than 2,700 new skills were learned, stretching from complex work to daily living tasks. Work tasks included: assembling skateboards, sailboat winches, electronic solenoids or computer terminal strips, to operating complex audiovisual equipment or stringing racquetball rackets. Daily living activities included: operating a washing machine and dryer, using a combination lock, making a peanut butter sandwich, frying an egg, and using proper eating etiquette (Galloway & LeCours, 1978).

Officials in Georgia, after learning about the California workshops, negotiated a statewide project; Mark Stricklett, an MG&A Company-trained man in the California Project, took the helm. Mark and a new crew built on the California experience and were equally successful in Georgia.

Next came the Ohio Project with Denis Stoddard as director. At this point, Marc was negotiating contracts in 19 states. So, for the next 3 years, he hired good project directors for assistance. When time allowed, he traveled across the continent and in many foreign countries, doing his renowned solos with the bicycle brake demonstration before large audiences.

Then Marc got cancer. Sometime in 1980, while in Georgia, Marc didn't feel well and went to a doctor and received the tough news. But unlike many who receive dire pronouncements and launch a series of practice funerals, Marc did his time in hospitals, took his radiation treatments, allowed for time to overcome the subsequent nausea, and then returned to conducting business as usual. His fight with cancer is mentioned here because he spoke candidly about it, and he approached his illness as he did his work: "Hang in there. There's got to be another way."

In the summer of 1982, more cancer appeared. It was worse than before. In September, Marc convened a meeting at his home in Urbana, Illinois, attended by 20 key employee representatives. Together, they scrupulously reevaluated everything they had been doing "in the light of new information learned while training in integrated workplaces [real industry, not sheltered workshops]" (Callahan, 1986).

Like their jazzman leader used to challenge old standard themes, they now challenged him, and he loved it. The group modified some of his most cherished principles. With Marc's blessing, they resolved to do the following:

See integration as being more important than acquisition of skills. They saw that training should be seen as a means for a job in industry, not an occasion for glorifying a training system.

Not train a "composite" employee. One can't train a person in one setting and then turn over the individual to a different setting in industry. This gave the employer the impression that only trained human service workers and not fellow workers could train people with severe disabilities.

De-mystify the writing of sequential steps in a task. Instead of writing countless steps, intended for general use, it was better to break the task down to the number of steps actually needed by a specific individual. The task could be broken down further as needed.

De-formalize the writing of task analyses. Filling out forms that covered every aspect of a job often amounted to needless paperwork. Each trainer should develop his or her own task analysis system and get moving quicker.

Stop selling standardized task analyses. The company possessed a "bank" of written steps for hundreds of tasks they had taught. The trainers came to the conclusion that many different task analyses could be written for the same job.

Training for adults should only take place in settings where it would be used. Another powerful movement in vocational training, headed by Lou Brown, had developed the "criterion of ultimate functioning" for persons having severe disabilities (Brown et al., 1976). The trainers eventually turned thumbs down to the procedure of using sheltered settings or even training rooms. The training needed to be done in what Brown called, "the real world—the real working place."

Train natural trainers as well as employees. The outside "artificial" trainer cannot be in the industry all of the time. Therefore, the most effective strategy would be to train "assisting persons:" other employees at the job-site who can coach or support the worker with a disability.

Use the natural assists and cues of an industry. Sometimes the cues brought by trainers from the outside tended to be outlandish, bringing too much negative attention to the trainee from other workers on the work floor. Many industries have their own natural training cues and assists that should never be ignored.

Take only as much data as necessary for the job. The overuse of forms, clipboards, and pencils by trainers tended to draw unnecessary attention to a learner from other employees.

Be aware that a systematic training procedure isn't the only way to work a person into an industry. Although the trainers' procedures often bordered on the brilliant, they learned that many industries have training procedures and resources of their own that should be considered as well.

According to later accounts by those who were present, they worked so enthusiastically that they failed to notice at first Marc's minor participation. He served only as an absorbed listener and good host. Although many of Marc's pet components were discussed and modified, he only registered amazement at how much he could learn from just one meeting. "This time," he said, "I didn't teach you anything. You taught me." He echoed that feeling many times with other colleagues and friends during the next 3 months before he died.

Although Marc had won his previous bouts of cancer, he faced another one on Friday, December 17, 1982. Doctors advised him on Monday to decide whether he wanted to resume the agonizing radiation treatments or to "choose an alternative." Rather than choosing the alternative of pain-killing drugs, everyone expected him to go for the radiation once more. He never made it. On Tuesday he died, not directly from the cancer, but from heart failure.

After losing their leader, many of the employees and colleagues met in small groups or talked to each other via long distance to discuss the future of MG&A. Was there a reason to continue the company? Did MG&A employees have the skills to pull off what Marc had done so well? Would the company be accepted by the field without Marc?

Finally, in October 1983, eight former employees took over the company; Michael Callahan was elected President and Katie Banzhaf was designated Chairperson of the Board. The Board Members were: Joy Upchurch, William Montooth, Stephen Zider, Lyndia Lewis, Nansi Rhoads, and Rita Brantner.

Today, according to the owners, MG&A has more business than it can handle, and their lively process of changing according to the times continues as well. There have been some recent modifications:

- The Company now calls their training approach *Systematic Instruction,* instead of the *Try Another Way* system. TAW, however, is mentioned constantly in MG&A's training programs because of its historic foundation and its openness to constant, leading-edge modifications.
- The company no longer conducts the 3-day, large-audience training programs. Instead, trainers insist on 5-day sessions with a maximum of 15 participants.
- The company focuses solely on *facilitating full integration* of the employee into "real work" in the "real world." MG&A sees training in sheltered workshops as a terrible dead end, even though most of the trainers began their work in such places. "Before my connections with Marc," Katie Banzhaf said, "I worked in a sheltered workshop in Ohio, and we never had a discharge to outside employment. Thanks to Marc and my colleagues, those days have ended for me."

*   *   *   *   *

Now come a host of people who have been trained or employed by MG&A. They stand on the current leading edge, casting fresh light on an unbelievably rich seascape of technology and just-plain-common-sense to help people get employed and to stay employed.

Even though "Try Another Way" has been retired as a formal term, Marc's undying optimism and his always-be-ready-to-try-another-way approach can be found in this book. The later modifying spirit of Marc's followers enriches this book as well.

This is a new book for a vast new era that has suddenly begun to unfold before us. "If Marc had lived, he would have loved what is happening to people with disabilities in industry," said Charlie Galloway as he reflected on this manuscript. I agree. For example, I doubt if Marc ever used terms like *supported employment* or *job coaching* as we understand them today. The rich array of skills now used for developing jobs in real industry, the way job developers now converse with managers of industry, the way employers now can recognize employees with disabilities as valued members in their production forces: all this would have amazed Marc. Marc would have taken the job tasks outlined in this book and developed them into the most elaborate, minutely detailed task analyses he had ever done. His colleagues would have modified and simplified these tasks analyses until only the necessary steps needed to accomplish each task remained. But Marc—never feeling the need to circle his wagons, make rigid dogma out of his own accomplishments, defending them to the death—would have let these later modifications happen. I think he would have gloried in the advances this book describes.

Robert Perske
Author of *New Life in the Neighborhood,*
Hope for the Families, Show Me No Mercy,
and *Don't Stop the Music*

REFERENCES

Brown, L., Nietupski, J., & Hamre-Nietupski, S. (1976). The criterion of ultimate functioning. In M.A. Thomas (Ed.), *Hey, don't forget about me!* (pp. 2–15). Reston, VA: Council for Exceptional Children.

Callahan, M. (1986). *A technology evolves: What happened when "Try Another Way" met the real world.* Syracuse: Marc Gold & Associates, P.O. Box 6135, Syracuse, NY 13217.

Galloway, C. & LeCours, R. (1978). *Try another way in California.* Syracuse: Marc Gold & Associates, P.O. Box 6135, Syracuse, NY 13217.

Gold, M. (1973). Research on the vocational habilitation of the retarded: The present, the future. In N.R. Ellis (Ed.), *International review of research in mental retardation* (Vol. 6). New York: Academic Press.

Gold, M. (1975). Vocational training. In J. Wortis (Ed.), *Mental retardation and developmental disabilities: An annual review* (Vol. 7). New York: Brunner/Mazel.

Gold, M. (1980). *Did I say that?* Champaign, IL: Research Press.

Hollander, E. P. (1958). Conformity, status, and idiosyncracy credit. *Psychological Review, 65,* 117–127.

Hollander, E. P. (1960). Competence and conformity in the acceptance of influence. *Journal of Abnormal and Social Psychology, 61,* 365–369.

Preface

This book was a joint effort, and thus it reflects many philosophies, emphases, biases, and prejudices. Yet, no one person was a greater influence upon concepts that underlie this book than Marc Gold. His work was seminal and one day may be viewed as classic.

However, we do not presume to have authored "the book that Marc Gold would have written." We have shaped the mission of this text to reflect our own perspectives on persons with severe handicaps entering work. We have very fixed ideas about their position in the work world, *as it should be*. Persons with severe handicaps have an equal right to share both the privileges and the pains of the growth that come from living and working in an integrated community. This uncompromising belief is based on the assumption that they have a capacity to cope with the strains and difficulties of life in our highly industrialized world of the 1980s. We are convinced that with appropriate preparation—which necessarily must begin in early childhood—people with severe handicaps can meet the demands of our society.

Mainstream living brings stress and difficulties even for the most able, and these hardships are most strongly felt by vulnerable members of the society. Persons labeled "severely handicapped" undeniably are one of the most vulnerable segments of our society. Additionally, there can be little disagreement that employment offers a major and positive life change for individuals who otherwise would be served by agencies throughout their lives. Their reserves are left untapped whenever their needs are catered to by totally sheltered environments. Only a minority of these persons are currently afforded integrated employment experiences. We believe that the *vast majority* of severely handicapped persons would benefit from employment in integrated settings.

In this 15-chapter book we investigate the processes involved in employing systems by which employment personnel can develop jobs in integrated settings, and methods for facilitating these opportunities for persons labeled "severely handicapped." In the first section we explore the style of "training" common to sheltered workshops. We demonstrate these workshops' inherent inadequacies based on an analysis of cost effectiveness and of programmatic philosophies. Our thesis is that sheltered work environments should systematically be depopulated in favor of employment opportunities in integrated settings. We analyze the criteria for describing "quality employment" and conclude that a fundamental goal of the process of employing is to obtain work as a contributing factor to enhancing the quality of life.

In the second section, which deals with job development, we describe practical job development activities, with a constant reminder that predating the **action** component of developing job openings must come some serious **thinking** about the agency's competencies, commitment, and overall philosophy. We provide the job developer with information about prospecting for leads in the regular job market. We cover job targeting, compiling and organizing information, obtaining referrals, researching prospects, developing a business attitude and vocabulary, and portraying a positive image to potential partners in the business world.

After prospecting for leads, the effective job developer must venture into the business world, where favorable initial and continuing impressions are extremely important. Job developers are provided with information about telephone contacts and introductory letters, "sales" presentations, and model responses to objections. Because job developers must also be effective negotiators, we illustrate multiple strategies for effectively negotiating integrated employment opportunities for persons labeled "severely handicapped." Additionally, because business-like follow-up cements arrangements and relationships, we describe systems for gathering and recording data, responding to objections and "stalls" that you are likely to encounter, planning plant tours, arranging job analyses and hiring, creative approaches to follow-up negotiations, and sealing-the-deal with formal agreements.

In the chapters addressing training-for-employment, we emphasize the processes of job analysis, skill acquisition, improving production rate, and methods for developing an independent worker. Practical approaches to analyzing potential job stations, tasks, and duties are considered. We also address ways of evaluating the company's own orientation and training program, "working the job," writing formal job analyses, and facilitating the worker's skill acquisition. One of the most challenging decisions for placement programs—the task of matching the potential employee to the job—is then discussed. We emphasize a criterion-referenced approach to evaluation and employee selection. We are convinced that determining *who* will be selected for employment opportunities must be a well-planned venture and be as close to normal business practice as possible.

Because the single most important objective of skill acquisition training is to enable the employee to perform tasks at the quality level required by the company, with minimal assistance from a trainer, we illustrate a variety of specific training strategies for facilitating workplace skill acquisition. A discussion of strategies for improving and maintaining adequate rates of production then follows. Emphasis is placed on methods of collecting and analyzing production data in natural environments. The section also deals with the transition of supervision and training responsibilities from the trainer to the company. Production rate training begins once the employee reaches the stage of skill acquisition; by then the worker is able to perform the job without trainer assistance and is striving to increase production rates to meet company standards. Thus, the last phase in the process of employing is developing a successful worker.

To restate our central thesis, we believe that human service personnel have an obligation through effective instructional strategies to prevent a new generation of sheltered workers. The undeniable conclusion is that there is no substitute for quality preparation when facilitating integrated employment opportunities for persons with severe handicaps.

Good intentions, sound philosophical orientations, and well-meaning efforts by themselves are insufficient preparation for employment. Quality training, as demonstrated by the learner's increased skills and competencies, is the necessary ingredient for integrated employment. Employment preparation involves sound analyses of the match between worker and job, an understanding and acceptance of the learner's abilities, and an unhesitating commitment to refine training strategies to ensure efficient learning.

The job developer who secures a job opportunity but who cannot deliver training services as needed is "all dressed up with no place to go." Equally, a skilled trainer who is unable to secure job stations can only practice those training skills within the sterile vacuum of a sheltered work environment. If nothing else, the reader of this book will recognize the possibilities that *currently* exist for encouraging increased employment opportunities for *all* persons with severe handicaps. We invite you to take your enthusiasm, your understanding of the job development process, and your skills in facilitating learning, and make a difference in the life of at least one person with severe handicaps—offer someone the chance to work, and the opportunity to experience the dignity that can come from working.

Acknowledgments

This book was made possible by cooperation with Marc Gold & Associates (MG&A), a staff training company in the human service field. Because it is relatively unusual to have an edited book without authored chapters, this book's format deserves a brief explanation. The concept for the book developed from worksheets, brief position papers, and procedural guidelines created to support the employment efforts of MG&A. As editors we refined the original materials by updating procedures, adding a wealth of new information, broadening the applications, and formulating a cohesive focus around employment in integrated settings.

Special acknowledgment must go to Katie Banzhaf for her assistance in reviewing the material. Additionally, we thank Joy Eason-Upchurch, Bill Montooth, Lyndia Lewis, Nansi Rhoads, and Ron Lecours for their tireless support and encouragement, observations, and generous insights that led to the completion of this project. We also wish to acknowledge our debt to many individuals—and also to apologize if their contributions are given insufficient credit. These colleagues include Penny Balicki-Johnson, Pam Bossert, Rita Brantner, Ann Buchholtz, Jude Fransen, Charlie Galloway, Debbie Gibson, Ed Guardnapo, Marion Jay, Phillip Jay, Rona Leitner, Harry McBride, Tom Moran, Connie Pelmonter, Marianne Roche, Kathleen Rutherford, Denis W. Stoddard, Darryl R. Townsend, and Steve Zider. We are pleased to thank these MG&A people for sharing their knowledge with us.

On a personal note, thanks go to Sydney, Jennifer, and to Colin for understanding and caring. And, of course, to Marc Gold.

We claim and fully accept complete responsibility for this book. All errors of interpretation are, of course, ours alone.

---

*This book is dedicated
to the memory of
Marc Gold*

I
STRUCTURES
VERSUS OUTCOMES

1

Sheltered Work Environments

A Dinosaur in Our Midst?

Thousands of adults labeled "severely handicapped" are currently enrolled in sheltered workshops, work activity centers, and adult day care programs. Their placement is not a function of their inability to learn the skills necessary to obtain and maintain employment in integrated environments. Rather, it is a function of *our* inability to design service systems that are responsive to their learning needs. In this chapter the inherent inadequacies of sheltered work environments are examined from the perspectives of cost effectiveness and programmatic philosophy. Our central thesis is that sheltered work environments should systematically be phased out in favor of employment opportunities in integrated settings.

RATIONALE FOR CHANGE

Historically, persons with severe handicaps have received vocational services in sheltered work environments. These programs, typically based within human service agencies, are known by a variety of titles, including sheltered workshops, work activity centers, and adult day care centers. Several authors have analyzed the implications of working in these sheltered environments and have compiled some fascinating statistics. For example, we know that across the United States there are at least 2,000 sheltered employment sites (Bellamy, Sheehan, Horner, & Boles, 1980), with approximately 100,000 persons labeled "handicapped" enrolled in their programs (Bellamy, Rhodes, Bourbeau, & Mank, 1986). Workshop enrollees labeled "severely retarded" comprise only 50% to 60% of the total sheltered work setting population (Bellamy, Rhodes, Bourbeau, & Mank, 1986).

These programs are costly ventures. We know that approximately $330 million was spent in 1980 to support the operation of sheltered employment sites (Bellamy, Sheehan et al., 1980); it is not unreasonable to suppose that since then this figure has risen dramatically. We also know that these efforts are not particularly fruitful in terms of money earned by their participants or placement rates. The average hourly wage of sheltered employees ranges from $0.34 to $1.56 per hour (Wehman, 1981; Whitehead, 1979), and their average yearly earnings approximate $666 (Bellamy, Bourbeau, & Sowers, 1983; U.S. Department of Labor, 1979). The placement rate for individuals transferred from sheltered work environments into integrated employment is about one in eight (Bellamy, Rhodes, Bourbeau, & Mank, 1986; Rusch & Mithaug, 1980; U.S. Department of Labor, 1979), with nearly three-fourths of these individuals moving in their initial year of enrollment (Bellamy,

Rhodes, Bourbeau, & Mank, 1986). The likelihood of their maintaining integrated employment for more than 2 years is less than 3% (Bellamy, Rhodes, Bourbeau, & Mank, 1986).

These statistics depict a rather inefficient system for providing training and employment to persons labeled "severely handicapped." DeFazio and Flexer (1983) further illustrate this inefficiency by describing the nature of "employment" in sheltered settings:

> The typical mentally retarded adult has significant habilitative needs, but he or she has few if any options as to where work is performed or services are received. Usually, he or she is assigned to work in degrading, segregated, and inefficiently organized work settings that are isolated physically, philosophically, and technologically from the normal work world of nonhandicapped persons. The employees of these facilities characteristically perform borrowed, unchallenging, frivolous work of marginal habilitative or social value and transferability for use in industry or for other valued community work settings. Typically, work is performed with cast-off and often inappropriate equipment and supplies, at an artificially imposed, substandard rate and under conditions that most nonhandicapped workers would reject as being dehumanizing. (p. 157)

CONTEMPORARY MYTHS

Farber (1968) observed that human service agencies continually perpetuate the misperception that persons with severe handicaps constitute a *surplus labor force*. This analysis translates the practices of vocational training from the realm of an individualized service into a larger, societally based context. The practices of human service agencies, for better or worse, tend to reflect the overriding beliefs of society (Garner, 1985). Stated another way, past and present practices in the facilitation of integrated employment opportunities reflect a societal expectation that persons labeled "severely handicapped" cannot be considered as productive, contributing members of society. Yet, there seems to be no logical and systematically determined plan to change these misperceptions.

The mission of human services personnel involved in employment preparation should be very clear:

> *To demonstrate that persons labeled "severely handicapped" can be productive in the integrated, profit-oriented environments of business and industry and therefore should not be restricted to noncompetitive, maintenance-oriented, segregated environments.*

Acceptance of this mission has several implications for the future of sheltered work environments and employment training efforts. First, a negative *image* of these workers is prevalent in most sheltered settings. The debilitating nature of this image has been embodied in the principle of normalization. Wolfensberger (1972) discussed in great detail the counterproductive nature of *negative image juxtapositions*, i.e., surrounding devalued persons with objects and images that denote triviality, want, separateness, and hopelessness. If DeFazio and Flexer's (1983) previously cited observations about activities performed in sheltered work environments are correct, then the continued existence of these programs serves only to perpetuate negative societal perceptions of persons with severe handicaps.

A second concern centers on the *safety net syndrome* that surrounds sheltered work environments. This phenomenon is evident in such statements as "Well, if they don't acquire the skills necessary for employment, they can always go to the sheltered workshop." By continuing to accept and support a perception of need for a system of sheltered work environments, human service practitioners have little real motivation to create a cadre of workers for entry into integrated employment. The typical justification for sheltered work settings is a classic example of circular thinking. The continued existence of sheltered work environments creates a situation in which there is no urgency to teach persons with severe disabilities to perform functional, productive, and marketable skills. The safety net is always there for *our* training failures.

A third and related implication focuses upon professionals' expectations. In this regard, take a few moments to ponder your own reaction to the following question:

> *Given appropriately designed training and support, can all persons labeled "severely handicapped" acquire the skills necessary to perform meaningful work in integrated employment settings successfully?*

When reacting to this statement many of you might focus upon the word *all* and think of the heterogenous group of people who have traditionally been labeled "severely handicapped." This concern about the word *all* typically is followed by a response that contains elaborate qualifiers, such as "except for . . . ," "all but . . . . ," "with the possible exception of . . . ." Your own answer to this question is a clear guide to your philosophy and actions.

Consider the consequences of stating that some persons with severe handicaps *cannot* be prepared to perform meaningful work in integrated settings. This position automatically eliminates from employment some individuals and, thus, discriminates against and devalues them. Persons thus categorized typically carry *labels*, such as severely or profoundly mentally retarded, autistic or deaf-blind. If specific individuals are excluded from the group that is considered to be employable, it is very unlikely that agencies will strive to prove their expectations wrong by working to place the "unplaceable" person.

In contrast, if the position is taken that *all* persons labeled "severely handicapped" *can* be provided with the skills necessary to engage in meaningful employment, then agencies have a responsibility to generate effective job development strategies; design and implement data-based training and support systems; and manage, coordinate, and apply available resources effectively. So, when pondering this important question, consider the consequences of being *wrong*, rather than of being *right*. To answer "Yes" and be wrong is far less harmful than to say "No" and be wrong. To say "Yes" requires a serious commitment; to say "No" requires only complacency and acceptance of the *status quo*.

The fourth implication relates to a perceived role conflict that undergirds the entire system: integrated employment *versus* contract procurement/production. In many sheltered work environments there is a strong emphasis on "attitude development," with little emphasis on job development or employment training. Others emphasize the procurement of subcontract work, meeting customer deadlines, and approximating an industrial work setting. In still others, there is a *bona fide* internal conflict between these two roles.

Ownership of the "Handicap"

Recently, when consulting in a sheltered work environment, we noticed that many of the workers were performing a rather routine assembly task placing pads into styrofoam trays that later would be used to package poultry. One particular worker was performing at a remarkably fast rate that was much quicker than his peers and possibly competitive with industrial work rates. When he was asked why he preferred this assembly task to entering integrated employment, the young man gave a rather alarming answer, "Because there is *big* money in chicken trays!" Big money turned out to be 33¢ per hour! It was quite clear that his fast work rate was absolutely critical to meeting the contractor's deadlines for the workshop, and therefore, he was not targeted for placement into an integrated employment setting. It is also likely that he is still earning "big money" assembling chicken trays in that sheltered work environment. Was *he* too disabled to leave the sheltered work setting, or would *it* be handicapped by his loss?

Production versus Placement

Pomerantz and Marholin (1977) provided an excellent review of the production *versus* placement conflict that plagues sheltered work environments. Their data, along with information provided by other researchers, indicate that most sheltered work environments fail miserably when measured by the traditional yardsticks of the business world (Greenleigh Associates, 1975; Whitehead, 1979). Often, they fail because they stay within the budgetary allowance of a public agency, as opposed to reflecting the demands of operating from a profit motive. Unfortunately, the job placement records of sheltered work environments are equally unimpressive (Bellamy, Bourbeau, & Sowers, 1983; Bellamy, Rhodes, Bourbeau, & Mank, 1986; Rusch, 1983). It would seem, therefore, that sheltered work environments lack both a specific mission and direction. We believe that the time has come to re-evaluate our reliance on a system that fosters dependence, maintenance, and passivity.

Many professionals feel seriously threatened by the suggestion that sheltered work environments should be depopulated in favor of a concentrated movement into integrated employment. Responses to this position range from comments asserting impractical idealism and ivory-tower thinking to disparaging remarks about the mental health of the proponent! Yet, for the reasons already outlined, this transition is both warranted and necessary if persons labeled "severely handicapped" are to receive opportunities for fullest integration into their communities: opportunities to engage in normalized work environments, opportunities to interact with a variety of fellow community members, and opportunities to exercise control over important decisions made about one's life.

Sheltered work environments once may have served a valuable purpose. However, the time has come to step forward and take very seriously our obligation to enhance the limited range of expectations held by many professionals. Through a commitment to the provision of integrated services, as opposed to bricks and mortar, *presently available* budgetary allotments can be realigned to bring about significant vocational opportunities for persons with severe handicaps. Certainly, such a realignment will take time. But the time to start is now!

2

Work
A Means or an End?

This chapter analyzes the varying perspectives that may be used to describe integrated employment for a person labeled "severely handicapped." Traditional concerns have tended only to focus on the features of wages, working conditions, and work tasks. As human service personnel strive to facilitate employment and training opportunities, further efforts are needed to define the parameters of integrated employment, opportunities to engage in longitudinal interactions with nonhandicapped co-workers, opportunities for choice and decision making, work activities that are culturally valued and status enhancing, the payment of a reasonable wage, and ultimately, definition of work as a contributing factor to enhancing the quality of life. This chapter proposes that the value of work goes well beyond any arbitrary listing of criteria; ultimately, the value of work is measured in the quality of life experienced by the worker.

CONTEMPORARY PERSPECTIVE

In recent years *integrated, competitive,* and *supported employment* have become the buzzwords of employment service personnel. Despite the widespread acceptance of integrated employment as a valued goal for persons labeled "severely handicapped," its operational parameters still remain somewhat hazy. For this reason it is often difficult to delineate the specifically desired outcomes expected from vocational training and job placement. Certainly, full employment has traditionally been the ultimate goal, and an emerging perspective views employment as the basic goal of "vocational" preparation services. What continues to be at issue, however, are the conditions under which employment takes place.

Most frequently, desired outcomes are defined according to a monetary perspective through analyses of the number of hours worked, hourly earnings, and taxpayer cost savings (Bellamy et al., 1984; Brown, Shiraga, York, et al., 1984; Garner, Zider, & Rhoads, 1985; Martin, Schneider, Rusch, & Geske, 1982; Schneider, Martin & Rusch, 1981; Wehman & Hill, 1983). Although the financial benefits of earning a living cannot be minimized, we propose that employment training personnel must look beyond the criterion. Financial criteria cannot be the sole measure of the value of employment because most workers derive benefits from working other than the earnings reported on a wages and tax statement. These benefits and the motivation to work can be realized in a remarkable variety of ways.

A *quality job* is one that meets the personalized needs of the worker. In this chapter, we analyze the varied considerations that affect the definition of a quality job—considerations that apply to *all* workers, those considered normal, as well as those labeled "severely handicapped." These guidelines can be used when employment training personnel are faced with the decision of whether to pursue a particular worksite.

HISTORICAL PERSPECTIVES:
EVOLVING PERCEPTIONS OF THE WORKER

When the North American economy was still primarily agricultural, high value was placed upon the skills and productivity of the individual worker. For this reason, there was a direct relationship between the amount of work performed *by the individual* and the availability of food, shelter, and other necessities. The worker's profit margin was directly attributable to the amount of work performed. The consequences and rewards of working, and the implications of not working, were an integral part of daily life, as work was a means of survival. It is certainly relevant to compare that situation with many of today's workers who, as employees of megacorporations, see little relationship between their level of productivity and the profit margin shown by their employer.

With the advent of industrialization, workers' roles changed significantly. They became extensions of the machines that they were hired to operate. This perception is well illustrated by the early time-and-motion studies (Gilbreth & Gilbreth, 1924; Taylor, 1895, 1903), which reduced the worker's role to one of merely facilitating efficient machine operations. Man and machine were seen as one—inextricably linked. Such factors as worker satisfaction, worker attitudes toward the job, and the effects of work on the overall quality of a worker's life were given minimal consideration. Industrialization, despite its benefits, inevitably leads to a devaluation of the worker-as-a-person.

The roles and perceptions of the worker underwent another significant change around the year 1930. This change was related primarily to three factors: (1) Social critics were calling attention to the perception that workers were, indeed, expendable as though they were "machine components"; (2) there was an increasing awareness that job designs were changing and that there was a need for greater numbers of skilled and motivated workers who could perform a variety of complex tasks at their own pace; and (3) labor unions assumed the role of articulating the workers' needs (Bass & Barrett, 1981). These events, in combination with an evolving body of research on the effects of work conditions on productivity, provided workers with a new and improved status. Recognizing that the psychologically satisfied worker is a productive worker, industrial management began to reconceptualize and place greater value on the psychological aspects of worker performance.

In recent years the role of the worker and the worker's satisfactions with the varied aspects of job performance have become important concerns for the decision makers of business, industry, and commerce. Most large companies now provide a variety of support services for their employees as a means of promoting their physical and mental health. These include health insurance plans, physical fitness programs, and extracurricular clubs and social organizations subsidized by the company. In addition, exemplary organizations in business and industry have made serious commitments to redesign and continually upgrade employees' roles in the performance of specified job tasks. Peters and Waterman (1982) describe this philosophy as follows:

There was hardly a more pervasive theme in the excellent companies than *respect for the individual.* That basic belief and assumption were omnipresent. But like so much else . . . it's not any one thing . . . one assumption, belief, statement, goal, value, system, or program . . . that makes the theme come to life. What makes it live at these companies is a plethora of structural devices, systems, styles, and values, all reinforcing one another so that the companies are truly unusual in their ability to achieve extraordinary results through ordinary people. . . . These companies give people control over their destinies; they make meaning for people. They turn the average Joe and the average Jane into winners. They let, even insist that, people stick out. They accentuate the positive. (pp. 238–239)

The worker and the worker's satisfaction with the job have become important factors in realizing a successful business venture. The fact that satisfaction with work goes beyond the paycheck has taken on a new and added significance.

EMPLOYMENT FOR PERSONS LABELED "SEVERELY HANDICAPPED": EXPECTATIONS, TECHNOLOGY, AND SERVICE MODELS

The design of vocational training and employment services for persons labeled "severely handicapped" has changed dramatically over the past two decades. Before 1965, persons with severe handicaps were summarily considered to be unemployable. That is, placement in a sheltered workshop or any other institutional setting was considered both appropriate and necessary. Research or demonstration activities that dealt with vocational training were conducted solely within sheltered workshops, work activity centers, or institutions (Albin, Stark, & Keith, 1979; Crosson & Pine, 1979). Although these original research endeavors did *not* clearly demonstrate that persons labeled "severely handicapped" could indeed take their place in the employment market, they did provide a basis for a technology of training.

The emergence of a training technology provided professionals with direction and effective procedures for facilitating employment (Garner et al., 1985). It became possible to demonstrate that persons labeled "severely handicapped" who received systematic training could learn to perform complex, vocationally relevant tasks (Bellamy, Peterson, & Close, 1975; Gold, 1972; Hunter & Bellamy, 1976; Rusch & Mithaug, 1980). Further, researchers and practitioners began to realize that the systematic training of handicapped persons, formerly restricted to sheltered environments, could be equally effective in the integrated workplace (Martin et al., 1982; Wehman & Hill, 1983).

This realization led to a second phase in the evolution of employment training services for persons labeled "severely handicapped": the development of integrated and supported employment options. During this second phase, training and employment services have had four foci: (1) social integration in employment environments; (2) demonstrations that employment training can be a cost-effective alternative to sheltered employment; (3) the development and refinement of job development, placement, training, and support strategies; and (4) the provision of a data-base that substantiates the benefits of integrated employment.

Although employment and training practices have enhanced the employment opportunities potentially available to persons with severe handicaps many unanswered questions remain. The most pressing of these relates to a definition of the operational parameters of employment. On first examination this observation may sound somewhat strange. The prevailing practices of human services agencies, however, reflect wide diversity of opinion on this issue. Many agencies and professionals argue that enrollment in a sheltered or work activity center *does* constitute employment. Others contend that employment can *only* be realized if it satisfies a specifically defined set of criteria, such as wages, integrated work environment, and fringe benefits. It is difficult to mount a movement for system-wide change when professionals in the field are themselves divided over this fundamental issue. If dramatic changes are to occur in the employment service delivery system and if the employment opportunities available to persons with severe handicaps are to increase, consensus must be reached on the definition of employment.

Some of the prevailing definitions of work and employment are presented in Table 2.1. Although these definitions vary slightly, there are several factors considered centrally important by their originators: (1) performance of work activities in settings that provide for ongoing interactions with nonhandicapped workers; (2) payment of wages; (3) opportunities for job satisfaction, advancement, and the ongoing support of nonhandicapped workers; and (4) work activities that are culturally valued and status enhancing. A commitment to the provision of these features should result in improvement in the worker's quality of life. Each of these perceived criteria, even though they are reasonably self-explanatory, requires further definition if they are to be incorporated within a vocational/career decision-making process. In the following pages, we examine each of these criteria and their potential impact and the corresponding employment service delivery system for persons labeled "severely handicapped."

Opportunities to Engage in Ongoing Interactions with Nonhandicapped Co-Workers

For most people, one of the hallmarks of the work experience is the opportunity to establish and maintain interactions with co-workers. Through this process the worker establishes friendships, exchanges information, learns job-related skills, and makes arrangements for social activities outside the workplace. These considerations apply equally whether or not one is disabled.

As we have previously discussed, opportunities for adolescents and adults labeled "severely" handicapped traditionally have been defined as placement in sheltered work environments. By definition, these environments are segregated and only provide services to persons labeled handicapped (Bellamy, Bourbeau, & Sowers, 1983; Bellamy, Rhodes, Bourbeau, & Mank, 1986; Elder, Conley, & Noble, 1986; Flexer, 1983). Consequently, opportunities to engage in interactions with nonhandicapped co-workers are either extremely limited or nonexistent. We propose that this criterion is one of the most critical dimensions for selecting a potential worksite and that it should never be violated or be compromised by employment training personnel. Integration is indeed the cornerstone of the competitive employment movement. This position was described by Lou Brown and his colleagues (1984) in the following terms:

> The position here is that if citizens with severe handicaps are to be absorbed into the fabric of their communities, they must function in ways that maximize rather than minimize acceptance, tolerance, and understanding of their complex needs. To accomplish this they must be given the resources to demonstrate publicly that they can perform in the real world. For too many years it has been hypothesized that extremely few adults with severe handicaps could perform meaningful work, and that even

Table 2.1.   Prevailing definitions of work and employment

Competitive employment is working for at least minimum wage or better, with nonhandicapped co-workers, at a job that provides room for advancement in settings that produce valued goods or services (Rusch, 1983, p. 504).

Meaningful work refers to a series of actions that, if not performed by a severely handicapped person, must be performed by a nonhandicapped person for pay (Brown, Ford, Nisbet, Shiraga, et al., 1983, p. 4).

. . . enable an individual to earn a living wage and other normative reinforcers associated with working (Gold & Pomerantz, 1980, p. 432).

The opportunity to work, the process of working, and the community opportunities created by the resulting income are all critical to integrated adult lives in our society. Adults with severe disabilities should have the same work opportunities as others in a community. Further, the quality of employment . . . should be judged by the same criteria to evaluate the employment of others in our society: income level and the resulting opportunities created by that income; quality of working life, including integration of the workplace, safety, and access to challenging work; and security benefits, including job mobility, advancement opportunities, and protection from lifestyle disruptions to illness and accident (The Association for Persons with Severe Handicaps, 1983, pp. 1–2).

Integrated employment is employment in a regular, non-human-service setting in which a person with disabilities works alongside and interacts with co-workers, supervisors, and if appropriate, customers, who are not disabled, in the performance of tasks typically performed in the workplace. The number of persons with disabilities employed at the site is not so great as to cause all persons to be treated as a group (Callahan, 1986).

Sheltered workshop or *workshop* means a charitable organization or institution conducted not-for-profit, but for the purpose of carrying out a recognized program of rehabilitation for handicapped workers, and/or providing such individuals with remunerative employment or other occupational rehabilitating activity of an educational or therapeutic nature. (*Federal Register,* May 17, 1974, p. 17509).

Work activity center shall mean a workshop, or a physically separated department of a workshop having an identifiable program, separate supervision and records, planned and designed exclusively to provide therapeutic activities for handicapped workers whose physical or mental impairment is so severe as to make their productive capacity inconsequential. Therapeutic activities include custodial activities (such as activities where the focus is on teaching the basic skills of living), and on any purposeful activity so long as work or production is not the main purpose. No individual worker whose productivity substantially exceeds 50% of minimum wage average shall be employed at less than the minimum wage under a work activity center certificate (*Federal Register,* May 17, 1974, p. 17509).

(*Supported employment* is) . . . paid work in a variety of settings, particularly regular work sites, especially designed for handicapped individuals (i) for whom competitive employment at or above the minimum wage is unlikely; and (ii) who, because of their disability, need intensive, on-going support to perform in a work setting (*Federal Register,* September 25, 1984, Section 102, [11], [F]).

those who could would only be able to do so in segregated environments. As a result, they have been devalued, undertaught, their lifespaces have been tragically constricted, and many negative generalizations have become embedded in the minds and hearts of millions of experientially deprived nondisabled persons. The label "severely intellectually handicapped" is not an exemption from the world of real work. On the contrary, those so labeled have the human right to be given every reasonable chance and resource to learn to perform in integrated environments. (p. 266)

A guiding principle in the movement toward integration into the mainstream of society is the concept of *natural proportion* (Brown, Ford, Nisbet, Sweet et al., 1983). This principle dictates that the number of persons labeled "severely handicapped" in any given environment—for example, in an employment setting—should never exceed the corresponding proportion of such persons in the general population. Approximately 1% of the population is severely handicapped. For employment training and placement personnel such a statement has significant implications. Worksites should not be overly populated by workers or groups of workers who are labeled "severely handicapped" for such a practice defeats the intent of integration.

Several writers have identified social skill deficits as the major reason why employees who are severely handicapped are terminated from their jobs (Manchetti, Rusch, & Lamson, 1981; Rusch, 1979, 1983; Rusch, Schutz, & Agran, 1982; Wehman, 1981). Assuming this to be true and accepting the inherent value of employment integration, social skill training must be a primary consideration for training personnel. There are emerging indications *in a variety of work settings* that integration can greatly enhance the social skill repertoire of persons labeled "severely handicapped." Movement from a segregated environment to an alternative integrated worksite inevitably brings changes in performance expectations (Gold, 1980a, 1980b). Certainly, a worksite in business or industry provides the worker with more normalized and valued role expectations and models than sheltered work environments (DeFazio & Flexer, 1983). These expectations can reasonably be translated into improved behavioral competencies through the application of systematic training (Gold, 1980a, 1980b, 1980c).

Our uncompromising position is that sheltered work environments are indefensible on a number of dimensions. Clearly, they do not provide sufficient opportunity for persons with disabilities to engage in interactions with nonhandicapped co-workers. The segregated nature of the sheltered work environment also inhibits the realization of socially valued roles for persons labeled "severely handicapped." For these and other reasons, integration *must* be a primary concern when developing and selecting employment sites. Worksites that segregate, congregate, and isolate persons with handicaps from ongoing interactions and relationships with nonhandicapped co-workers should be excluded from consideration.

Wages

Remuneration has long been the primary justification for sheltered employment as the preferred option for persons labeled "severely handicapped" (Brown et al., 1984). Yet, the opportunity to work in business or industry typically enhances the worker's earning power when compared to the meager remuneration available in most sheltered settings (Bellamy, Bourbeau, & Sowers, 1983; Garner et al., 1985; Martin et al., 1982; Rusch, 1983; Wehman & Hill, 1983). The central question, therefore, is what constitutes a *reasonable wage* when evaluating the advisability of a potential worksite? Are the wages permitted by regulations of the U.S. Department of Labor (DOL) flexible enough to provide persons with severe disabilities access to employment and to maintain or improve their quality of life? The answer to this latter question appears to be a resounding "Yes." Using this flexibility to the full is the task of employment training and employment personnel (Bellamy et al., 1984; Brown et al., 1984). Decisions in this area ultimately affect the future of employment and training efforts for persons labeled severely handicapped.

In 1980, Marc Gold proposed a direct relationship between work and nonwork activities. He suggested that their individual options for leisure pursuits and further independence increase proportionally with increases in their wages. Although this maxim is true in the real world of employment, it does not apply to the sheltered setting. In a sheltered work environment, the worker has little opportunity to experience the relationship between wages earned and opportunities that can be realized. For example, if the amount of contract work decreases in a sheltered work environment, do workers have concerns about how to pay their bills, or where their next meal is coming from, or whether or not they will be able to pay the rent? The universal answer to each of these questions is demonstrably "No."

In a sheltered work environment, contingencies for establishing the work-benefits relationship are practically nonexistent. Individuals in the wider society who are employed in business, commerce, or industry learn quickly that meeting the employer's specified performance standards leads to a paycheck. Conversely, extended absences, shirking of responsibilities, and shoddy performance invariably lead to reduced working hours, potential job termination or layoff, and, ultimately, reduced income levels. The relationship between employment and the ability to pay the bills (or participate in leisure or luxury pursuits) is a constant reminder of the need to work.

The issue of wages is complicated by receipt of Supplemental Security Income (SSI) and other forms of state and federal subsidy for persons labeled "severely handicapped" (Bellamy et al., 1984; Brown et al., 1984). We speculate that many adults with disabilities have often been discouraged or prevented from working due to the potential loss or reduction of SSI payments and the related benefits of Medicaid insurance. This is a legitimate concern and should not be minimized by human services professionals. Although parents and families are often criticized for not supporting a job placement on these grounds, in many cases it is simply that they see employment as a gamble that might later result in unemployment through layoff or firing with the loss of an otherwise guaranteed income.

Lou Brown and his colleagues (1984) have sought to balance the need for employment resulting-in-remuneration and employment for other reasons. Their analysis indicates a belief that "in a hierarchy of important values, there are many instances in which earning money should be ranked much lower than many other values associated with work" (p. 263). The values hierarchy of these authors is best expressed in their own words:

> **First,** a worker with severe intellectual handicaps should be placed in a nonsheltered environment that offers access to meaningful work and a variety of individually enhancing quality of life phenomena;
> **Second,** after a worker is placed in an enhancing environment, all reasonable efforts designed to develop the performance of meaningful work should be made; then
> **Third,** the provision of direct pay for the performance of meaningful work should be arranged. (Brown et al., 1984, p. 263)

Employment training personnel should endeavor to seek the highest wages possible for the people they represent. Yet, we propose that the consideration of what constitutes an appropriate wage must be a personalized decision based upon the individual needs of each person. A reasonable wage must be evaluated in terms of: (1) the effects that wages may have on a person's supplemental sources of income and support; (2) the prospects for extended employment resulting from a negotiated, flexible payment arrangement; and (3) the relative importance of wages in relation to other benefits that may be derived from the work experience, such as involvement in an integrated environment with nonhandicapped co-workers. The implications of these considerations should always be discussed with the potential employee and with his or her family or advocate. The ideal job brings a level of re-muneration that balances the issues outlined above in the most optimal way possible for the individual. We propose that employment in an integrated setting for minimal wages is *always* superior to continued placement in a sheltered work environment.

Opportunities, Job Satisfaction, Advancement, or Change

Advancement is not frequently discussed in the professional literature, but should be an important consideration in the process of employing. Advancement refers to possibilities for job enlargement, promotion, and lateral or vertical movement as new job possibilities and opportunities for retraining occur within the organization (Gold & Pomerantz, 1980). This concept is important to job stability and the individual's ability to retain a functional relevance to the changing needs of the employing business or industry.

It is totally naive to assume that once an employment placement is made that the worker's job responsibilities will remain stable and unchanged. Employment personnel must be aware of the availability and quality of in-house training, the potential for job changes in light of the employer's needs, and the possibility of a transfer to a new job should the current job role be eliminated. Although specific information in each of these areas may not be readily available, you must keep these factors in mind because they may affect the employee's longevity in employment.

A good example of job advancement or change is illustrated by the experi-ences at the Motorola Corporation in Austin, Texas of a young electronics worker who was labeled "mentally retarded." He was trained on his job through an employ-ment project of Marc Gold & Associates. After 2 years of successful employment, his employer's needs changed, and he was transferred to their plant in Phoenix, Ari-zona. Training on the new job was conducted by Motorola's own personnel. Based upon his exemplary employment productivity record, this worker was viewed as an asset to by the company, which felt that it would be a good financial investment to provide retraining in the new work location. It is important to note that the success-ful retraining and continued employment were facilitated by the employer and assis-tance by a human service agency was not required (P. Bossert, personal communica-tion, August, 1985).

When considering the issue of advancement, consider the first job oppor-tunity as an *initial phase* in career development. Job changes, layoffs, and transfers *will* occur—these realities are part of the contemporary employment and career de-velopment process for all people. Remain aware of these realities and design services accordingly.

Work Activities that are Status Enhancing and Culturally Valued

To a significant degree in our society the value of tasks performed at the workplace reflects a person's perceived value. One of the first questions that many of us ask new acquaintances is, "What kind of work do you do?" Therefore, it is important to make every effort to ensure that work activities performed by persons labeled "severely handicapped" are status enhancing and culturally valued to the maximum extent possible. Unfortunately, traditionally this work has been of little consequence to so-ciety (DeFazio & Flexer, 1983; Farber, 1968; Gold & Pomerantz, 1980; Pomerantz & Marholin, 1977).

Research and model programs have demonstrated clearly that persons labeled "severely handicapped" can learn to perform tasks effectively that are considered status enhancing (Bellamy et al., 1975; Garner et al., 1985; Hunter & Bellamy, 1976; Karan, Eisner, & Endres, 1974). The challenge is to translate these findings into common practice when providing placement opportunities. Sole reliance on the easiest-to-find, entry-level positions does little to enhance the image traditionally attached to persons labeled "severely handicapped." However, in the pursuit of status-enhancing jobs, agencies must be careful not to create a new method of excluding persons with severe disabilities from integrated employment. Job development efforts must balance the need for high-status jobs with the need that thousands of persons have for work.

Quality of Life

The opportunity to earn a living leads to independence, the ability to exercise personal choice, and an array of nonmonetary benefits. Martin et al. (1982) describe the story of two young men and the effects that employment ultimately can have on the quality of life:

> Three years ago, Steve and Murphy, who were diagnosed as being mildly to moderately mentally retarded, were working in a typical sheltered workshop and living in a nursing home for mentally retarded adults. Their morning routine consisted of being awakened by service attendants, waiting in line to use the restroom, eating cafeteria-style in a large dining hall, and traveling to the sheltered workshop with other residents in a yellow agency schoolbus. After being directed to their work stations by supervisory aides, Steve and Murphy assembled and later disassembled objects, menial tasks that lacked correspondence for competitive employment. For their efforts, Steve and Murphy were paid well below minimum wage, approximately $0.76 per hour. During their workday, they talked with other retarded individuals or the few staff members.
>
> After the day's work, Steve and Murphy returned to the nursing home to watch television in the day room with other residents. Usually after dinner they once again watched television, talked with other residents, or were entertained by local community volunteer groups. About once a week they went on a planned social outing to a nearby discount store to buy miscellaneous and needed personal care items. On returning to the home, Steve and Murphy found little privacy. Even after they retired for the evening, staff entered their room for bed checks throughout the night.
>
> Today there is a dramatic difference in the quality of life of one of their lives. Unfortunately, Steve's life is not different. His daily work routine has changed little, if any . . .
>
> Murphy, on the other hand, is experiencing a new and exciting life. For the past 3 years, he has been employed as a kitchen laborer in the food services division of a local university and lives in his own apartment. During Murphy's recent visit to Steve in the nursing home, they discussed Murphy's job, some new items he bought for the apartment with the money he made, and the girl he met at work. Murphy told Steve about his new assignment at work—operating the new dishwashing machine. Next, he invited Steve over for dinner to show off his new toaster oven and coffee maker. Finally, he talked to Steve about going to the movies with his new girlfriend. As Murphy said goodbye, Steve commented that he, too, would like to become involved in a similar training program so that he could have money to spend at the movies and live in his own apartment. (p. 59)

This vignette illustrates well what is, perhaps, the most critical factor in the facilitation of employment opportunities for persons labeled "severely handicapped": the resulting improvement in the quality of life. The final outcome of an employment and training effort is the new employee's first opportunity to take advantage of many of the experiences available in the community. Employment can open the door for persons labeled "severely handicapped," a door to fuller integration into community life.

What measures can be used to evaluate the quality of a person's life? Because quality of life must be viewed and weighed on an individual basis, it is important to identify factors that cut across individual differences, such as preferences, needs, wants, and values. For example, within the context of this discussion, we have proposed several criteria for a quality job and ultimately the quality of life (i.e., a reasonable wage, opportunities to engage in interactions with nonhandicapped co-workers, opportunities for advancement, and work activities that are status enhancing and culturally valued). This listing, although certainly not exhaustive, *can* provide an initial basis for establishing a quality-of-life experience for people labeled "severely handicapped." This list can be shortened or grow. Remember, the *individual* must be provided with the *opportunity* to choose the determinants of his or her quality job—and a quality life.

3

The Elusive Concept of Employability

For too many years, persons labeled "severely handicapped" have been evaluated in relation to a nebulous criterion: **employability**. These vocational evaluations have often deemed many individuals to be unemployable; as a result, these individuals have had extremely limited prospects for obtaining appropriate vocational training services and integrated employment opportunities. Traditional vocational evaluation strategies and the limiting expectations that often result are critically reviewed in this chapter. In addition, specific approaches for identifying employment-related skills are outlined in a manner that can readily be translated into practice by employment and training personnel. Our central thesis is that the concept of employability must be expanded through the provision of systematic training and support to include all persons with severe handicaps. Training and support can provide constructive alternatives to the "sorting process" that is inherent in traditional vocational evaluation processes.

CATEGORICAL DECISION-MAKING MODEL: ROOTS OF THE PROBLEM

Human service programs traditionally have received a major portion of their financial support from public funds (e.g., state and federal funds, tax levies, matching support, United Way, grants-in-aid, telethons). These funding mechanisms have fostered categorical decision making in the operation of program services. Under this model, prospective participants—also known as clients, trainees, and residents—are screened and evaluated according to established sets of entry criteria. They are, for example, measured for an intelligence quotient, assigned a medical diagnosis, or given a DSM-III psychiatric classification, a diagnostic classification system devised by the American Psychiatric Association. Those who meet established criteria are considered eligible for services from the agency. Those who do not meet the established criteria are excluded from services and are referred to a "more appropriate" service provider. The use of categorical decision-making models has prevented most persons with severe disabilities from receiving employment because they are considered ineligible for services.

The field of special education provides a case study in the evolution of a categorical decision model (Bricker, 1977). Over the last century, professionals in that field have generated exhaustive policies, practices, and procedures that dictate the particular nuances of the special education service delivery process. Myriads of administrative criteria determine who does and who does not qualify for services; how they will be classified and categorized for service delivery purposes; and which programs will qualify for local, state, or federal funding. Over a decade ago, Hobbs (1975) summarized the dangers of a categorical decision-making model in this way:

> Categories and labels are powerful instruments for social regulation and control, and they are often employed for obscure, covert, or harmful purposes: to degrade people; to deny them access to opportunity; to exclude undesirables whose presence in some way offends, disturbs familiar custom, or demands extraordinary effort. (p. 11)

In this analysis Hobbs captured one of the most controversial effects of the categorical decision-making model: the practice of excluding from services certain individuals who are deemed to be incapable of profiting from instruction. This issue of *educability*—by which is meant the ability to profit from education or training— has been considered for many years by many of the most respected professionals in the field (see, Baer, 1981; Burton & Hirshoren, 1979; Cruickshank, 1960; Noonan, Brown, Mulligan, & Rettig, 1982; Sontag, Certo, & Button, 1979; Stainback & Stainback, 1983; Tawney & Smith, 1981). The two diametrically contradictory positions on this issue were articulated by Noonan et al. in 1982:

> Opponents of educability for all handicapped persons generally focus their argument on certain characteristics of this population to demonstrate a rational basis for the ineducable level. . . . The opponents of educability . . . argue that the ineducability, and thereby different class status of severely handicapped, provide a rational status to exclude some handicapped persons from education. The first rationale for exclusion is that the profoundly handicapped would fail to benefit significantly from education. (p. 5)

The crux of the debate, therefore, rests on an invalid criterion—or a lack of one—for determining whether a given individual is perceived to be capable of learning. The debates continue with no clear end in sight. In the vocational training field, similar debate centers around the issue of *employability*.

TRADITIONAL VOCATIONAL EVALUATION: A PROCESS FOR SORTING AND SELECTING

The process for determining employability generally has proceeded as follows. Those individuals who meet certain criteria, either real or imaginary, are considered to be employable and are prepared for placement in an employment setting. Those individuals who do not meet the specified criteria for employability are placed in a sheltered setting. Of significance here are the professional beliefs and practices that underlie this potentially arbitrary, debilitating, and dignity-limiting decision-making process.

The first step in determining whether an individual is to be considered employable often is the administration of a standardized vocational evaluation. Most vocational evaluations include routine educational and psychological test batteries, rating scales, work samples, and situational assessments (Flexer & Martin, 1978). Proponents of this approach (e.g., Revell, Kriloff, & Sarkee, 1980) describe the purposes of the evaluation process as follows:

> Vocational evaluation, *as an assessment of inherent vocational potential,* identifies an individual's assets and liabilities. It is not proposed that this evaluation mechanism supplant traditional assessment programs developed for developmentally disabled indi-

viduals; rather, data resulting from this process should be used to complement, and subsequently expand, the direction of existing information *so that realistic vocational training plans can be developed for this population. The primary objective of vocational evaluation is to provide an assessment technique that will identify vocational potential.* (Emphases added, p. 73)

This definition points clearly to two pervasive beliefs that guide traditional evaluation processes: (1) that vocational evaluation instruments and techniques can predict the likelihood of success for a person with severe disabilities in employment—a measure of the evaluation's predictive ability—and (2) that vocational evaluation instruments can measure an individual's "innate potential" to benefit from training, a measure of construct validity. However, the power of the instruments used in the evaluation to make accurate prognostications is rarely demonstrable, particularly for persons with severe disabilities.

We propose here that human service practitioners should presume that *all* persons labeled "severely handicapped" can be trained to take their place in the work world. It makes sense, both empirically and pragmatically, to use currently available resources for training, rather than for evaluating, labeling, eliminating, and categorizing.

Myths of Artificial Approximations and Prerequisites

It is particularly disturbing to see the credence with which many human service practitioners regard the results of vocational evaluations. An example of the denial of opportunity resulting from traditional evaluations occurred recently during a series of staff training sessions with educational personnel responsible for job development, training, and placement. During the course of these training sessions, these personnel were asked to participate in a simulation activity and were given the following directions:

> You have been contacted by Mr. William Jones, President of Allied Electronics. This locally owned company is involved in the development of electronic circuitry components and wants to hire one of your trainees to assemble printed circuit boards (demonstrations of circuit-board assembly provided through slide presentation). In your small groups, make a list of the necessary prerequisite skills for successful performance of this job. Once the list is completed, go back and determine strategies for evaluating these prerequisites. (Lecours & Garner, 1982, p. 7)

A representative sample of the prerequisite skills and evaluation activities that were generated by these groups is presented in Table 3.1. In every instance, the prerequisites and their respective evaluation activities depended upon the use of *artificial approximations* (Brown, Branston, Hamre-Nietupski, Pumpian, 1979) of the ultimate task: the assembly of an electronic printed circuit board. None of the participants suggested that the best or only way to determine learner skills would be through actual training on the specified task.

As a postscript to this experience, we want to assure you that the job described was not a hypothetical example. A young woman labeled "severely handicapped," who demonstrated *none* of the *perceived* prerequisites, subsequently was trained to perform this complex task to acceptable company standards. This was accomplished through the skillful application of available training technology in the actual work location, not through a developmental approach to facilitating the acquisition of "prerequisite skills."

Table 3.1.   A representative sample of perceived prerequisite skills and evaluation activities for assembly of printed circuit boards (as reported by groups of work-study coordinators)

Prerequisite skills	Evaluation activities
1. Finger dexterity	1. Pegboard activities
2. Shape/texture discrimination	2. McCarron-Dial Work Sample
3. Eye-hand coordination	3. Valpar Work Sample
4. Color discrimination	4. "Construction paper" color test, e.g., "Touch red"
5. Spatial relations	5. Puzzle assembly
6. Judgment	6. "If . . . then" interviews
7. Self-motivation	7. Teacher observation
8. Speed/accuracy of work	8. Practice sessions (unspecified)
9. Sociability	9. Role-playing activity
10. Following steps in sequence	10. Work sample, e.g., fold and staple

Facilitate Opportunity—Not Just Train and Test!

Despite the widespread use of vocational evaluation instrumentation, many professionals have questioned its utility with persons labeled "severely handicapped." Gold (1980b), for example, charged that the vocational evaluation literature is replete with statistical significance but devoid of any practical significance. He challenged the utility of evaluation processes in the following observation:

> Testing and labeling have practical limitations. . . . For instance, the trainer usually has little interaction with the . . . examiner who diagnoses and evaluates the client. And because the examiner seldom sees the treatment or training activities (s)he bases evaluation on a limited number of skills and tests. Both are denied important information about the learner by this system. . . . The most effective demonstration of a learner's ability and personality will naturally occur when (s)he is actively engaged in learning. Because the trainer is constantly adjusting to changes in the learner's behavior, (s)he is continually evaluating while teaching. (Gold, 1980a, p. 4)

Thus, Gold encouraged professionals to invest their time and effort in training, rather than testing. Pomerantz and Marholin (1977) supported this position by observing that: (1) vocational evaluations, even if valid and reliable, are not germane for those individuals given no opportunity to enter the integrated job market and (2) although vocational evaluators are frequently the most highly trained staff persons, they spend most of their time generating data that never will be used. Is it reasonable to speculate that the entire vocational evaluation process may be a sophisticated way of assuaging the conscience of human service practitioners? For, by saying that an individual is unemployable there is no reason to stretch the limits of our training technology.

AN ALTERNATIVE TO TRADITIONAL TESTING SYSTEMS

An alternative to standardized norm-referenced vocational evaluations is to use criterion-referenced training activities. Whereas standardized norm-referenced measures provide an opportunity to evaluate *inter*individual performance, criterion, ecologically referenced systems add a further dimension. These measures can also determine an individual's learning profile. Consequently, they allow for the comparison of a person's subskills, one with the other. Thus, we can evaluate *intra*individual differences. Although norm-referenced systems provide for a final or *summative* analysis, criterion systems add to this end-product by creating additional options for *formative* analyses. As a direct result, ecologically referenced approaches can provide analyses of both the process and the outcome. Procedures typically used in such a system include:

1. Identify the tasks and routines required for a particular job.
2. Analyze and subdivide the tasks into discrete, teachable components.
3. Develop specific instructional and feedback strategies.
4. Initiate training on the specified task using the task analysis.
5. During the course of training conduct a natural assessment to determine whether the person is learning the task as presented.
6. If the person is not learning the task or is finding it difficult to acquire, modify the training strategies.
7. Continue the training and adjustment process as dictated by derived performance data.

Criterion-referenced approaches focus primarily upon the facilitation process. Information that results from training is more valuable and valid than any predictions that could be made from the results of a standardized evaluation using approximations of the real task. One assumption that underpins the criterion-referenced approach is that, if the learner does not acquire the identified skills, then the trainer is using insufficient *instructional power*. Gold (1980b) defines instructional power as "the amount of intervention, assistance, or demonstration required by the trainer in order for the learner to reach criterion" (p. 6). Thus, this approach places responsibility on the trainer, rather than apportioning blame on the learner for any perceived learning inadequacies.

Concepts of employability typically are used in reference to individual persons, but can as easily be used to describe instructional efficacy. If a particular training strategy proves to be ineffective with a particular learner, who is to say whether the strategy was inappropriate or whether the learner is "to blame." Is this not a case of the labeler describing the limits of his or her own instructional power? In essence, the labeler is saying, "Here is where my instructional effectiveness stops," "Here is where I give up," or "Here is where I stop applying resources." The point we are making is that *employability* cannot really be determined unless we assume no change in instructional practices or resources. As instructional power is enhanced through improved training technology, employment opportunities are enhanced as well. The time has come to eliminate the term "employability" from the vocabulary of human service providers and work trainers. If an individual is considered unemployable it is only because trainers have failed to design and implement appropriate training strategies.

4

Structures versus Outcomes
Service Models for
Training and Employment

This final chapter of the first section outlines a clear direction for facilitating integrated employment for persons labeled "severely handicapped." Employment and training services first must focus upon outcomes. By this we mean that they must attend to the characteristics of the final product before attempting to delineate the structure of the service delivery options.

PERSPECTIVES IN TRANSITION

Within the past decade, there has been a dramatic shift in thinking about the vocational potential of persons labeled "severely handicapped" (Bellamy et al., 1975; Bellamy et al., 1984; Conley, Noble, & Elder, 1986; DeFazio & Flexer, 1983; Garner et al., 1985). The philosophical and programmatic principles that underpin the system of sheltered work environments have been thoroughly re-examined (Brown et al., 1984; The Association for Persons with Severe Handicaps, 1983; Wehman & Kregel, 1984; Whitehead, 1979). Unfortunately, in the context of human services such shifts in thinking are not as rapidly translated into action. Thus, tension exists between historically vested sheltered programs and those advocating integrated employment for persons labeled "severely handicapped." This tension can only be eliminated if the human services community focuses its collective attention on two primary areas of concern: structures and outcomes. The provision of integrated employment requires agencies to focus on the outcomes of their services to individuals, rather than merely on the structure or model of the services.

SIGNIFICANCE OF STRUCTURES AND OUTCOMES

Structures refer to the organizational frameworks or models used to provide vocational training and employment services to persons labeled "severely handicapped." These organizational frameworks may include a variety of subcategories, such as administrative hierarchies (boards of directors, executive officers, and organizational structures), personnel (vocational trainers and support staff evaluators), budgetary priorities (capital costs, such as "bricks and mortar," and human resources), and policies and procedures (personnel practices, supervisory structures, and governmental regulations).

However, any analysis of structures must primarily be focused upon the *quality* and *quantity* of services that are provided. It is distressing to note that the quantity of services provided often is interpreted as the primary indicator of the service's quality. For example, often an annual report of a human service agency may simply be a numerical catalog of services provided during the preceding fiscal year, which are displayed in terms of the number of clients served, the number of staff members employed, and the number of bus miles traveled. Although these statistics provide a picture of the agency's fiscal responsibility and capacity, they do not necessarily reflect the impact of its services on the lives of its consumers. The qualitative structure of human services cannot adequately be assessed without a simultaneous consideration of desired outcomes.

In this discussion, *outcomes* refers to meaningful integrated vocational opportunities for persons labeled "severely handicapped" that are realized directly or indirectly as a result of training and facilitation. This definition implies that outcomes are planned and future oriented; there is a direct relationship between the development of skills and competencies and opportunity; and the attainment of desired outcomes is directly attributable to effective facilitation.

What appears to be at issue among human services professionals are the criteria that should be used to evaluate the relative value of alternative outcomes. Although professionals frequently espouse valued philosophies for service outcomes, such as the principles of normalization and integrated employment, the interests of consumers are often considered secondary to the needs of the service system. In the final analysis the outcomes selected, the philosophies that guide their selection, and the degree to which those outcomes are achieved by consumers are the ultimate measures of program effectiveness. When designing a vocational training and employment service system, structures and outcomes must be viewed in terms of their impact on the consumer.

Given this perspective, it becomes apparent that structures and outcomes interact in a variety of ways. First, in much the same way that "form follows function," structures should indeed follow outcomes. The outcomes selected by and for the consumers of vocational training and employment services must dictate the types, quantities, orientations, locations, and intensities of the available service structures. To do otherwise is to minimize the vital role of consumer needs in the design and implementation of the service system. Outcomes should be the destination toward which vocational training and employment services are directed. Structures are the vehicle for reaching that predetermined goal.

Second, outcomes can be used as evaluative tools to determine the relative value and success of program structures. In this regard, consider the many sheltered programs across the country that have an *expressed* commitment to integrated employment. As a means of program evaluation, several key questions can be posed to determine these agencies' degree of success in meeting their stated outcomes:

- How many individuals—frequency expressed in percentages or in actual numbers—have successfully made the transition from a sheltered program environment to meaningful work in integrated settings?
- How long do they remain employed?
- To what extent are agency personnel advising the recipients of these services about their option to enter an integrated work setting?
- What types and quantities of resources have been allocated toward facilitating integrated employment?

- What decisions, energy, and financial resources have been allocated toward perpetuating sheltered work environments as an alternative for the recipients of agency services?

Such questions as these provide a method for making the vocational training and employment system accountable for its actions. By monitoring an agency's stated goals and objectives (i.e., outcomes) and their corresponding services (i.e., structures), advocates and consumers can facilitate the development of service systems that are more responsive to identified needs.

Quite often, service systems participate in the practice of *progressive status quoism* (Farber, 1968; Gold, 1980a). This malady involves two simultaneous actions on the part of the service system: The service system gives the appearance of grave concern over a pressing social issue or problem, such as employment opportunities for persons labeled "severely handicapped," but it does little, if anything, to solve the identified problems. Progressive status quoism can easily be deterred through analyzing the ongoing interaction between structures and outcomes.

Finally, when considering the relationship between structures and outcomes it is imperative to tie them both to emerging technological and philosophical advancements. Structures and outcomes have little validity if they do not represent the best practices of available technology and innovative experiences, e.g., research findings, demonstration projects, etc. If either structures or outcomes are philosophically or technologically outdated, the results are equally dated and questionable.

The consumers of vocational training and employment services are entitled to the very best available in job development, employment, training, and support. Although currently there is no legally enforceable mandate for "quality" in vocational services, we propose that there is a clear ethical mandate that professionals ensure that meaningful and high quality vocational services are delivered. This obligation must be taken seriously. The relationship between structures and outcomes is a reflection of professional skills, competencies, and degree of commitment to the ever-changing standard of quality in human services provision.

ANALYSES OF THE STRUCTURES FOR PROVIDING VOCATIONAL TRAINING, SUPPORT, AND EMPLOYMENT SERVICES

Until very recently, discussions regarding vocational training and employment services for persons labeled "severely handicapped" focused solely on theoretical issues, such as the debilitating nature of sheltered work environments and the "employability" of labeled persons. Fortunately, these discussions are now being translated into action. Selected human service agencies are developing and implementing vocational training and employment systems that encourage meaningful work opportunities. This trend has been encouraged and reinforced by federal agencies responsible for special education and rehabilitative services (Bellamy, Rhodes, & Albin, 1986; Elder, 1984; Conley et al., 1986; Will, 1984). Now that employment is becoming a valued outcome, practitioners are devoting their attention to developing new and innovative structures for providing vocational training.

Two major structures have emerged: *transitional employment* and *supported employment*. Each of these options is a systematic approach to providing varied degrees of training, support, and follow-up services (Bellamy et al., 1984; Martin et al., 1982; Wehman & Kregel, 1984; Wehman, Kregel, & Barcus, 1985; Will, 1984). Further, each of these structures views the movement from a school or a sheltered work environment into employment as a transition that requires careful planning before implementation (Kiernan & Stark, 1986). Will (1984) captured the spirit of this transition with the following observation:

> Transitions are an important part of normal life. As roles, locations, and relationships change, all of us must adapt, and we do so with more or less disruption or stress. The transition . . . to working life called for a range of choices about career options, living arrangements, social life, and economic goals that have lifelong consequences. For individuals with disabilities, this transition often is made more difficult by limitations that can be imposed by others' perceptions of disability and by the complex array of services that are intended to assist adult adjustment. (p. 2)

Transitional Employment

As a means of providing a transition from schools and sheltered workshops to integrated work environments some persons with severe handicaps may benefit from intensive, though time-limited, assistance. Will (1984) further described this competitive employment process as "an outcome-oriented service process encompassing a broad array of services and experiences that leads to employment. . . . Transition is a bridge between security and structure and the opportunities and risks of adult life" (p. 1).

Transitional employment is a time-limited service structure; that is, the availability of the service decreases after a specified period. These processes, included in competitive employment, involve:

1. Survey of the community to establish appropriate relationships with employers and to identify potential employment locations, i.e., job development
2. Analysis of available positions with regard to their match with the identified characteristics of a "quality job"
3. Complete analysis of the duties, tasks, and responsibilities required by specific jobs and by clusters of jobs
4. Job match between a potential applicant and an employment opportunity
5. Provision of on-the-job training and facilitation services
6. Time-limited follow-up services
   (Belmore & Brown, 1978; Gold, 1980a, 1980b; Martin et al., 1982; Rusch, 1983; Wehman, 1981; Wehman et al., 1985)

Planning and the effective coordination of services are key elements of competitive employment. It is critical that vocational training and employment personnel actively respond to the numerous factors that can impede the process of employing, e.g., parental or family concerns, potential loss of Supplemental Security Income and Medicaid benefits, transportation problems, agreements with the potential employer, etc. Good intentions are no substitute for systematic planning when facilitating employment opportunities (Chapters 10–12 and 15 provide further considerations of these and associated factors).

As an example of competitive employment services in action, consider data recently generated by the Manpower Demonstration Research Corporation. In a study of 250 adults labeled "mentally retarded," 42% made the transition from a sheltered work environment to competitive employment. The average worker in this group worked a 29-hour week at a wage of $3.63 per hour. The mean cost of training was $7,550 per participant. Similar data by other researchers (Hill & Wehman, 1981; Martin et al., 1982) also have demonstrated that competitive employment can be a legitimate and cost-effective alternative to sheltered employment.

Supported Employment

For many persons with severe handicaps, competitive time-limited employment training services are not long or intense enough to facilitate meaningful work opportunities. As a result, the concept of supported work services has emerged *both* in the professional literature *and* in federally mandated regulations. For example, the *Developmental Disabilities Act of 1984* provides the following definition of supported employment:

> . . paid work in a variety of settings, particularly regular work sites, especially designed for handicapped individuals (i) for whom competitive employment at or above the minimum wage is unlikely; and (ii) who, because of their disability, need intensive, on-going support to perform in a work setting (*Federal Register,* Sept. 25, 1984, Section 102 [11], [F]).

In a recent joint publication prepared by the Rehabilitation Research Training Center at Virginia Commonwealth University and the Specialized Training Program at the University of Oregon (1985), this legislation was analyzed as follows:

> It is a *type* of employment, not a *method* of employment preparation, nor a type of service activity. It is a powerful and flexible way to ensure normal employment benefits, provide ongoing and appropriate support, create opportunities, and achieve full participation, integration, and flexibility. (emphases added, p. 1)

This analysis specifies six essential features of the supportive work services:

1. Employment with all the typical outcomes associated with working, e.g., wages, job security, benefits, appropriate working conditions
2. Ongoing support where necessary throughout the working career of the consumer
3. An emphasis on jobs, not services
4. Full participation
5. Social integration
6. Variety and flexibility in the types and quantities of services provided

The emergence of the supported work model is extremely significant. Combined with the complementary components of competitive employment, it is now conceivable that we may realize full employment opportunities for *all* persons labeled "severely handicapped" (Bellamy, Rhodes, & Albin, 1986). Service delivery options can be matched to the needs of the individual, and exclusion from services can no longer be tolerated.

Mank, Rhodes, and Bellamy (1985) have proposed four alternatives for the provision of supported work. In the *supported jobs alternative* a single individual is placed in a work setting—much like the competitive employment model—but is provided continued assistance. The *enclave* alternative provides for a work group of from six to eight individuals performing real work in a real work setting, with supervision and support provided both by the host company and the human service agency (Rhodes & Valenta, 1985). In the *mobile work crew* model a group of workers provide a specific service, such as lawn care or maintenance, in varied locations throughout the community (Bourbeau, 1985). The *benchwork* alternative is directed toward the completion of contract work (Boles, Bellamy, Horner, & Mank, 1984) in what perhaps could be considered a small, segregated work setting, with ongoing access to interactions with nonhandicapped persons in the immediate neighborhood; for example, work location in an integrated industrial park, shared use of public transportation, and eating lunch in a neighborhood restaurant. These alternatives provide flexibility within the supported employment model. Individual consumers can be provided with opportunities for work within these alternatives dependent upon their individual needs, interests, and aspirations.

Wehman and Kregel (1984) recently provided a component-based analysis of the supported work model that can be superimposed on the alternatives described by Mank et al. (1986). These components apply equally to each of the above described alternatives and specify the kinds of professional activity that typically occur during the implementation process:

- *Job placement* during which time arrangements are made for a worksite, transportation, final details relating to Social Security/Medicaid benefits, worksite adaptations, etc.
- *Job site training and advocacy,* which involves task analyses, the design and implementation of training strategies, and effective communication with supervisory and line personnel
- *Ongoing monitoring* of the worksite, review of worker performance, retraining as needed, and communication with company personnel
- *Follow-up and retention* services to ensure the continued employment of the consumer

A commitment to the supported work services model necessarily entails a commitment to implementing each of these program activities.

One recurring objection to the supported work model is the cost involved in the provision of lifelong services. An obvious response to this criticism is the fact that lifelong services are currently being provided to persons with severe handicaps within the context of sheltered work environments, but with little, if any, positive return on the financial investment. Interestingly, however, in a recent study by Rhodes and Valenta (1985) that described the supported employment experience of eight adults with severe handicaps, $1.26 was earned for every $1.00 invested in vocational training. Additionally, project participants each paid a total of $2,425 in federal taxes! For skeptics, these data present a cogent argument for adopting the supported work model as a viable alternative for persons with severe handicaps.

Structures exist currently for bringing about the organized depopulation of sheltered work environments. The remaining ingredient, however, is more elusive—the initiative needed for human service agencies to put into practice an emphasis on integrated employment. Structures, no matter how sophisticated or innovative, become empty promises without a parallel degree of commitment to the outcomes they are designed to achieve.

Effective service coordination requires a commitment from both generic and specialized service providers. Traditionally, service coordination has been interpreted only to include two basic activities: referrals from one agency to another and the drafting of interagency agreements on cooperation. Yet, neither of these approaches has been shown to be particularly effective in meeting the needs of persons with severe handicaps. This inefficiency becomes most apparent when human services agencies are unable or unwilling to provide a specified service because it "sets a precedent for future endeavors," or "goes beyond the scope of the agency's charter or perceived role in the community." Put bluntly, the agency using these rationales is unwilling to "go the extra mile" to facilitate meaningful employment for a handicapped person. Once again, the practice of progressive status quoism has reared its ugly form.

We are certain in our belief that effective service coordination must focus upon the individual's needs, not the needs of the service system.

ANALYZING THE OUTCOMES OF VOCATIONAL TRAINING AND EMPLOYMENT SERVICES

As we described earlier, outcomes refer to those interdependent skills, competencies, and opportunities that are to be realized by persons labeled "severely handicapped." Meaningful outcomes are *the* reason that vocational facilitation and employment services exist. These services are not designed to provide employment for administrators, job developers, employment trainers, psychologists, and bus drivers. Such a distinction, often taken lightly, is fundamental and should guide every program decision.

The issue of quality in vocational training and employment services is discussed extensively in other sections of this book (see for example, Chapters 2 and 10). If you review that material you will see some pragmatic ways to establish specific criteria for creating an agency-wide philosophy of integrated employment. Yet, this is only the first step. What remains is your initiation of specific planning strategies to ensure that *all* of the *structures* in your program/agency reflect and reinforce the exact nature of the *outcomes*.

II

JOB DEVELOPMENT

5

Approaches to Planning

Effective job development must be preceded by effective planning. As you venture into the world of business to secure employment opportunities for persons with disabilities, you must be able to portray the philosophical and programmatic orientations of the human service agency in a clear, concise, realistic, and honest fashion. Doing so requires planning that focuses on the types of assistance to be provided; the needs, skills, and preferences of the people to be employed; the operational parameters defining employment; and the agency's commitment to support potential employees.

This chapter provides a practical orientation to the planning required for job development activities offered through a human service agency. Before providing employment opportunities for people labeled "severely disabled," consideration must be given to all the necessary components and strategies that constitute a successful employment service. Many of these components have no direct counterpart in traditional human service programs. Therefore, much of this information, especially in the area of job development, has been developed from techniques used in the mainstream business world. Additional information has been gained from the *application* of these techniques to the process of employing people with severe disabilities. Finally, for those people who require more extraordinary measures to become successfully employed, innovative and effective techniques are included that are compatible with typical business practices and yet meet the particular needs of persons with more severe disabilities.

The first rule of planning is that it should complement and encourage action, rather than stifle it. Too many agencies spend months and sometimes even years "getting ready" to offer job opportunities. In the succinct words of the awareness-enhancing button: *Pre* (e.g., vocational) can mean *never*. We invite you to make a commitment to get started; place strict limits on the amount of time you invest in planning, and stick to those limits. Remember it is always possible, perhaps it is even preferable, to learn-while-doing and to revise as necessary. However, several critical issues should be addressed before ever calling on an employer.

The objectives of planning are to:

1. Decide on a philosophy that describes how the people you represent are to be presented to potential employers. This value-laden decision will affect virtually all aspects of the process of employing.
2. Determine the specific approach or alternative approaches that you will follow in securing employment.
3. Outline the range of services that you offer both to the employee and the employer.

4.   Determine your agency's competence and commitment to provide employment to persons with disabilities.
5.   Develop vocational profiles on the people to be employed. This information is vital for matching individuals with jobs.
6.   Consider recruiting an advisory board comprised of local business persons.
7.   Select or hire appropriate personnel to provide the representation and training.

PHILOSOPHY OF REPRESENTATION

The philosophy presented here is that all people labeled "mentally retarded and severely disabled" are fully capable of participating in typical places of business and industry as employees (see also Bellamy, Bourbeau, & Sowers, 1983; Bellamy et al., 1984; Brown et al., 1984; Rusch, 1983; Wehman & Hill, 1983). These individuals, when given effective representation and powerful training, can meet most employers' "essential needs," and many may even be able to produce at the standards expected of nonhandicapped workers. Every agency involved in job development needs to develop a statement of philosophy, understandable by all those involved in employment, *before* calling on employers. The media, presentations, correspondence, and actions of the agency and its staff should follow this philosophy in a consistent manner.

Many traditional approaches to job development, such as *Hire the Handicapped*, focus on the disability as a reason for hiring a worker. We view these approaches as demeaning and patronizing, for they send confusing messages to employers why a person should be considered for employment. A more positive and dignified approach would be to represent people with disabilities as fully capable of meeting or of learning to meet the employer's essential needs. Some of these essential needs, which have been identified from experiences with many employers, focus on these components: quality work performance, safety, and dependability; value of work output exceeds wages paid; customer relationships are not compromised; and relationships with co-workers are cooperative.

This list gives a job developer clear competencies to discuss with a prospective employer and also allows for the flexibility necessary to employ individuals with significant disabilities. Once it is established that the employer's essential needs can be met, you can then "seal the deal" by focusing on the unique characteristics of the job applicant and on the services offered by your agency.

The agency's representation philosophy not only affects the relationship with the employer but also the needs of the person being employed. The job a person obtains is not merely an *end* in itself, but is also a *means* to many other opportunities. Therefore, providing work in an integrated setting should be an overriding goal for vocational employment services. In developing an operating philosophy for an employment service, personnel should give serious consideration to the following features of integrated employment:

- Opportunities for interaction with nonhandicapped co-workers and supervisors
- Status-enhancing and culturally valued employment
- Opportunities for personal choice in job selection

- Appropriate compensation for work performed
- Employment in natural, non agency settings that are not populated with others who are disabled
- Opportunity to develop networks and meaningful personal relationships with people outside human-service agencies

These features must be considered if an agency is to balance the needs of employers with the needs of people who are to be represented. You must ensure that both the employer's needs and the individual employee's needs are addressed in the development of any given job.

APPROACHES TO EMPLOYMENT

Competitive Employment or Supported Work

To decide the approach to employment that will be used, ask this question: Will the employee be expected to perform all the components typically expected of any employee for the job (usually referred to as *competitive employment*), or will the performance of typical job responsibilities be modified, redefined, or lessened through negotiation with the employer (referred to as *supported work*). Traditionally, competitive employment has been the employment approach used for persons with disabilities. However, after numerous attempts to employ persons with severe disabilities, particularly during the early part of this decade, it has become evident that a requirement to perform *all* components of a job to typical standards represents a barrier to integrated employment for many people with more significant disabilities (Brown et al., 1984). Most agencies serving people with severe disabilities probably need both competitive and supported employment as options for employment. Then, depending on the individual, the job developer can select the best approach.

It is important to note that an initial selection of either of the approaches should not in any way "lock" you into seeking a particular format or style of employment. Flexible options can often be negotiated for persons who are not able to meet all the standard requirements of a given job, and persons performing supported work often can have their responsibilities increased to full competitive employment status. Even where changes in the employment expectations cannot be negotiated, it is almost always possible to develop another job opportunity in the same site or at another company.

Single Applicant or Multiple Applicants

A further distinction that must be made during planning is whether the job developer will represent a particular applicant to an employer or a group of potential applicants. Generally, the following perspective has proven to be true: *The more severely disabled a person is, the more that person requires individualized representation to be chosen for a job.* However, many people who are being served in programs for persons labeled "severely handicapped" are able to compete successfully when applying for a job.

There are many ways by which a job developer may offer prospective applicants an opportunity for employment. Figure 5.1 describes this issue from two perspectives: the number of applicants represented and the level of assistance offered. Job developers may choose from four alternatives using this matrix.

Number of Applicants Represented for a Job Opening	Level of Assistance	
	Direct	Referral
Multiple	Direct representation	Referral
Single	Direct representation	Referral

Figure 5.1.   Representation strategies.

Single Applicants   Since the advent of the supported work concept in the mid-1980s, many programs have chosen the strategy of representing one individual at a time for each job. The job developer either seeks a particular job that seems to match the needs, skills, and desires of an applicant or looks for several jobs and then offers positions to specific individuals for whom the job seems to fit. The single-applicant strategy for job development is most effective when an applicant:

- Needs a particular set of employment conditions in order to be successful
- Expresses a preference for a particular type of job or place of employment
- Has applied for several jobs under a multiple applicant strategy and has not been hired

Representational strategies should not cause applicants to become frustrated or to feel that they are less valued than others.

Multiple Applicants   The multiple-applicant strategy of representation is based on the system used most by businesses and is therefore the more natural of the two choices. Once a job has been secured by the job developer, an announcement of the opening is posted or otherwise communicated to people interested in employment. The job posting/announcement must contain all the information necessary to help an applicant and his or her family make a decision whether to apply for the job (see Appendix 15, Sample Job Posting). Applicants then follow the instructions contained in the posting to apply for the position. Appropriate levels of assistance may be offered to the applicants for the completion of resumes, filling out application forms, reading the posting, and similar components of the job-hunt process. The employer is responsible for interviewing a group of applicants and making the final employment decision. The main difference between this and a company's typical application process is that the applicant pool is limited to the group represented by the job developer. Other differences may also be tailored into the process, as approved by the employer.

     This strategem provides applicants an opportunity to experience a natural sequence of events in seeking employment. It also allows them to make decisions about various types of work, rather than accepting jobs that have been developed for them. The job developer must carefully weigh the potential costs and benefit before choosing a representational strategy for a particular person.

Direct Representation or Referral

There is a general assumption that most people who have been labeled "severely handicapped" and "unemployable" require the assistance of a "professional" job developer in order to become employed. And, until many more people with severe disabilities are employed, this is probably the case. The job developer is employed to seek out, evaluate, and secure job opportunities. These activities are performed in lieu of teaching the applicants how to represent themselves, which replaced a reliance on existing generic services, such as Job Service and Vocational Rehabilitation. In addition, job developers too often act as a substitute for the natural, family-based networks that are so effective in getting most people their first job. Job developers undoubtedly would be more effective if they considered ways to incorporate and use generic services and family networks, rather than replacing them.

Job developers do, however, perform three vital roles in the direct representation approach: (1) They "lend their competence" to people with disabilities until employees are able to learn their jobs; (2) they can be held accountable for facilitating job opportunities; and, (3) they can scan a community to target jobs about which applicants might otherwise not have knowledge or access.

Traditionally, vocational rehabilitation counselors used a referral method of representation to inform applicants of potential job openings but then provided little assistance to applicants in securing a job. This approach, used in its purest form, represented a substantial barrier for persons with severe disabilities. Therefore, most agencies that serve such persons have chosen to utilize a direct representation strategy almost exclusively.

Although most experienced job developers would agree that direct representation is a crucial component of employment services for persons with severe disabilities, there are many instances in which a referral might be just what is needed to find a job. Referrals can be made by family and friends, by the local employment service, and by the job developer. It is important to remember that referral is the manner by which most people obtain jobs, particularly their first job. Additionally, many people employed in segregated work settings probably could find work if someone counseled them that it was appropriate for them to do so.

Who is the Apparent Customer: The Applicant or the Employer?

As long as an agency is specifically funded to provide services to persons with disabilities, there should be no question as to who is the "ultimate consumer" of an employment service. The primary client is always the individual with a disability. However, in some cases it may be advisable to act as if the employer, rather than the applicant, is the customer. In every case experience has shown us that the needs of employers must also be considered if people are to enjoy long-term employment.

Probably there are as many ways to conceptualize and define the various approaches one might take in seeking job opportunities as there are people to represent. These approaches involve a myriad of issues and alternative strategies. For the purpose of this discussion, two fairly distinct approaches are contrasted. The first of these is the *business consultant approach,* which takes the view that the employer is the ultimate consumer and that the employee benefits from the successful relationship developed between the placement agency and the employer. In the *employee represen-*

tative approach the potential employee is the customer. The employer benefits from the performance promised by the agency representative and the output manifested by the client.

Employee Representative Approach   This is the most typically used approach in the employment of persons with disabilities. Information from the potential applicants is used to construct a profile of each applicant's needs, skills, and preferences regarding employment (see Appendices 13 and 14 and later in this chapter for further information on profiling). Based on this information, the job developer tries to secure a position that fits the profile. This approach can be used to develop both competitive jobs and supported work. The job developer needs to initiate and maintain a close relationship with people who are represented—the "clients" of the service (Figure 5.2).

Business Consultant Approach   This is an emerging approach that is now being used by many vocational rehabilitation counselors, also referred to as the employer Account Strategy (Galloway, 1982). This approach focuses on developing relationships with a number of employers in a community who become the "accounts" of the job developer (Figure 5.3). Employers are encouraged to contact the job developer whenever a job becomes available. The job developer then communicates the opening to a pool of potential applicants or selects a certain applicant from the pool. Employers are made to feel that their recruitment and productivity needs are the most important consideration in the relationship.

Job developers must weigh multiple factors in planning for an effective employment service (Figure 5.4). Elements of each approach need to be combined to produce the hybrid necessary to suit funding or other program objective purposes. Thus, it is clear that agencies must decide on the particular "mix" of approaches that best meets the needs of the people to be represented, rather than on "either/or" choices. Indeed, often the only pragmatically acceptable approach is one that takes the stance of the business consultant approach, but that has as a hidden agenda a primary loyalty to the employee. All of the approaches we describe are applicable for people labeled "severely disabled" and otherwise unemployable.

EMPLOYEE REPRESENTATIVE APPROACH

(Transitional Employment Service)

Job Sources   **Employee Sources**
Selected employers (employer account   Single assigned applicant and/or multiple
  strategy)   assigned applicants
Random employers

Typical Training Offered: Wide range of time-referenced services, which can include off-site classroom training of general or specific job-related skills, OJT, and training after employment. Services may be offered to the employer in exchange for consideration in hiring your clients.

Follow-Up Services: These are considered in Chapter 9.

Operating Premise: The agency has assigned people to represent. The agency determines the clients' vocational preferences and tries to find them jobs that they are willing and prepared to accept. The assigned person is the primary client.

Figure 5.2.   Employee representative approach.

BUSINESS CONSULTANT APPROACH

(Transitional Employment Service)

Job Sources	**Employee Sources**
Single company	Random identified applicants or single
Selected employers (Employee account	applicant identified by the employer
strategy)	Employee is not your client
Random employers	

Typical Training Offered: On-the-job training (OJT) and training-only employment (time-referenced).

Follow-Up Services: These are considered in Chapter 9.

Operating Premise: The agency finds a job and offers it to a number of people previously identified as applicants to be served. The company is the primary client.

Figure 5.3. Business consultant approach.

RANGE OF SERVICES OFFERED

An important step in the planning process is determining the range of services that your agency will offer, both to the people to be employed and to the employer. Merely listing these services is only a first step. Agencies must complement the list with a structured, detailed description for each service so that "clients," families, staff, and employers will know what to expect.

Possible Range of Services to **Employee**:

- Development of a vocational profile describing needs, skills, and preferences concerning employment
- Assistance in locating and securing a job
- Assistance in preparing for the application and interview phases
- Nondiscriminatory assessment of the applicant's ability to perform on the job
- Effective and individualized training based on a structured, detailed analysis of the tasks to be performed
- Facilitation and support in dealing with work-related and nonwork issues that affect job success
- Assistance in securing transportation, housing, and parent/guardian support
- Assistance in dealing with problems that might occur with governmental benefits, company benefits, and notification of governmental agencies once the individual is employed
- Assistance in finding a new job if the employee quits, wants another job, is laid off, or is fired

Possible Range of Services to **Employer**:

- Assurance of meeting the employer's "essential needs"
- Identification, notification, and prescreening of applicants represented by the agency
- Input and assistance in the interviewing and selection of employees hired through the agency

THE FLOW OF EMPLOYMENT

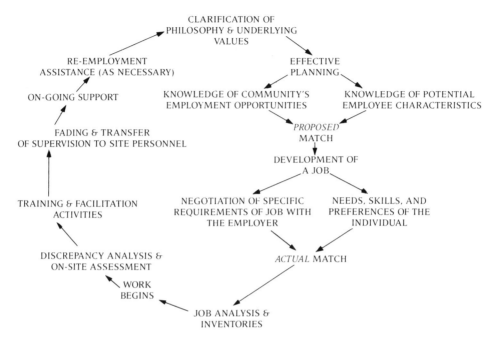

Figure 5.4. The flow of employment.

- Comprehensive job analyses and inventories of the job(s) to be performed
- Provision of instruction and support, either directly to the employee or indirectly to co-workers and supervisors, that are sufficient to ensure that the employer's "essential needs" will be met
- Assistance in acquiring tax incentive reimbursements and other subsidies that may be available to the employer
- Advice on barrier removal, job modification, and other reasonable/innovative forms of accomodation
- Provision of long-term support to the employer to ensure continued success of the employee
- Technical assistance on affirmative action issues
- Preparation of all documentation, forms, and data required by funding/monitoring sources related to the employee

Many local factors influence the particular range of services an agency chooses to offer. Funding, staff expertise, the availability of generic services, and the needs of the people served all determine the final list of services. Agencies should be careful not to overextend their resources or to agree to offer assistance in technical areas, such as on affirmative action issues, about which they lack experience.

AGENCY'S COMPETENCE AND COMMITMENT

This phase of planning is possibly the most critical. Does the agency and its staff have the capability to perform the services it is offering to the employees and their employers? According to Charles Galloway, author of *Employers as Partners* (1982), there are two ways of ensuring the *non*success of an employment service: (1) the agency is completely unable to deliver the service promised to the employer; or (2) although the capacity is there, the agency is unable to deliver on promises on a timely basis.

It is important to remember that employers operate from a *business* perspective, rather than a *human service* perspective. If employers are promised outcomes that are not delivered and if services are rendered in a shabby and ineffective manner, not only does the current employee suffer but other people with severe disabilities may also be denied future opportunities both at the particular worksite and with other employers who hear about such problems.

Before any employers are contacted, several questions need to be posed, evaluated, and answered affirmatively by the agency:

- Are training and facilitation techniques adequate to ensure that employees will meet the "essential needs" of employers?
- Do personnel have the ability to provide assistance, directly or indirectly, on all the items listed in the agency's Range of Services?
- Has information been gathered on the people to be represented that is as comprehensive as possible concerning their needs, skills, and preferences regarding work?
- Do personnel have the necessary business experience to identify, understand, and respond to the needs and problems of employers?
- Is there an expectation on the part of all agency personnel that people with severe disabilities can be successful in integrated work settings?
- Is there a solid commitment by agency personnel to the concept of integrated employment for all persons with disabilities?
- Has the agency developed a strong philosophical operating statement that describes how the people served are to be represented and treated?
- Does the agency have a commitment to facilitate employees' nonwork areas of need that affect their success at work?
- Are the job trainers/coaches willing to work in a variety of work settings, on various shifts, and possibly on weekends to ensure success?

Develop Vocational Profiles

An important activity before the initiation of job development efforts is to gather all meaningful information possible on the needs, skills, preferences, and experiences of the people who are to be employed. This information serves as the basis for successful job matches. Traditionally, it has been derived from standardized assessment procedures or through time-limited, simulated evaluations performed in sheltered workshops. However, in most cases, rather than describing the needs, skills, and preferences of the persons being assessed, these evaluations resulted in pronouncements of who was, and more usually who was *not*, "employable." Because we assume the employability of all persons with disabilities, we consider the bulk of the information obtained by such evaluations to be worthless (see Chapter 3).

What job developers really need to know about the people to be represented can more easily and more effectively be discovered through the development of a vocational profile. This profile is a narrative description of the relevant skills, needs, preferences, and experiences of each individual to be employed. Rather than relying on standardized procedures, job developers utilize interviews with prospective employees, their families or caregivers, teachers, agency personnel, friends, and, where possible, former employers. Records, IEPs, and program plans are reviewed and people are observed at work, at leisure time activities, and in their homes. This activity yields a "picture" of each individual that can serve both as a guide to potential worksites and as a measure of any discrepancy between existing sites and potential employees.

A sample vocational profile for an adult who is severely disabled is presented in Appendix 14. Furthermore, Lou Brown and his colleagues (1986) have developed an ecologically based strategy for evaluating the "vocational milieu" of workers with severe handicaps. It evaluates the needs of workers across 19 dimensions, which range from transportation to work performance to toileting procedures.

Form a Business Advisory Board

Numerous employment projects report that the development of an advisory board comprised of business persons from the local community has contributed to their success. This board can offer valuable ideas and suggestions that are particularly crucial during the planning phase. Suggested guidelines for recruiting and encouraging the involvement of a business advisory board are presented as follows:

1. Select enough members, say 8 to 12, so that if several are absent, a board meeting can still be held. Avoid recruiting too many people, however, for some members may lose interest if they only have restricted opportunities for input.
2. Target mid-management people in large companies and owners/managers in smaller companies. Members experienced in decision making are usually preferred.
3. Select a cross-section of the local community's employers, both in size and type of business.
4. Set meetings about once every 2 months or, at the most, once every month. Remember, most of these people are busy with their jobs and families, and many serve on other similar boards.
5. Spend part of every meeting educating the board on the concept of employment for persons with severe disabilities. Just as important, spend part of every meeting listening to the members.
6. Set precise time limits for each meeting and stick to those limits.
7. Consider having a meeting schedule with variable times; breakfast, lunch, and afternoon times meet the scheduling needs of different members.
8. Develop informal operating procedures so that board members know what is expected of them and how long they are expected to serve.
9. Decide in advance what the ground rules will be about asking members for jobs for the agency's clients. It is *not* a good idea to promise that members will never be approached for job openings; rather, assure members that they will not be pressured into providing job sites.
10. Do ask for referrals and assistance from board members for locating potential job sites.

Select and Hire Staff

Personnel must certainly be selected before initiating any employer contacts or job site training. Agencies are faced with at least three vital issues when employing staff: (1) Will the staff who are responsible for developing the job sites also be expected to provide the job training and facilitation, or will those roles be separated? (2) What are the specific skills required of job development and job training personnel?, and (3) Should staff be specially trained professionals with experience in the human service field, or should they be recruited from outside the field—specifically from employees and supervisors who have experience in the world of work? These important questions have emerged only relatively recently because of the new-found commitment to integrated employment.

Separation of Roles   Perhaps the easiest way to answer the question whether the roles of job developer and job trainer should be performed by the same or different individuals is to follow the maxim: "The more severely disabled a worker is, the more likely it is that the worker will require or benefit from the continuity offered by having the same person develop the job and train him or her for the job." Of course, this is not an iron-clad rule. Many agencies report success using both approaches. However, when the job roles are separated, effective communication between the job developer, the employer, and the job trainer is crucial to success.

The Role of the "Job Coach"   The skills required of personnel representing and training people with severe disabilities include 12 prerequisites:

1. Job coaches must be able to respond to the unique components of a variety of community-based work settings. Dress codes, behavior, jargon, and the particular "culture" of a worksite vary from company to company. Traditional agencies impose a single approximation of what service providers feel is a typical work setting. Job coaches must be careful not to expect community worksites to be similar to sheltered programs.

2. Depending upon the structure of the supported work service, job coaches may be responsible for developing the worksites at which the training and employment will occur. The relationship that one develops with an employer for the purposes of securing a supported work position is quite different from the more typical subcontractor relationship common in sheltered programs.

3. Job coaches must be able to capture all the requirements and needs of a particular job; this activity is often called job analysis. Additionally, for the provision of supported work services, the analysis must include all the related and subtle skills that affect the employee's success in that job.

4. Job coaches might be required to restructure jobs to facilitate the success of a worker with severe disabilities. This task requires negotiation with the employer for approval of any restructuring of work routines.

5. Job coaches must possess systematic training skills sufficient to assist persons with severe disabilities, including persons with inappropriate behaviors and/or accompanying physical limitations, to perform their identified jobs successfully. These skills must include effective strategies

for fading assistance to the least degree possible while maintaining acceptable worker output.

6. Job coaches must be willing to participate actively at the worksite whenever necessary to ensure the meeting of the production criterion, to relieve the worker in emergencies, and to encourage the employee with disabilities to assume gradually increasing job responsibilities.

7. Job coaches must be able to facilitate relationships between the co-workers and supervisors, and the person with disabilities. This activity might well be the most vital one for ensuring lasting success.

8. Job coaches are expected to implement strategies for the provision of training and support by co-workers and supervisors. Job coaches must strike a balance between the needs of the worker with disabilities and the degree of cooperation and assistance available in each individual worksite.

9. Job coaches must provide services on an ongoing basis, for as long as necessary for each assigned worker. To do so, they must develop as many individualized agreements with employers about the form of the ongoing support as there are assigned employees.

10. Job coaches must be prepared to offer assistance and training for needs and skills outside the worksite. Conceivably, these needs may include transportation, financial assistance, resolution of family/personal problems, and similar non-workplace concerns.

11. Job coaches must communicate regularly with the employee and his or her family or residential provider and promote communication between the employer and the person's home. Effective job coaches recognize that a person's work life and life outside work are inextricably connected. Traditional services have often promoted a disconnection of these two fundamental arenas.

12. Job coaches must be able to "troubleshoot" problems that occur in worksites, such as production problems, the method of performing tasks, relationships with co-workers, boredom, frustration, attendance, and the like.

Recruitment of Staff   The final question, that of the direction of recruitment efforts, is interesting for it is a product solely of the integrated employment movement. *Berkeley Planning Associates* noted a growing controversy surrounding this question in their 1985 report to the Office of Special Education and Rehabilitation Services. Currently, there is a lack of consensus whether experienced workshop staff or employees from community settings make better job developers and job trainers.

There is no straightforward answer to this question. Agencies need to hire appropriate personnel to provide the representation and support necessary to assist persons with severe disabilities to be successful on integrated jobs. Certainly, there are exemplary staff members currently employed in work activity centers, residential programs, and institutions. Yet, agencies must carefully screen staff to be sure they are not carrying "unwanted baggage," such as preconceived notions about the employability of people with severe disabilities. Agencies have reported remarkable successes in hiring supervisors and regular employees from community businesses. Star Center in Norwalk, Connecticut, for example, has hired over 10 job coaches directly from local business settings. The agency reports satisfaction with these employees; however, each job coach is offered a comprehensive initial staff development workshop and continuing support. The chief personnel problem at this agency is that job coaches recruited from the business world may be more easily lured away by the higher salaries offered by business employers at the sites in which they are training than human services workers earn. Indeed, this is a potential problem for all effective job coaches and job developers.

6

Practical Prospecting

The pursuit of job opportunities requires that job developers learn to maneuver in what is generally considered to be foreign territory to human service workers: *the world of business.* To be effective, the job developer must commit time and energy to learn the needs, language, customs, and whereabouts of those in business. Consider the advice of Willie Sutton, a renowned safecracker. When asked why he robbed banks, Willie's response was very simple and straightforward: "Because that's where the money is!" Perhaps this seems to be an irrelevant analogy. Yet, if job developers want to be effective, they must learn how to "be" where businesses are.

Prospecting is the phase in the process of employing during which job developers learn about local businesses and decide which ones to contact as they develop an overall view of an area's employment situation. The representational approaches decided upon during the planning phase dictate to some degree the depth and breadth of the prospecting effort. If an employer account strategy is chosen, for example, the prospecting efforts are focused on several high-potential employers. In an employee representative approach, a much larger list of businesses need to be compiled and researched. In any case, the number and types of employers in a given area must be narrowed down to a working list.

After a comprehensive picture of employment is developed and a working list of potential employers has been targeted, information on the targeted companies must be gathered and organized for effective decision making. The success of prospecting efforts is facilitated by efficiently documenting each piece of information learned about an employer and using that information when considering job matches between employers and applicants. This research should also give an indication of the particular language and "buzz words" used by various types of businesses. The prospecting phase is also the best time to begin asking for and using referrals for information and leads for possible employment opportunities. Finally, agency staff should closely examine their own human service vocabulary and replace jargon with plain language.

Although prospecting is presented here as occurring early in the process of employing, it is a never-ending activity for agencies that offer integrated, community-based employment to the people they represent. The approaches described in this chapter should prove helpful for job developers in new agencies, as well as those in established services. Topics considered include targeting, compiling, and organizing information; obtaining referrals; researching prospects; developing a business attitude and vocabulary; and portraying a positive image to potential partners in the business world.

These specific objectives should be accomplished during the prospecting phase:

1. Develop a picture of all the employment opportunities available in a community.
2. Develop a comprehensive working list of potential businesses to contact.
3. Target a call list of employers for initial calls.
4. Research the targeted businesses to obtain information necessary for successful negotiations and matching.
5. Identify already existing linkages that may be helpful in efforts to target more narrowly potential jobs.
6. Develop a system/strategy for compiling and organizing information on employers.
7. Obtain and use referrals that can assist in securing appointments and job opportunities.
8. Develop and *use* a business vocabulary and strive to view employment issues both from a business *and* human service perspective.

DEVELOP AN OVERVIEW OF A COMMUNITY'S EMPLOYMENT PICTURE

A key to the successful provision of vocational opportunities for persons with severe disabilities is developing a thoughtfully selected, continually updated list of employers on whom to call. These employers are chosen because they possess specific characteristics that make their businesses ideal places for people with disabilities to work. However, before such a list can be developed, the job developer must strive to obtain an overall picture of the employment opportunities available in the local area. Failure to do this may result in agencies seeking the same types of employment for all the people they represent or, even worse, may result in fewer jobs being developed due to the narrowness of the job development approach.

To obtain a broad picture, job developers need to be aware of all the various categories of employment in a given community. These job categories generally can be found in most communities:

- Manufacturing: light and heavy
- Service industry: restaurants, hotels/motels, transportation, communication, information, services to individuals and business, such as plumbing, accounting, and lawn care
- Hospitals
- Education
- Schools and universities
- Governmental: state, county, and local offices and services; libraries; parks; federal facilities
- Clerical
- Retail and wholesale outlets
- Construction
- Regional and local employment: agriculture, fishing, timber, and ranching.

Such a list as this can help a job developer ensure that all potential employment areas are being considered. Additionally, the concept of supported work, which allows job developers to identify parts of jobs to be performed by persons with disabilities, opens for consideration new segments of the labor market, such as clerical jobs.

Another effective way to develop a picture of employment in a community is to seek out a comprehensive listing of employers. Various agencies can assist you in targeting the jobs that you wish to pursue. The logical starting point for job developers is the local Chamber of Commerce. Most will readily share their list of local members with agencies that provide employment representation for people with disabilities. However, many of these lists are not comprehensive, but only include the larger and more civic-minded employers. Additionally, most members of the local Chamber of Commerce are private employers. Public employers, such as schools and governmental units, may not be listed.

Some job developers have reported that simply thumbing through the *Business-to-Business Yellow Pages* yields a comprehensive list of a community's employment opportunities. Although the *Yellow Pages* is an instant and easy-to-use reference—the businesses are already divided into categories—this source is far short of ideal. It may not list all the employers in a given area; zip codes are usually not provided, which are necessary for mailing letters of introduction; and the name of a contact person is rarely given. Therefore, additional research on employers found from this source is often necessary. Employer directories, the R & D Center in your area, Private Industry Councils, and local business and civic organizations are all excellent sources for leads.

Is there a comprehensive list of businesses that offers up-to-date and complete addresses, telephone numbers, *and* names of contact persons? Some communities do have such a list. Local offices of the United Way, which can be found in almost every community in this country, usually maintain one of the most comprehensive listings available to employers anywhere. Their lists are often computerized, separate businesses into useful categories and size groupings, contain updated addresses and telephone numbers, and identify specific contact persons, typically those who coordinate United Way donations. Although we do *not* advocate a charity-based approach to the development of job opportunities for persons with disabilities, using such valuable information as the United Way listing is recommended. To turn our back on this valuable resource would be a clear disservice to the people we represent. For example, an agency in Pascagoula, Mississippi, a community of about 40,000 people, reports that the United Way list made available by the local office contained over *2,000* employers. The list contained all the desired information we listed above, *plus* the number of employees who worked at each location. A list of this type could prove very helpful to novice job developers in understanding the range of employment opportunities available in a community.

DEVELOP A COMPREHENSIVE WORKING LIST OF EMPLOYERS

Once the job developer feels comfortable that the agency's view of the local employment picture is comprehensive, the next step is to organize information into a format that is useful for deciding which employers might represent potential places of employment. Because the overall list may contain virtually thousands of possibilities, an organizational strategy is clearly necessary. The following suggestions should prove helpful in developing a working list of potential employers:

1. Target a number of individuals who will initially be represented for employment. One job developer can probably represent *no more* than 20 to 25 people at one time, and many professionals would say that people with severe disabilities require a much smaller ratio.
2. From the vocational profiles of the applicants (see Chapter 5), develop a general listing of the *types* of employment that were indicated as needed and wanted.
3. Plot on a map the places of residence for all the people represented. Draw circles of proximity around individuals or groups of applicants' residences to indicate the limits of transportation access to work.
4. Decide on a sufficient total *number* of employers to comprise the working list. A reasonable number would be four or five employers for every person represented.
5. Begin a matching and listing process that considers: (1) employers close to potential applicants; (2) a cross-section of large to small employers; (3) a cross-section of types of employment that meet the needs and preferences indicated in the vocational profiles of the applicants; (4) employers felt to be "sure bets" for job openings; and (5) any employers identified by family, friends, or others as potential sources.

Keep in mind that the most important goal of prospecting is to identify companies that:

- Are now hiring or soon will be hiring
- Meet the needs of the placement approach you selected (size, type of jobs, location, etc.)
- Have growth potential both in the short and long run
- Offer their employees fairly certain career growth and development opportunities
- Use processes that will require human labor in the foreseeable future

These suggestions are not intended as a prospecting "cookbook." Rather, they are offered to alert you to all the necessary considerations of prospecting. You are encouraged to evolve your own sequence and lists of considerations that suit your particular situation.

It is also important to remember that the specific employers included on a working list will affect significantly other phases in the process of employing. Such issues as whether employers have predominantly entry-level or experienced-based jobs, the typical employee pay schedule, whether most workers work full- or part-time, the range of benefits offered, whether the work is seasonal or year-round, and the flexibility typically allowed by an employer must be considered in the development of the working list. Chapter 10 dealing with quality considerations for employment sites should also prove helpful.

TARGET A CALL LIST FOR CONTACTING EMPLOYERS

In this phase of prospecting a strategy is developed for ordering the working list so that the identified employers can be contacted in a rational and sequential manner. Employers at the top of the list will form the Call List that will be initially utilized by the job developer in obtaining appointments for the ultimate purpose of securing job sites. The most logical strategy to use is to call first on the employers who seem to be the most likely to meet any of a number of important goals. In other words, you are likely to select for first contact such employers as these:

- Employers for whom the job developer has referrals
- Employment sites that appear to match the needs of a targeted individual(s)
- Employers who are felt to be the most likely to agree to provide employment
- Employment sites for which transportation is the least problematic
- Employment sites in reasonable proximity to other existing and potential sites

Again, as with considerations for the development of the working list, we do not suggest a rigid formula-based strategy. The point we want to make is that there should be some thoughtful and logical process for deciding on which employers will be called on first and which ones are to be left to a later date. If this is not done, it is likely that an agency's overall job development efforts will lack clear direction and effectiveness. Furthermore, if there is no rationale for why certain jobs were targeted and developed, the people who are employed are likely to find themselves in ill-matched jobs that they did not want.

A strategy for determining the number of employers to include on the Call List is provided in Chapter 7.

RESEARCH THE TARGETED BUSINESS

After the Call List has been compiled but *before* calls are made on prospective employers, job developers should consider ways of gathering information on the targeted employers. The trick in the prospecting phase is to obtain enough information about the potential employee to make the decisions necessary for developing the working and Call Lists and to have sufficient knowledge to make an initial contact, **without spending too much time finding that information**. Useful and easy-to-obtain information on employers answers the following questions:

1. What type of work does the employer do (production, service, etc.)?
2. Who are the key personnel and decision makers?
3. What is the size of the business—how many employees?
4. Are there seasonal trends? Do they affect employment?
5. What are the typical hiring practices (off-the-street, personnel department, Job Service, employment agencies)?
6. What are key words or jargon used by the company?
7. Is public transportation close by?
8. Are the employees unionized?
9. What is the name of a potential contact person?

This information can be obtained from many of the same sources used to develop the working list of employers. Business, industrial, and trade directories, which are available in most public libraries, are very helpful. Local Chambers of Commerce, employees of the company, referrals, business people in the community, and friends can also offer valuable information. Company literature may be available from the company or from the local employment office. A great deal of information can be obtained from one quick telephone call as well. Newspapers and magazine articles are also sources of information about larger companies. And, finally, do not forget to ask the parents/guardians of applicants, especially if the employer is located in their neighborhood. For additional references on researching employers, we suggest that you refer to *Employers as Partners* by Galloway (1982), which offers an excellent in-depth discussion of precontract planning.

IDENTIFY ALREADY EXISTING LINKAGES

An often-overlooked aspect of successful employment services for persons with severe disabilities is the job developer's perspective about the way in which most people who are not disabled obtain their first job and, in many cases, most of their subsequent jobs. Rather than engaging in a formalized process of systematic job hunting, most people rely on informal contacts available through family and friends to land their initial jobs. However, traditional employment services for persons with severe disabilities often have operated as if the applicants dropped out of the sky! Actually, in some cases they did something close to that, if the applicants came from an institution to an area where they had no family or prior contact. In such cases the job developer is probably justified in acting as the primary representative of the applicant, without attempting to contact the parents of the individual for referrals.

However, the vast majority of persons who are represented for employment opportunities do have a network of family, friends, and acquaintances who can be utilized for providing leads, referrals, and suggestions about possible employment sites. Job developers should seek the assistance of these individuals when considering potential employers and types of employment. Parents have often been heard to comment, "If I had known you had wanted my input, I could have come up with several places where _____ could work!" An important function of prospecting is to communicate to the parents/guardians, family, and friends of applicants that long-term employment in integrated settings can be accomplished when *everyone* participates in finding and supporting employment.

COMPILE AND ORGANIZE INFORMATION

An efficient and well-organized system is needed for filing, storing, and retrieving the quantity of information collected on employers. An aggressive job developer is likely to develop a large number of prospective employers. This information needs to be cultivated, captured, updated, and refined as more and more employers are contacted.

The simplest system is usually the best. If the agency has access to a personal computer, many off-the-shelf data-based filing programs can be used to store employer information in formats that can be devised by the job developer. If there is no access to a computer, an excellent "pencil and paper" system for updating and documenting employer contacts combines an individual card file with a listing of contacts in the order in which they were made. All the preliminary information can be placed on 5" × 7" index cards. The cards can be filed alphabetically, monthly, by status, such as "hot lead," "maybe," or "no go," or by any other system that meets the job developer's needs. An index card system is flexible, efficient, easy to use, and inexpensive. Most importantly, it gives a visual overview for quick reference. Thus, it should contain only the information required for that purpose. See Appendices 1 and 2 for a sample contact listing and card file.

USE REFERRALS

Using referrals is a time-honored business practice that has almost no counterpart in human services. In business, referrals are used as keys to unlock the often tightly closed doors of potential customers. In the human service world, our doors are *supposed* to be wide open. Therefore, procedures and protocol for the use of reference people are somewhat foreign for those of us without business experience. Although it is not a "make-it-or-break-it" prerequisite to have a referral for every employer to be contacted, a well-placed recommendation can certainly help open the door.

Even though the use of referrals is a continuing process, the prospecting phase is the time to develop a habit of asking for and utilizing them. Everyone to whom the job developer—and for that matter, applicants, parents, and friends— talks about employment can provide leads and referrals. Make a point never to leave a discussion about the agency's services or an appointment without asking for a referral. Do not be pushy, but equally important **do not be afraid to ask**! Remember, people in business *expect* to be asked. If an employer is interested in your services, ask for a referral. If an employer is not interested, still ask!

If you find it difficult to ask for a referral, here are some examples of requests that have worked:

- "Can you give me the names of other employers whom you feel might be interested in our services?"
- "Do you think that any of the other local branches of this company might be interested in becoming involved in a project such as this? Whom should I speak to there?"
- "I am calling on the ABC Company next week. Do you know Joe Jones or anyone else there?"

When a referral is obtained, be sure to record who provided the referral and for whom it was intended. A commonly used method is to request the referring individual to write a short note on the job developer's business card. When a job developer is able to use the name of a mutual acquaintance, the prospective employer is much more likely to agree to an appointment. Referrals can also be obtained from parents, friends, and personal business contacts. When making presentations to civic organizations, professional groups, and others, always remember to ask for leads.

Sometimes, a referral is simply not available for an employer contact. Chapter 7 describes how to make a self-reference with a letter of introduction.

DEVELOP A BUSINESS VOCABULARY AND PERSPECTIVE

Most of the people whose job it is to facilitate the employment of persons with severe disabilities were themselves trained in the human service field. Therefore, many of us need to develop a vocabulary and a perspective that will be understood and ac-

Table 6.1.   Translation of common terms

Human service	Business
Competitive employment	Work, jobs
Supported employment	Parts of a job, performance of partial job responsibilities
Payment mechanism	Subminimum wage certificate allowable
Integration	Working around regular workers on regular jobs
Ongoing supports	Long-term employ(er/ee) assistance
Reinforcements	Things the employee likes
Client	Applicant, employee, trainee
Staff	Supervisor, boss, co-workers
IHP	Employee training program, job analysis
Remuneration	Pay, wages, salary
Service	Business, product line
Agreement	Contract
Placement	Employment, work
Evaluation/assessment	Employee appraisal
Agency/program	Plant, restaurant, store
Population to be served	Segment of the labor force
Administration	Management
Down-time	Lay-off, recession, strike
Behavioral outburst	Employee gets mad
Counsel	Talk to
Meaningful relationships	Likes other workers, has friends
Intake	Application process, interview

cepted by business. The following list of questions should be answered affirmatively before making employer contacts. This list is designed to focus your attention on the issues that will enhance your approach used to contact employers and to increase the probability of your success.

- Are you aware of the essential needs that most businesses have in common?
- Can you explain how you will help meet the essential needs of employers and the needs of the people you represent?
- Can you talk the language of the types of businesses you hope to contact through using such words as recruitment, hiring, quality, and productivity?
- Do you know the key words and jargon of the targeted companies?
- Have you translated the human service terms and jargon into plain language that a business person would understand?
- Have you identified and deleted from your presentations the human service agency terms that distract from your message or demean the people you represent?
- Have you closely observed business people who are representative of your targeted employers?

- Do you have a sound rationale for why you chose a particular employer for contact?
- Have you researched the businesses you expect to call upon?

Finally, in addition to developing a business attitude, job developers must strive to adapt to the particular language spoken by employers and to reduce the amount of human service jargon used to describe employment services. One effective way to do so is to make a list of commonly used human service terms and then identify business words that can be substituted for them. Try to use as many business terms as possible in your presentations, and explain the human service terms that you feel obliged to use. Study Table 6.1 and expand it to include other terms you use. Develop a more comprehensive list as contacts, and mistakes, are made.

7

Getting the Appointment

At this point in the process of employing, the job developer must actually venture into the business person's habitat. This step can never be taken lightly. Initial impressions ultimately affect the chances of developing employment opportunities for people with disabilities. This chapter provides information on how to use the call list that was developed during prospecting, the development of media, the techniques of telephoning and making person-to-person contacts, and effective responses to questions raised by employers. All these elements are focused toward a single goal—getting a face-to-face opportunity to discuss the employment of persons with disabilities. It is vital that job developers realize that the chance of securing an opportunity for someone as a result of a "cold" telephone call or brief encounter is practically nil. Both the job developer *and* the employer need the time that a scheduled meeting provides to make informal decisions. How to contact employers and convince them to free up 30 minutes or so of their valuable time for a face-to-face meeting is discussed below. Specifically, the chapter explains how to:

1. Implement a strategy for contacting the employers on the call list.
2. Develop the letters, brochures, and other presentation media that represent philosophy and the services of the agency and serve to introduce the job developer to the employer.
3. Decide on the type of initial contact to use to obtain an appointment for a face-to-face meeting.
4. Develop and use effective telephoning and person-to-person techniques to obtain appointments with employers.
5. Handle the common questions, objections, and "stalls" that are encountered when attempting to secure appointments.

STRATEGY FOR CONTACTING EMPLOYERS

At this point in the process, the job developer must actually start making contact with the employers on the Call List. Should all employers be contacted at once? How many contacts should be attempted at a given time? Is a one-at-a-time approach the best strategy for making contacts? These are questions with which many beginning job developers wrestle.

It is always tough to get started. It is also difficult to know *how* to get started. At this point it is perhaps most important for job developers to understand the following maxim:

The opportunity for persons with severe disabilities to work depends exclusively on your willingness to make employer contacts.

Such a statement as this has value because, if making initial contacts can be stressful even for experienced salespersons, which is well documented in sales and motivational literature, human-service-oriented staff may avoid altogether making such contacts. In order to overcome this natural hesitancy and to help you manage the number of calls that may be made, we suggest a strategy used by sales personnel for making contacts. Before developing a strategy, consider the following factors:

- Job developers have a *right* to call on employers. And, all job developers, even the best, have to face outright refusal at times.
- A sufficient number of employers must be contacted to have a good chance of getting an appointment.
- It is not a good idea to contact too many employers at the same time. Doing so may likely result in scheduling conflicts, and poor follow-up with employers.
- Allow sufficient time to prepare properly for the initial meeting (the next phase) with an employer.

With these considerations in mind, it is now possible to devise a contact strategy that will yield results. The process presented here is the same type of strategy that sales personnel use when they contact employers for sales meetings. Of course, we encourage job developers to develop their own strategy based on their experiences.

1. First week: (a) Target the first five employers on the Call List for contact.
                    (b) Mail letters of introduction, as appropriate, to each employer.
2. Second week: (a) Target the next five employers on the Call List for contact.
                    (b) Mail letters of introduction to them.
                    (c) Make initial contact with all five employers targeted during the first week to secure appointment [total contacted so far is 10].
3. Third week: (a) Target the next five employers on the Call List for contact.
                    (b) Mail letters of introduction to them.
                    (c) Make initial contact to all employers targeted during second week [total contacted = 15].
                    (d) Hold initial meetings with employers contacted during the second week who agreed to meet with you.
4. Fourth week: Repeat steps 3a–d and continue the process in subsequent weeks until a sufficient number of employment opportunities are secured.

It is not our intention to suggest that you adhere to a formula-based approach to job development. People with severe disabilities require more flexibility and individualization to become employed than is offered by any "cookbook" approach. However, because the area of employer contacts is one that so greatly affects the employability of people with disabilities and because human-service-oriented job developers may be reluctant to face potential rejection, a regimen for targeting weekly contacts may prove beneficial to novice staff. Once experience is gained, job developers will evolve a personal style of managing employer contacts that has proven to be effective for them.

A strategy such as the one we have just described will eventually result in job opportunities—*if* the job developer sticks with a schedule of contacts. The number of suggested weekly contacts—five—is based on experience. We consider this to be the *minimum* number of weekly contacts to program for success. Additional contacts can be attempted as long as the job developer does not overextend his or her resources. A large number of unsuccessful contacts could be viewed as a symptom of trying too much, too soon. The job developer experiencing mostly rejections should slow down and examine the targeted employers and the methods and media used, rather than simply increasing the number of weekly contacts. Employers have consistently stated that when human service staff contact them in an effective manner, they really try to meet every reasonable request.

DEVELOPMENT OF MEDIA AND LETTERS OF INTRODUCTION

Almost every employment service for persons with severe disabilities would benefit from more informative and attractive media. There are four types of media utilized most frequently by agencies offering employment opportunities: (1) standardized letters of introduction on an appropriate letterhead to employers; (2) brochures, business cards, and presentation materials; (3) forms and agreements that are a part of the employment relationship with the employer; and (4) information for consumers of the service and their families.

Regardless of how the particular type of media is to be used, keep these important considerations in mind:

- Bad media is infinitely worse than no media at all.
- Start with a flexible format until problems are "ironed out" and the agency has had some experience with response to the media. Being flexible protects against having to discard unsuitable media in which a large investment has been made.
- Balance information with "pizzazz."
- Know exactly how each piece of media will be used and what its purpose is.
- Do not try to meet too many needs with a single piece of media.
- Use an effective and efficient development process such as: Group input➤ Individual development ➤ Group approval➤ Individual final changes.

Standardized Letters of Introduction

In the absence of a referral and in most cases even when a referral is available, a letter of introduction can introduce the job developer to the employer and can pave the way for the telephone call that will be made to get the appointment. It makes sense to spend time developing a single standardized letter that can be sent to all employers, rather than composing individualized letters for each contact. The letter of introduction is recommended in all but the following instances of employer contact:

- If the employer is a good friend of the job developer

- If a formal letter would be viewed as out of place to the employer, as in certain types of work, or in the community, such as in some rural settings
- If the employer was previously contacted through a drop-in visit or through informal contact.

The purpose of the letter of introduction is simply to provide a referral that it is hoped will improve the chances for getting an appointment. The purpose is *not* to ask for a job and *not* to describe the service or to convince the employer to agree to participate; it is to obtain access to the employer. See Appendix 3 for sample letters of introduction.

As you construct your own letters of introduction, keep these content issues foremost in your mind:

- Know the purpose of the letter and stick to it.
- Be careful of labels. Decide how to describe the people to be represented.
- Try to catch the reader's interest.
- Do not try to "sell the service" in the letter.
- Identify your role as meeting the essential needs of employers.
- Do not use jargon.

Matters of format are equally important:

- Keep it short—*never* more than one page and preferably no more than three paragraphs.
- Send an *original copy* only—no copies or "type-ins."
- Insist on *neat typing*.
- *Type* the envelope; do not use labels.
- *Sign* every letter personally.
- Use a *postage stamp*; do not use bulk mail or even metered mail.
- *Double-check* everything—grammar, spelling, addresses, and names.

These last format suggestions help the letter "punch through," to use the jargon of direct mail specialists. If the letter is tossed in the wastebasket by a secretary or by the employer, even before it is opened, it does no good. These suggestions help ensure that your letter of introduction is opened and read by the employer personally.

Brochures, Business Cards, and Presentation Materials

These media are all important because they are the "advertising" and promotional materials an agency uses to establish credibility with employers. Brochures seem to be an obligatory part of a media package of virtually every employment program. Brochures can effectively describe the services offered by an agency, and they can establish a degree of credibility. Yet, they can also be poorly prepared and become rapidly outdated as procedures change. For these reasons, some agencies choose initially to develop a typed fact sheet that can be neatly duplicated on the project's letterhead. A fact sheet format can be a permanent substitute for a brochure, or it can temporarily serve in its place until sufficient money is available for a quality product and until the content of the services has become clear. See Appendix 4 for a sample informational handout.

The exchanging of business cards is so much a typical business practice that every job developer and employment trainer should have personalized business cards to offer to employers, applicants, and interested others. In addition to business cards, the agency should invest in compatible letterhead and envelopes that convey a positive message about the services offered.

Occasionally, an employment project may be associated with a parent agency whose name conveys negative or confusing images to employers. For instance, an employment project managed by an agency called "Helpers of the Handicapped" (not an actual agency, we hope!) would probably want to choose a new name for their employment services. In addition, do not use a traditional human services letterhead that lists service phrases, such as *The Helping Hands Agency*, and the names of the board of directors and large contributors.

Presentation materials for employment projects have typically consisted of slides of people at work. Although slides can be part of good presentation materials, they have limited use. It is not appropriate to walk into an initial meeting with an employer with a truckload of projectors, screens, and slide trays. However, certain slides that have been chosen because of their quality or message can be made into 8" × 10" photographs and used to develop a visual aid for initial meetings with employers. Photographs can be placed in presentation binders, available from any office supply company, in a sequence that is consistent with the description of the services (also see Chapter 8). The presentation binder should have clear vinyl pages to hold photographs, brochures, letters of recommendation from employers, and other forms that are vital to the employment relationship.

Forms, Agreements, and Other Employer-Directed Materials

Media for employment services also include materials that are vital to the relationship established with the employer. These materials should be neatly typed and copied, but they need not be printed. Examples of the kinds of materials a project might have include:

- Agreements of employment, or summary of expectations (Appendix 9)
- Job analysis and data keeping forms (Appendix 16)
- Subminimum wage forms
- Forms required by funding source, such as the JTPA
- Information for applicants and families

These materials are included in a separate category from brochures to reinforce our suggestion that an individual piece of media should not be used to fulfill too many purposes. Agencies can effectively communicate information about the project, the range of services offered, job openings, and project updates through typed and copied flyers. It is much more important that applicants and their families obtain the information than it is to have polished and expensive ways of getting them the information.

ALTERNATIVE APPROACHES FOR MAKING INITIAL CONTACTS

Job developers have three avenues for making initial contacts with an employer in an effort to get an appointment: telephoning, drop-in visits, and casual contacts.

Telephoning

Telephoning is probably the most commonly used approach. Using the telephone to follow up on a letter of introduction or a referral is an efficient and accepted business practice (Table 7.1). Most business people expect to be telephoned before a salesperson calls on them. The following suggestions and comments for securing the initial meeting should be helpful in telephoning employers.

- If a letter of introduction has been sent, be sure to give the letter time to reach the person.
- Remember the purpose of the call is to get the appointment. Do not try to "sell" the employer over the telephone.
- Estimate how much time will be needed for the meeting, request it, and promise to stick to it.
- Be prepared to answer any questions that the employer may ask. Even if you prefer not to do so on the telephone, you may have to answer in-depth questions.
- Do not ask employers if they received your letter. They may say "no" even if they have it. Refer to the fact that you sent it, and proceed from there.
- If you have a relevant referral, open with it.
- Be sure to have your calendar available so that you know when you can meet.
- If the employer asks you to set a time, do it—do not throw this choice back to the employer. Give the impression that you are as busy as the person you are meeting.
- Keep your talking to a minimum. Ask for an appointment and let the employer respond.
- Follow positive calls with a letter confirming the visit.

Drop-In Visits

Drop-in visits are another approach for making initial employer contacts. They have the *same* purpose as telephoning—to obtain an appointment. The value of a drop-in visit is that it is so much more difficult for employers to say "no" face-to-face. However, drop-in visits are limited to a relatively small number of appropriate situations:

- When local customs, familiarity with the employer, or the type of job targeted call for person-to-person contact
- When the person to be contacted is in a publicly visible job so that the job developer can determine a reasonable time for making a contact; exam-

Table 7.1. The telephoning approach for making initial contacts

Advantages	Disadvantages
Efficient	Easier for the employer to say "No" over the telephone
Typically accepted and expected by employers	Job developers may have a reluctance to make "cold calls"
Does not involve the time or financial investment of the other approaches	In certain situations, may be viewed as too "formal"

ples might be grocery store managers, restaurant managers, crew leaders, etc.

- For employers who are in public service positions where such a visit would be acceptable
- If in doubt, call

Drop-in visits are *not* acceptable approaches for employers who are out of public view, even if their employees are highly visible. Such employers expect to be contacted either by telephone or through the next approach, casual contact.

Casual Contact

Casual contact is probably the least known approach to human-service-trained job developers. For business people however, it is a viable avenue of making contacts and securing important appointments. In order to use informal contact as a strategy to get in the door, job developers must make a commitment to be where business people are; in other words, the nonbusiness contexts at which business people congregate. Joining civic clubs, country clubs, health clubs, and other similar organizations is certainly the traditional way of ensuring informal employer contacts. However, less inclined (and less wealthy!) human service job developers can increase the number of informal contacts simply by being aware of the many opportunities that are available through already existing relationships and circumstances. "Talk up" the services of the employment project to friends. Let people know what is required for an employment opportunity and ask for their help. The number of casual contacts will increase proportionately to your efforts.

EFFECTIVE TELEPHONE TECHNIQUES

The effective use of the telephone is a subject that has received a great deal of attention in the business world. We therefore searched the business literature for articles and techniques that were developed expressly for business people making telephone contacts to business people.

Stern and Zemke (1980) suggest that any initial call to an employer use a script. A script for a telephone contact is a brief written outline that:

- Establishes that the desired party is on the line
- States who is calling
- Begins with an opening statement that refers to the letter of introduction and/or a referral
- *Briefly* describes the service offered
- Ends with a request for an appointment

Three sample scripts are included in Appendix 5.

Most telephone calls do not end with a "Yes" at Step 5, because most employers will have questions to ask. They may probe and stall as ways of hedging on setting a time for an appointment. The remainder of the conversation will not follow a strictly prepared script, but rather it should consist of well thought-out responses to the likely questions raised by the employer, with a continuing reminder that what is really wanted is an appointment.

Employers will form a mental picture of the job developer and of the agency based on the letter of introduction, the referrals used, and the telephone call. The image created will, to a large extent, determine the nature of future interactions with the employer. The job developer is at the most risk for refusal during the initial call. The following suggestions are aimed at improving your telephone techniques:

- Write out the script part of the initial call.
- Brainstorm a list of potential questions, objections, and stalls that may be raised by employers. Write down for future reference any unexpected ones that are actually raised by employers.
- Consider effective responses to all potential and actual questions, objections, and stalls.
- Practice the script and responses with another staff person.
- Be positive and calm before the call. Practice speaking in a relaxed manner so that the script sounds natural.
- Try not to ask questions that might result in a negative response, such as "Do you need any new employees?"
- Remember the purpose of the call is only to get an appointment. Do not try to develop a job on the telephone.
- If a call ends without an appointment, think positively. Consider sending a follow-up thank you letter, with literature on the project, and promise to call back in the future.

"Phone-O-Phobia"

Occasionally job developers are reluctant to pick up the telephone and call a potential employer. This comes from what Stern and Zemke (1980) call the "hot stove" syndrome. One too many telephone calls ended in a "No" response, or even worse, the job developer fears that the call *might* end negatively. It is understandable that after a particularly negative experience, most people are apt to become somewhat "telephone shy." If a job developer experiences a prolonged bad streak with no successful outcomes, "phone-o-phobia" might develop. Excuses are found everywhere to avoid picking up the telephone. Although this malady may seem amusing on the surface, it has important implications when it strikes a person who is responsible for developing employment for people with severe disabilities. If the calls do not get made, employment opportunities simply do not get developed.

There are several ways to overcome phone-o-phobia. The first approach is to attack the cause. Consistent rejections experienced by job developers are probably due to lack of sufficient preparation. A remedy is to re-examine carefully the procedures outlined in this chapter. The job developer will most likely discover that a number of vital components had not been considered.

If the caller is prepared but is still reluctant to call, practice in less stressful circumstances may prove helpful. Telephone calls should be role-played first with co-workers, then with friends, and finally with a business contact who is willing to be of assistance.

It would probably help all job developers to become more systematic in their calling. A powerful tool for overcoming telephoning reluctance is to impose a set of procedures that ensures that calls are made. The following steps are especially recommended for people suffering from phone-o-phobia:

1. Decide on the number of contacts that you wish to make on a given day. Post that goal over your desk and ask your supervisor or a co-worker to remind you of your commitment.
2. Target a script or several alternative scripts that you have practiced and with which you are comfortable.
3. Write out your scripts on index cards.
4. Type up a list that you will tape over your desk that contains several reinforcing statements. We suggest the following:

   - "I have a right to call on an employer and develop a job."
   - "An employer may say 'No,' but if that happens, I'll just make another call."
   - "If I don't call, then the people I represent simply can't work."
   - "If I keep calling, someone *will* say 'Yes'."
   - "It's just a person at the other end of the line."

5. Mentally picture yourself calling. Run through a mental rehearsal of possible questions, objections, and tough points.
6. Review your list of responses to the expected concerns of the employer.
7. Ask someone to listen while you *make the call.*
8. If you are successful in getting the appointment, celebrate! But, first, review the call and see what seemed to make the difference and write it down so you can use that technique again.
9. If you did not get an appointment, cheer up! Go over the call with a listener and try to determine the reason why you were not successful.
10. Get ready to make another call.

Your final response to call reluctance as a job developer is to change your approach entirely for getting the appointment. Try using drop-in visits and informal contacts until you reach an appropriate level of confidence needed in dealing with employers.

Avoiding Mistakes in Using the Telephone

Inexperienced job developers are likely to make the telephone errors common to all novice callers. These mistakes routinely result in a lack of success in getting appointments and can lead to phone-a-phobia. Telephone prospecting expert, Thom Norman, lists the following common mistakes in his self-study guide, *Telephone Prospecting for Greater Success*:

- Using an inappropriate tone of voice: It is generally better to act friendly and conversational.
- Speaking at the wrong speed: Avoid sounding as if you are reading a script.
- Talking to the wrong person: Check out the contact's name first.
- Calling for the wrong purpose: Do you want a job opportunity, or do you want a subcontract for the workshop?
- Giving too much information: Remember, all you want is an appointment.
- Not giving the employer reason to listen: Is your opening boring or poorly delivered?

- Not listening to the employer's comments
- Assuming that you understand the employer: Some problems are subtle and complex, so agree to learn about employer concerns.
- Assuming that the employer understands you: Have you used jargon or concepts with which the employer is not familiar?
- Failing to determine the employer's availability to talk

QUESTIONS, OBJECTIONS, AND STALLS

Job developers must expect that employers will try to learn all they can over the phone to avoid having to spend valuable time meeting in person. There will be a friendly battle between you and the employer, with you wanting to say the least possible and get the appointment, and the employer wanting to obtain the most information possible so the appointment will not be necessary.

An effective job developer is prepared to answer the questions, objections, and stalls raised by the employer in such a way that the concerns all are answered, but without fully exploring each point. Remember, the goal is to land a face-to-face meeting. Every job developer should make a list of all the toughest employer concerns *and think through potential answers to them.* The following is a list of questions, objections and stalls that have commonly been raised by employers who were contacted about developing employment opportunities for people with severe disabilities. Responses to selected concerns are listed in Appendix 6.

- "We have no openings at this time."
- "Shouldn't they be in a workshop instead of working?"
- "The work we do here is too dangerous/too complex/too demanding/too . . ."
- "Our employees wouldn't want to work next to people who are mentally retarded."
- "What about my liability? I might be sued if something happens. Isn't that right?"
- "We hire all our employees through the union/the employment office."
- "With so many others out of work in this country, why should we work with you?"

Finding answers to these and other similar questions may be difficult, and it is necessary to deal with each of them in a serious manner. Attempting to offer glib or rote responses will be easily detected by employers. For questions without a straightforward answer, job developers may have to admit that they do not know all the answers, but that they can always offer to do research about it. Furthermore, responses that work well in one part of the nation may not be relevant in other locations. Be particularly careful about quoting solutions, even ideas found in books such as this, without first checking them out locally.

We wish you good luck in getting the appointment. Take this process seriously, and remember that persistence is often the key to success.

8

Cutting a Deal
The Initial Meeting

By now your prospecting, research, telephone calls, and letters have resulted in a face-to-face meeting with a captain of industry. The process of employing now moves into the realm of selling and negotiations. In this chapter, multiple strategies on how to prepare for, present, and successfully close negotiations with employers are described. This phase of job development involves the skillful application of "sales" techniques to: (1) convince the employer of the benefits that can be derived from hiring those individuals whom you represent; (2) facilitate agreement on the conditions of employment, e.g., wages, working conditions, training and follow-up services, etc.; (3) maintain the philosophical and programmatic goals and capabilities of the human service agency. Of course, employers' concerns must also be addressed through careful negotiation.

The initial meeting with an employer is another crucial milestone in the effort to secure employment for persons with severe disabilities. An interesting feature of this meeting is that the best outcome, typically, is that the process of negotiation **continues**, and the worst outcome is an employer's clear **refusal to become involved.** Job developers rarely get a firm "Yes" at the initial meeting, but they might get a firm "No." At the conclusion of a successful initial meeting, the employer will have gained information about what is to be offered and what is sought and the groundwork will have been laid for a relationship that will eventually culminate in an employment opportunity for a person with severe disabilities.

In considering objectives of the initial meeting, job developers must focus on the preparation for it and the techniques required to keep the development process moving in a positive manner. A concise set of objectives for this phase is:

1. Plan thoroughly for the initial meeting, focusing on fulfilling all its critical components.
2. Develop a proposed outline and "flow" for the meeting. Central to this objective is the initiation of a relationship upon which interactions can be developed.
3. Get ready, practice for, and conduct the initial meeting after having identified the key decision makers.
4. During the meeting, determine the employer's interest by recognizing and dealing with the negotiation stance used. A "Yes/No" decision should *not* be sought at this time. The main task is to explain your services and why the employer should want to be involved with what you are doing.
5. Negotiate a follow-up meeting, establish a process for handling the follow-up meetings and negotiations, and obtain appropriate referrals to other employers.

PREPARATION FOR THE INITIAL MEETING

Job developers must invest energy and time in preparing for their first meeting, as you did when prospecting and making initial contacts. *Before* having a face-to-face meeting with an employer, pay attention to these two areas: (1) ensuring a successful meeting and (2) ten essential considerations for a successful meeting.

Ensuring a Successful Meeting

The initial meeting with a prospective employer offers you the first real opportunity to explain *in detail* the services you wish to offer. Remember, the business world is an extremely pragmatic marketplace; it operates on the principle of mutual benefit. Unfortunately and typically, the "old boy" network is denigrated by those on the outside who fail to realize how it creates opportunities that otherwise would be unavailable. Mutual benefit means that *both* parties in a transaction win. Thus, it helps you create the right atmosphere for the initial meeting if you do not simply and solely ask for favors, but rather, emphasize that the agency and the people you represent can also offer a valuable service to the employer.

In addition to having the right focus, the initial meeting should have the right "feel." The following points should help you accomplish that goal:

- Get to know your contact better by beginning the meeting with a nonbusiness topic of conversation. Most business people prefer to have friendly and rather informal meetings, rather than sit through stiff and formal presentations. Keep the conversation goal-directed but pleasant.
- Scrupulously limit your presentation to the agreed-upon time. Develop a reputation as someone whose word can be trusted—there is no more valuable a currency in the business world than time. If you arrive at 1:40 P.M. (on time, of course!) having said that you need 20 minutes, then leave as the clock strikes 2:00 P.M.
- Try to be an unexpected surprise to employers by being a human service worker who is *prepared*. Have your presentation and materials prepared, organized, and professionally polished.
- Dress in the manner expected by the company. Reflect the code of their workplace, rather than your workplace.
- Be consistent in presenting your philosophy of the employment of people with severe handicaps. If you say one thing, yet reflect another perspective entirely by how you say it, you will be described as one who speaks from both sides of the mouth—though not, of course, until you have left the office! More importantly, doing so may cause irreparable harm to the people you represent.
- Identify yourself with the business world. Think their thoughts, use their language, analyze problems from their perspective, *but* always remember whom you primarily and ultimately serve.
- Be enthusiastic and confident—but in a calm manner. Although you are "selling" the services of those you represent, you do not need the employer to think of you in the same light as the Girl Scout cookie seller. You must be sensitive to the subtleties involved in employment decisions.
- Be able to recognize and deal with as many as possible of the different types of negotiations. This is not feasible until you gain an education in the

world of business, industry, and commerce. And, an education always has to be earned. It is always tough learning something new, so recognize that until you gain that education you will clearly appear naive to those "in the know." Are we saying, try to reflect some humility? Yes, yes, and yes again!

Job developers must also deal with the pressures of achieving closure on employment sites. Although a reasonable amount of pressure is probably helpful, we advise that you do not try to accomplish too much, too soon. Because it is highly unlikely that a lasting and valuable relationship can be sealed in a single 20- to 30-minute meeting, it is counterproductive to attempt to make that your goal. The typical result of a "get-it-all-done-today" attitude is a "No, thanks" response by the employer. It is also likely that the relationship being negotiated will require the eventual coordination and involvement of several areas of the business—personnel, production, management and, possibly, employee training. Therefore, it is usually not a good idea to press for a "Yes" or "No" answer during the first meeting. Rather, try to keep the meeting on a positive note. Of course, if the employer indicates that a deal is imminent, go for it! Just remember that there is a great deal of information that must be imparted before you have laid a stable foundation for successful employment opportunities.

Ten Essential Considerations for a Successful Meeting

The initial meeting with an employer should be simple and straightforward. However, in order to accomplish that simplicity, you must orchestrate multiple variables that affect the outcome of the meeting. Ten essential considerations for a successful meeting are:

1. Time required for the meeting
2. Names of contacts
3. Jargon/business language
4. Research
5. Gathering information
6. Getting referrals
7. Conditions to expect
8. Materials
9. Dress
10. Attitudes

Time Required for the Meeting   The amount of time requested is perhaps one of the most critical factors in determining whether an employer agrees to meet with you. If too much time is requested, say 45 minutes or an hour, many employers may simply be unwilling to meet. Time means money for business people. On the other hand, if an unreasonably short time is requested, from 5–10 minutes for instance, it will be impossible to cover all the points that need to be discussed. Additionally, the employer might be skeptical of such a request, knowing that the meeting will probably run longer. Based on our experience, we suggest that a reasonable time to request for the initial meeting is 25 minutes. This amount of time is almost 30 minutes, but it sounds considerably shorter, just as $99 seems significantly less than $100. Most importantly, it is possible to make an effective initial presentation in this time frame. When the time is up, be prepared to leave. An effective way to draw attention to the fact that the time commitment has been met is to say to the employer, "The time we agreed to is up; however, if you have any more questions I would be happy to stay and answer them."

Names of Contacts   Everybody at the employer's place of business is a potential ally or enemy. Take a tip from successful business people and find out the names of the secretary, the person behind the front counter, key employees, and others who might affect the employer's decision to participate. Often, being able to remember the secretary's name is just the "door opener" that is needed to have your calls returned. Recalling a person's name is always a compliment. Remember, many business leaders have chosen their secretaries because they trust their judgment; thus, the business person may well ask his or her secretary to confirm or refute an initial opinion of you. This small investment of effort needed to impress a secretary can yield important results.

Jargon/Business Language   Using business jargon or buzz words can be positive *if* they are used correctly. For example, clothing manufacturers refer to themselves as being in the "needle trades." Hotels and motels may refer to their building as a "property." Correct use of jargon indicates a level of awareness and preparation that will be respected by the employer. However, do not throw buzz words around randomly. If in doubt, leave them out. The best way to research business jargon is to *listen* to employers. As experience is gained with certain types of businesses, job developers will be able to use words and phrases confidently that are commonly used and accepted.

Research   Before attending the initial meeting, have at least a general idea of the employer's line of business and the type of jobs that are performed. In preparation for this initial meeting, information that you compiled during prospecting is studied in order to find out as much as possible about the company, develop a meeting format to accomplish your objectives, and outline and practice the content of the presentation. The prospecting research is often sufficient.

If you have been referred by someone, then ask your referral source to give you information about your prospective contact, their company, and the industry of which it is a part. Trade journals in the company's own lobby readily trigger up-to-date conversational topics. Plan to arrive 5 to 10 minutes early, but not much more, to take advantage of this sort of information and the impressions you can gather by being there.

There is some important information that you will not be able to obtain in advance. Prepare questions, to be asked during the initial meeting, that will elicit the necessary information. Yet, try to ask questions in a way that does not give the impression that you are unprepared. That is, try to ask questions from an informed, rather than a naive, position.

Example: *"Mrs. Jones, I understand that your plant is a leader in the manufacture of breaker boxes. Do you usually have more job openings in fabrication or in assembly?"*

—or—

"I understand your plant is a union shop. Is the union the United Textile workers, or is the Amalgamated Clothing and Textile Workers?"

Gathering Information   A close cousin to research is the activity of gathering information once the job developer is at the job site. A host of impressions, names, jargon words, job titles, and facts must be remembered in order to make a quality decision for employment. An Employer Information Sheet (Appendix 7) is recommended as one way for collecting this quantity of important information. A note pad can also be used for jotting down impressions and keeping a narrative log of meetings. Using an open pad for note taking is acceptable while meeting with an employer. However, refrain from filling out the information sheet until you are back at your office.

Obtaining Referrals   This component is so important that it is built into the "flow" of the initial meeting. Examples of ways to ask for referrals are described in Chapter 6. The timing of asking for a referral is crucial. It is usually best to wait until the meeting is nearly over and several "next step" questions are being covered. If the subject is raised too soon, it may cloud the purpose of the meeting. Above all, do not be shy about asking for a referral. Act as if it were an expected part of the meeting. If a referral is given, be sure to establish the ground rules for using the referral and stick to them; for example, can the referrer's name be used?, should a particular person be contacted?, or will the referrer agree to call the person referred?

Conditions to Expect   This is perhaps the most sensitive component of the initial meeting. Under what conditions will the meeting be held? During the first employer contact you should strive to communicate that a private business meeting is desired. Doing so is not as easy as it might sound. If certain conditions are too clearly stipulated by the job developer, the employer may feel insulted at being instructed on how to hold a business meeting. However, there are conditions under which an effective presentation is impossible. A job developer may be asked to meet in a noisy lobby when it is clear that the person has a more private meeting place available. This is a subtle but clear message about the employer's feelings concerning the meeting. In such cases, the job developer is justified in saying, "It looks as though I caught you at a bad time. I'll call you back later and we can set a time when we can meet more privately." Experience has shown us that many times such a statement results in the employer immediately suggesting a more private place to meet. If not, then at least 30 minutes of your time was not wasted.

It is important for us to remember that some employers routinely hold business meetings in rather public places. Many restaurant managers, for instance, ask to meet in the dining area during the morning or mid-afternoon slow period. Such customary meeting places should be considered appropriate unless you feel that efficient communication is simply not possible.

Materials   Effective presentation materials help express the business-like attitude of the agency and the service. Your prepared materials also offer valuable information for your contact. They assist the employer in deciding whether to give any additional consideration to offering a job opportunity to individuals represented by your agency. Presentation materials appropriate for the initial meeting are business cards and brochures, letters of referral, a presentation portfolio of photographs of people who have been employed through your agency, and other such informative materials. Note that slide presentations, videotapes, and overhead transparencies are *not* included on this list. These materials take too much time to set up and use for the initial meeting. Furthermore, the sight of someone coming through the door with an armload of audiovisual aids might be an immediate turnoff for the employer as they quickly realize that the commitment for a 25-minute meeting could never be met. A key question to ask yourself is, "Do business people use this type of sales material?" If the answer is "Yes," then and only then consider using it. Slides, overhead transparencies, and videotapes may be helpful and appropriate in follow-up meetings, but at a later date (see Chapter 9). When you do plan to use audiovisual materials, be sure that your contact is aware of the type of presentation you have in mind. You may even want to suggest that a group of people view the presentation as a means of informing various departments about your proposal.

It is critical that your materials appear professional and that they convey exactly the same philosophy of employment as your letter of introduction, telephone call, and the verbal content of your presentation. Unsophisticated approaches are viewed unfavorably by those in business so leave anything that smacks of "home movies" at home! If you are unsure how the presentation or the materials will go over, then pick out the most cynical, uncharitable, and pessimistic person in your agency and demand that they be candid about your presentation!

Dress   Dressing appropriately is a symbolic way of establishing a common ground between the job developer and the business world. The type and style of clothing to wear to the initial meeting depend upon the person with whom the meeting is held and the type of work the company does. Meetings with company managers, owners, and personnel directors invariably require a coat and tie— preferably a suit—for men and equally formal attire for women. The Golden Rule in this case is: If it is expected for (and *by*) them, then it is equally expected of you.

For more informal sites, say a restaurant or a service station, more casual dress clothes are appropriate—a shirt and tie for men and "office" clothes for women. However, even if strictly informal work settings are visited, such as construction sites or outside work crews, dress should never be too informal. Wearing work clothes and jeans may send the wrong impression to the employer. The perception by the employer that the job developer is capable of negotiating and making business-like decisions may be compromised if the visitor is too closely identified with line workers.

Attitudes   Business decisions are often made as much on the basis of feelings and symbols as on facts and information. Realizing this, the job developer needs to conform to the conditions that are comfortable for business people. One way to do that is through dress; another is to develop and project a business attitude through observing, practicing, and experiencing the procedures and practices of business people. Here are some ways you may do this:

- Aim at translating terms and concepts from human service language to business language.
- Use business language with your colleagues.
- Role-play business presentations with your colleagues.
- Join and attend professional and civic organizations that are frequented by business persons, such as the American Society for Training and Development, Chamber of Commerce, or your state's manufacturer's and retailer's associations.
- Observe closely the language and behavior of business people in the community and during presentations.

The investment in these activities is minimal, but the typical return is phenomenal!

OUTLINE AND "FLOW" FOR THE INITIAL MEETING

The actual content of the meeting depends on decisions made by the agency during the planning stage. Job developers must be thoroughly versed in the range of services offered to employers and employees, the training techniques utilized, and the people who are represented. It helps, however, to have a framework in which to present this information. The following ten steps describe the flow of a typical meeting:

1. "Break the ice" with informal conversation. Not everyone feels comfortable chatting informally, but it can be an effective strategy to create a friendly atmosphere. Keep this part of the meeting brief; remember, you only have 25 minutes.
2. Explain who you are and how you were referred. Be ready to explain why you chose that particular company.
3. Discuss your reasons for being there: what you want, who you represent, what you can offer, what is expected of the employer, and past performance data.
4. Allow for questions from the employer.
5. Ask questions.
6. Determine the employer's negotiation position (See the section on negotiations).
7. Consider whether to ask for a job or to ask for another meeting.
8. If numbers 6 or 7 are positive, then establish lines of communication; decide who is to be the continuing contact person, when it is best to call, and similar considerations.
9. Request a plant tour for a future date (see Chapter 9).
10. Ask for a referrral.

PREPARATION: PRACTICE FOR HOLDING THE INITIAL MEETING

Although experience and success make each subsequent meeting easier, initially, preparation and practice of the meeting content are necessary. We suggest that you follow a sequence of steps, such as the one outlined below, so that you can gain sufficient confidence and polish.

1. Rehearse your presentation with a co-worker or on audio- or videotape. Play back the tape and check for length of time, points covered, objectives met, vocabulary, and flow.
2. Leave yourself plenty of time to get to the meeting. If you are early, you can either drive around, rehearse in your car, or use the time effectively at the company site (see steps 4 and 5).
3. Before you leave your car at the time of your appointment, make sure that your business card is crisp and handy and that you have a pen, note pad, calendar, and presentation materials. Go over your premeeting checklist, and then relax for a minute or so.
4. Announce yourself appropriately to the reception person, who will vary

widely depending upon the type of business. Wherever they are available, browse through any trade journals and company literature; note their titles for future reference.

5. If there is a secretary or receptionist, consider asking a few questions while you are waiting. For instance, it is appropriate to confirm the correct title of your contact. The people you will routinely be dealing with are upwardly mobile individuals, and you will want to be familiar with their latest promotion. You might also want to introduce yourself and find out the names of people who generally receive visitors.

A checklist that lists all the critical considerations for the initial meeting can be a valuable tool for job developers who are just getting started. Figure 8.1 is a general framework for a personalized list to be compiled by individual job developers.

All the preparation, practice, and research finally culminate in a face-to-face meeting with an employer. If the job developer has invested the energy and time to cover the topics discussed in this and the preceding chapters, the meeting should have a good chance of resulting in employment opportunities for persons with disabilities. However, the introductory handshake is only one of the necessary steps in a continuing process. The initial meeting presents the job developer with an entirely new set of challenges.

DEALING WITH NEGOTIATIONS

In *Employers As Partners*, Galloway (1982) described his own conceptualization of the negotiation process developed by Michael Schatzki (1981) in the book, *Negotiation: The Act of Getting What You Want*. Schatzki said, and Galloway emphasized, that the key to success in striking a bargain is to be able to anticipate the kind of negotiation to be entered. This is of particular importance to job developers because securing an employment opportunity for a person with severe disabilities results from a negotiated process.

To assist in the recognition of the subtleties of negotiation, Schatzki describes an employer's three different responses to a presentation:

Oh-Boy!   *Show-Me*
Negotiations   *Negotiations*

Oh-No!
Negotiations

The valuable feature of Schatzki's model is that understanding the particular negotiation stance chosen by an employer is about as simple as the names imply. To clarify these three positions, consider some descriptions and examples taken from everyday life.

Oh-Boy!

In this stance both parties stand to win if they go through with the deal. Imagine that you want to buy a house, and you see your dream home advertised in the newspaper

---

Initial Meeting Checklist

1. ____ Is your business card crisp and easily accessible?
2. ____ Do you have your presentation materials handy and neat?
3. ____ Have you prepared mentally (practice, relaxation, "psych-up," review)?
4. ____ Are you dressed in a manner to make a positive impression?
5. ____ Do you know how to ask for the privacy that you need?
6. ____ Is your presentation concise, clear, and well-organized?
7. ____ Have you practiced your presentation?
8. ____ Do you know how long your presentation will take?
9. ____ Do you know what information you need from the company?
10. ____ Do you know how you will ask for and record that information?
11. ____ Do you know how to request a tour and when to schedule it?
12. ____ Do you have the name(s) and title(s) of your contact and other important employees?
13. ____ Have you thoroughly planned for how to respond to the usual questions, objections, and stalls?
14. ____ Do you have a complete packet of the materials to be left with the employer?
15. ____ Do you have the name of the person who referred you?
16. ____ Do you know how to ask for a referral?
17. ____ If you get a "Yes," do you know when services can start?
18. ____ Have you received, and committed to memory, a general outline of the initial meeting?

Figure 8.1.   Initial meeting checklist.

for $100,000. That is more than you want to pay, so you decide to offer $90,000. When you call on the owner, you find that the price has been reduced to $85,000, for quick sale. You check out the house and immediately decide to buy. This is an example of an *Oh-Boy!* negotiation. Both parties got what they wanted because the deal, from each party's perspective, contained everything that was needed.

Show-Me

In this scenario, one party clearly has much to gain, but the other party is not so sure that it is a good deal for them. Imagine that you have been approached by an insurance salesperson who claims that you can make a lot of money by cashing in your whole life insurance policy and converting it to term insurance and investing the difference in mutual funds. You have never heard of this approach, but you might be interested because you like the thought of making money. However, you have faithfully paid on your whole life policy for 15 years. In this situation, the insurance salesperson clearly has a commission to gain, but it is not clear whether you gain. In

order to complete the deal, the salesperson must deal with a *Show-Me* stance of negotiation on your part, and the *Show-Me* stance must be converted to an *Oh-Boy!* position before both parties can win.

Oh-No!

In this form of negotiation one party has a great deal to gain, and the other is not at
all interested in the deal. Imagine that the telephone rings and a fast-talking person
begins discussing the marvelous things that the new "Wonder Product of the 1990s,"
the Cyclone vacuum cleaner, can do. "And it's only $499.99 or $19.99 per month for
3 years! There's even easy credit acceptance if you have your major credit card
ready." But, you realize that you just bought a trusty upright for $80, and it is doing
just fine—and besides, you hate telephone sales pitches. You say, "No, thanks!" and
hang up. This is an example of *Oh-No!* negotiation. There was no way that you were
willing to move even to a *Show-Me* position. The caller made an error by not probing
for your needs and by not offering a compelling reason for you to change your mind.

In the process of contacting employers, job developers can expect to encounter each of these stances of negotiations. By considering the employer's viewpoint, it
is possible for you to be better prepared for the initial meeting.

The position most likely to be taken by employers when contacted about employment opportunities is the *Show-Me* stance. Employers will want to know who
the people are, why you feel that they would be good workers, and the answers to
countless other questions. They may also use objections and stalls as a way of putting
off making a decision about offering a job. Thorough preparation is required in order
to answer effectively all the employer's questions and convert the *Show-Me* stance to
Oh-Boy! However, it is not necessary to seek a "conversion" during the initial meeting.
That is a job best left for subsequent meetings. The primary goal of the initial meeting
is to identify the stance chosen by the employer and to decide what to do next.

Occasionally a job developer immediately encounters an *Oh-Boy!* negotiation
stance from an employer. This may happen in any of several ways. It is possible that
during the initial contact, on the telephone or in person, the employer says, "This is
great! I need some workers right away. Bring someone round tomorrow." Or, half-
way through the initial meeting, the employer might say, "I've heard enough, this
sounds great! When can you start?" Both of these situations, as nice as they might
seem, can present real problems to the job developer. In order to have a true *"Oh-
Boy!"* stance, both parties need to have all the facts. Employers may respond
positively without being aware of the flexibility and conditions that a person with
severe disabilities may require in order to be employed successfully. If a job developer feels that the *Oh-Boy!* position has been arrived at too fast, we suggest that
you make an attempt to slow down the negotiations until all the information is on
the table. Of course, when job developers are in a desperate situation for employment openings, this can be *very difficult* to do!

Sometimes it is difficult to determine if an employer's stall represents a *Show-
Me* or an *Oh-No!* stance. As long as the employer is not giving an outright "No," it is
probably worth pursuing for a while. A confusing *Oh-No!* negotiation can arise in
situations where a mid-level manager of a company gives a clear "No," and later a
higher-level employee or the owner hears of the project and wants to become involved. This sticky situation needs to be handled very carefully, because the person
to feel the real impact of the change is the person who is disabled. Also, we do not

suggest that job developers try to convert an *Oh-No!* stance to a *Show-Me* by going over the head of the initial contact person. Inevitably, bad feelings will result from such a move.

The least likely stance encountered by job developers is the *Oh-No!* type. One by-product of effective targeting is a reduction in the incidence of *Oh-No!* confrontations. Yet, there are certainly employers in every locality who do not even want to discuss the employment of persons with severe disabilities. It is probably best to try to change this type of attitude by the quality performance of workers in other businesses, rather than by confrontive negotiation or attempting a "re-education" of the errant business person.

Actions speak louder than words—let the success of those you represent at other business settings speak for itself. Try hard to avoid getting on a soapbox, and certainly think twice if you see yourself turning into a business person's educator proselytizing about the intrinsic value of all humankind, including those labeled "handicapped." A "bleeding heart" approach might elicit door-to-door donations for charity, but it certainly does not score jobs.

Perhaps the best response to an *Oh-No!* stance is to thank the employer for the time you have taken, leave as graciously and professionally as possible, send a packet of information with a cover letter if the refusal occurred over the telephone, and move on to other employers. Reluctant employers can be contacted at a later time, perhaps 6 months or a year later. It is possible that conditions, attitudes, or personnel will have changed by then.

Careful attention to these established principles of negotiation generally leads to successful conclusions. Through experience, both positive and negative, job developers become adept at selecting negotiation strategies, judging the success of their application, and developing hybrid strategies that are even more effective than those described in this chapter. In any case, it is vital for the job developer to savor every "victory" and to regroup whenever positive outcomes are not immediately realized.

NEGOTIATING FOR A FOLLOW-UP MEETING AND ESTABLISHING PROCEDURES FOR FOLLOW-UP

It should be clear from these discussions on various types of negotiations that it is very likely that additional meetings will be necessary to secure an employment opportunity from most employers. When time is running short at the initial meeting and it seems that a *Show-Me* relationship is emerging, the job developer can close the meeting successfully by landing an opportunity for a subsequent meeting. Several strategies are effective for this type of closure:

- The job developer can take the lead and suggest directly that another meeting is warranted and ask if a date can be set.
- A tour can be requested, which can serve as a way of returning to the company. The more often a job developer can get into a place of business, the greater the chance of landing a job.
- Materials, such as the portfolio of photographs, can be left with the employer to share with others. Because it is necessary to return to pick up the material, it may be possible to discuss employment prospects further at that time.

- The job developer can offer to make a multimedia presentation to a number of managers and employees. This can be particularly attractive to an employer who is concerned about the reactions of co-workers to hiring people experiencing severe disabilities.

It may seem that some of the approaches we have described for getting another appointment are somewhat "sneaky." However, these all are typical and accepted business procedures. In order to be successful, the job developer *must* keep the process moving in a positive direction toward final closure—the development of an employment opportunity. This is not a time for wavering. If an employment site looks like a good place for a person to work, any reasonable and moral procedure should be considered to make it happen.

If an employer agrees to meet again, the job developer needs to establish some procedures agreeable to both parties. Keep in mind these commonly encountered issues:

- Carefully set the date and meeting time. The follow-up meeting may need to be longer. The job developer now has some extra credibility to ask for additional time.
- Make sure you know the points on which the employer wants additional information. If you are not sure, then ask!
- Be sure that a tour is on the itinerary. It is necessary for identification of jobs and for making job creation observations.
- Try to target other employees who need to be present at the follow-up meeting, such as direct supervisors and key co-workers.
- If another person will be providing the job training, let the employer know that the job trainer will be attending the next meeting. Also, do not forget to inform the job trainer of the meeting date and time.
- And certainly do not fail to send a note of thanks to the employer that also reminds him or her about the follow-up meeting.

9

Sealing the Deal with Follow-Up Negotiations

This chapter discusses the many features that still remain unfinished even after a successful initial meeting with an employer: activities necessary for closing a deal with an employer, the importance of business-like follow-up procedures, how to handle the objections and stalls that you are likely to meet, touring the employment site, some creative approaches to follow-up negotiations, how to target a job, different types of employment agreements, and an alternative approach to developing a relationship with an employer. Effective follow-up is essential if the job developer is to cement the deal with an employer after the initial presentation has been made.

Follow-up meetings differ from the initial meeting in several important ways:

- Additional appointments are much easier to negotiate. The main barrier to be overcome is finding a convenient time to meet with the employer.
- They generally last longer. More time is required to discuss and answer questions. However, it is a good idea to limit the time to no more than 1 hour, so as not to impose on the employer.
- As relationships develop, meetings generally become less formal. This is positive, but keep in mind the importance of maintaining a professional, business-like relationship.
- You may elect to show slides, videotapes, or overhead transparencies at a follow-up meeting. However, be sure to inform the employer if you wish to do so.
- You need to ask very specific questions and give specific information. Write down the important points and double-check them for accuracy. The cardinal rule is: **Never promise what you can't deliver.**
- More people become involved in the process of employing. You need to get to know the management and the lines of communication and responsibility. The employer needs to get to know the employment trainer and any other people who may be involved from your agency.

Finally, establish your competency and professionalism and the competency of the people you represent.

The bottom line for follow-up negotiations is to secure an integrated employment opportunity for a person with severe disabilities. The objectives that are necessary to accomplish that goal are:

- Offer in-depth information about the training, facilitation, and support procedures that are to be offered to the employer.
- Learn about and assess the company.
- Handle the negotiation stance taken by the employer.
- Target and define the job to be performed.
- Gain approval for employment and set a date for the job analysis and hiring.
- Finalize an agreed understanding with the employer to list expectations or by signing a formal employment agreement.
- Consider an alternative approach for making contacts with difficult-to-reach employers.

DEVELOP CONTACTS PROFESSIONALLY

Follow-up is an expected and necessary business practice. It is a good idea to send a first-class letter within 48 hours of your presentation to thank your contact for meeting with you, to send any promised materials, and to confirm the date for the next meeting. See an example of a follow-up letter in Appendix 8.

It is imperative that you remember, for use in your follow-up contacts, relevant names and titles mentioned during the initial presentation. Make sure you address your contact by the title reflecting his or her latest responsibility. An outdated title given on your follow-up letter could be taken negatively. If a telephone call was requested, be sure to call at the proper day and time.

OFFER IN-DEPTH INFORMATION

Follow-up meetings offer the job developer the opportunity to explain fully the procedures used to ensure the successful employment of a worker with severe disabilities. The following topics may be discussed in a follow-up meeting:

- Concept of job creation and supported work
- Who the prospective employee is, where he or she is currently employed, and past employment experiences
- Initial and possible long-term flexibility concerning working hours and wages
- Agreement to meet certain "essential needs" of the employer
- Way in which the job analysis and training are to be performed
- Long-term supports to be offered to the employer and the employee
- Other agencies that may have an interest in or affect the employee's work, such as vocational rehabilitation, the Social Security Office, or the residential program
- Responsibilities expected of the employer and co-workers
- Past experiences of employment of persons with severe disabilities, e.g., information on quality, training time, relationships with co-workers
- Brief information on the flexibility that may be required in order for the employee to be employed (e.g., if the potential employee has inappropriate behaviors or physical limitations, the accommodations that may be

necessary can be discussed. It is *not* recommended that the job developer discuss every conceivable detail of a potential employee's problem. Doing so may create unfair expectations and may also halt the negotiations for that person's employment.)

Some agencies capture all the general information that needs to be communicated to an employer on a fact sheet or Summary of Expectations (see Appendix 9 for a sample). This information can be presented early in the negotiations and can be amended, as necessary, before final agreement.

Employers also need to be made aware of the selling points of the proposed relationship, which the job developer offers as reasons for the employer to become involved. Once again, Galloway (1982) presents a useful strategem for sorting out the various selling points for employment of persons with disabilities. He suggests that the positive features and services of the proposed employment relationship be assigned to one of three categories:

1. *Inherent Selling Points*: These are positive features or services of the relationship that are automatically guaranteed, no bargaining is necessary to get them.
2. *Sweeteners*: These are additional features or services that might not be expected by the employer *but* that may increase the attractiveness of the deal.
3. *"Hole Cards"*: These are features or services that are not typically offered to employers, are costly, and are used only as a last resort to secure an opportunity. The overuse of "hole cards" may cause a negative perception about the inherent quality of the feature or service being offered.

Using this framework, a job developer can separate the range of services developed during planning and other features into useful bargaining points. A presentation plan might look something like this when representing persons with severe disabilities.

1. *Inherent Selling Points*
    (a) The employee meets "essential needs" of the employer.
    (b) Quality is always the first consideration.
    (c) Employer has the final right of approval for all processes used.
    (d) Long-term support is available to the employee.
    (e) On-site trainer performs job analysis and initial training.
2. *Sweeteners*
    (a) On-site trainer provides assistance to co-workers in general training skills.
    (b) Step-by-step procedures, useful for all new employees, are developed for every job performed.
    (c) Transportation is initially provided for the new employee.
    (d) A bonus is available to an identified current employee to function as an assisting co-worker for the new employee.
3. *"Hole Cards"*
    (a) The trainer ensures production at a given rate until the new employee learns the job.
    (b) The agency pays the employee's first month's salary while the job is learned.

(c) Long-term transportation is provided, i.e., in a supported work model.

LEARN ABOUT AND ASSESS THE COMPANY

In addition to imparting information to the employer necessary for securing an opportunity for a person with severe disabilities, the job developer needs to find out as much as possible about the company. This information allows the job developer: (1) to target a job, or possible job modifications, that the new employee will perform; (2) to learn about the "culture" of the company—the rules, procedures, degree of flexibility available, and interactional styles of co-workers; (3) to assess the general suitability of the site for a person represented by the agency to work; and most importantly, (4) to make the final determination about the suitability of the match between the employment site and the potential employee (see Chapter 10).

The job developer can learn this information through several avenues:

1. Ask questions during meetings with the employer.
2. Observe the manner in which employees interact and the way that procedures are followed.
3. Take a comprehensive tour of the employment site.
4. Talk to employees and others who have information about the company.

Undoubtedly, the most direct way to obtain information is to ask questions of the employer. A list of questions should be compiled by the job developer to fill in all gaps of information. Although the actual list will vary from agency to agency, detailed information is commonly required on these subjects:

*   Information requested on the Employer Information Sheet (see Appendix 6)
*   Exact specifications or expectations that the employer has for the job, including productivity, range of responsibilities, quality expectations, etc.
*   Way that reimbursement will be handled
*   Company's probationary policies, employee appraisal, and grievance policies
*   Names of all the immediate supervisors and co-workers
*   Chain of command in management
*   Acceptable procedures for handling minor and major problems
*   Requirements for agency trainers, substitute trainers, and visitors
*   Photographic restrictions
*   Security and safety procedures

Recording the information obtained during the initial meeting is vitally important because making the decision to continue negotiation with the company will be based upon the results of this meeting. An accurate account of facts, impressions, and possible problems discovered during the initial meeting is essential.

The atmosphere of the follow-up meetings allows direct questioning of the employer. It is appropriate to write down the responses at the same time, rather than waiting as you did in the initial meeting. The system used to record the information should be as simple as possible. An effective, inexpensive, and very simple system for recording information is to use the Employer Information Sheet along with a notebook for each employer negotiation. The information sheet can be used for filing purposes and quick reference, and the notebook can contain all the responses and observations made during negotiations. Notebook contents can later be shared with the employment trainer for reference. See Appendix 9 for sample memos containing such observations.

Your style of questioning and recording needs to be determined in advance. By all means consider asking if it is acceptable to take notes, but avoid using an "interview" questioning style, i.e., going point by point down a list. Try to build your questions into the body of the presentation:

> *Example:*   *"Because the people we represent will be giving up government benefits when they become full-time employees, we try to find jobs in companies that offer their employees a complete benefit package. What benefits does your company typically offer?"*

Careful observation can unearth information about employment sites that might not otherwise be available. No one, especially an employer, wants to admit his or her shortcomings to outsiders. However, these shortcomings can affect greatly the success of an employee who has disabilities. Observation can yield interesting data about both positive and unfavorable aspects of a company:

- How employees relate to management and vice versa
- How co-workers relate to each other
- How "loose" or "tight" is the general atmosphere
- Who the *un*official leaders are
- Who is friendly and who is not
- How closely that established procedures are being followed
- How closely what the job developer is told matches with what actually occurs at the work area

Begin making observations at the initial meeting, and continue to make them. A separate section of the notebook can be assigned for impressions and observations. You can later decide whether to share this information, for it is possible that impressions made one day will later change. Rather than allowing concrete impressions to be based on idiosyncratic observations, look for consistently recurring themes before becoming concerned.

A tour of the company can offer an excellent opportunity for observing the items outlined above. But it provides much more than that. The tour usually provides the job developer with the first chance to observe closely the range of jobs available in a company. Even for employment sites where many of the workers are in the public view, the tour provides a much more comprehensive view than otherwise would be available.

The most important outcomes of the tour are to begin to identify a job (or a part of job) that could be modified into a supported work position and/or assess if a job identified by the employer is suitable for a person with severe disabilities.

The tour needs to be arranged during the initial meeting and scheduled as a part of the first follow-up meeting. The job developer and the employment trainer, if the positions are separate, should both take the tour. This is an excellent opportunity to introduce the trainer to the employer. Also, try to make sure that the contact person from the initial meeting is a part of the tour. Of course, tours might cause an interruption in the work of employees—so refrain from talking to workers unless you are encouraged to do so by the tour guide.

It is important to limit the number of persons on the tour. The job developer and the employment trainer should normally be the only representatives from the agency. Parents and other agency employees should not attend. A tour is also *not* the best time to introduce the prospective employee. Remember, this is only the first view of the company, and an agreement has yet to be reached about employment. Additionally, it is important to remember that information gained during the tour may result in a different person being targeted for the site. Prospective employees may be given a tour at a later date (see Chapter 12).

If permission can be obtained, it can be helpful to take photographs or otherwise record impressions with a micro cassette recorder. However, it is crucial to ask the employer's permission *before* the tour. Certainly, do not wait until the tour is about to begin to request permission. Many companies have strict rules against taking any photographs or making on-site recordings. Equally importantly, be sure to ask an employee if it is permissible to take his or her photograph.

Talking directly to employees and others can yield valuable information, particularly about the way people feel about an employment site. A request can be made of the employer for an opportunity to speak with certain employees. When talking with employees be sure to keep the questions positive. Be careful to avoid giving an impression that only negative information is being sought. If an employee volunteers negative information, listen, but do not encourage it, or act excited. Also, look for consistent patterns of negative responses. Many employees just like having someone to complain to, regardless of the severity of the problem.

Job service counselors can offer objective advice about a potential employment site. They have probably sent numerous applicants to the site for employment, and they will have received feedback on the working conditions and the reasonableness of the employer's demands.

Your friends, acquaintances, and colleagues can also provide helpful information about an employer. Finally, do not forget the parents of the potential employee and your business advisory board. There is almost no end to the amount of information that is available on most employers.

The following situation illustrates the importance of obtaining information from outside sources when making a decision about an employer:

> Marc Gold & Associates conducted a project in Mississippi several years ago that obtained employment in integrated jobs for people from work activity centers who had been labeled "unemployable." A job was developed in a small community with a company that processed timber. Everything seemed fine with the site until an employee of the local work activity center stopped the job developer one day and said, "That place you found is awful! Nobody in this town works there unless they have to. I know several people who work there now and they have been looking for other jobs almost since they started." The job developer checked out the observation with other people and found the employee's statement to be true. Negotiations were discontinued with the employer the next day.

NEGOTIATE WITH THE EMPLOYER

As we noted in the previous chapter, most employers assume what Michael Schatzki (1981) calls a *Show-Me* negotiation stance. They raise questions and objections and may stall on closing the deal. In fact, in a *Show-Me* negotiation the employer may be raising an objection about a hypothetical problem to see how you respond and how well you are able to offer solutions. Keep in mind that the employer might be testing how well you "troubleshoot" problems. Both of you, if you are being honest, know that future problems are likely, and the employer wants to see how well you can help overcome a problem situation.

These reactions are a normal part of every business interaction. They must be accepted and dealt with calmly and professionally. A job developer can do this by listening carefully, by focussing on meeting the employer's needs, and by seeking out solutions to problems.

Questions

To answer the employer's questions effectively, you must develop an intimate knowledge of the services offered and listen, rather than assume. Many job developers glibly jump right into answering an employer's question, even before the question is completed. A competent negotiator, however, carefully ascertains what the employer is asking and responds in a measured and accurate manner. If the answer to a particular question is, "I don't know," you should admit it and offer to find an answer by the next scheduled meeting.

If certain questions are particularly difficult to answer, bring the subject up *before* it is asked by the employer. This approach, which is often used by trial lawyers in court cases, can deflect a point from becoming an objection. The following statement is an example of this strategy:

> Job Developer: *"Many employers are concerned that their current employees will resent the fact that a person labeled "mentally retarded" has been hired to work with them. However, we have found that when the people we represent begin to do their jobs, their fellow employees become very supportive and enthusiastic. Many even develop close friendships with our trainees."*

A listing of the most commonly asked questions and responses should be developed, just as with the initial contact and meeting. It may even be helpful to type a standardized question-and-answer handout that could be left with the employer at the end of the initial meeting (See the sample handout in Appendix 4).

Objections

Objections, which are a normal part of every business presentation, must be accepted as such and dealt with calmly and professionally. You can do this by becoming a problem solver and need satisfier.

Most of the objections you are faced with can be defused or even avoided by doing some advance research. Make every attempt to relate your presentation to the prospect's needs by choosing to talk in terms of end results and benefits to the company. A sincere interest and some careful monitoring with all your senses—eyes, ears, and intellect—help establish confidence in you and reduces their objections.

Objections are questions that have become potential sticking points. Even more attention is required to deal with an objection than with a question. After all, the initial response to the question was not answered sufficiently well to satisfy the employer! You must now rethink the response more carefully. The best way to avoid objections is to answer the original questions carefully and completely. The following is an example of how a question becomes an objection:

> *Employer:*   *"We've had dealings with 'rehab' agencies in the past and we didn't have very much luck. Why should I agree to work with you?"*
> *Job Developer:* *"Oh, well that's a different agency."*
> *Employer:*   *"It's my experience that you guys are all about the same. I just don't think that it is worth my time."*

It is clear from this conversation that the job developer created the objection with a stumbling response that insufficiently answered the original question. The employer has almost decided not to become involved, and it will be very difficult for the job developer to turn this situation around.

Objections may occur at various times during the process of negotiations. Some typical objections include the following:

- "We can't afford it."
- "We don't need it."
- "We don't have any openings right now."
- "I need to discuss this with . . ."
- "We have no jobs that are cyclic and stable."
- "We have no jobs they can do."
- "We'll get back with you later on."
- "Our work is too dangerous for handicapped people."
- "Check back with me at the first of the year."

Before you begin calling on employers, have thoughtful answers prepared for all these potential objections. It is an equally good idea to brainstorm with fellow placement staff for additional potential objections. Friends and acquaintances in business may also be able to offer valuable assistance in developing a list of possible objections.

The timing of the objection may give the job developer a clue about how to defuse it effectively:

1. *Early objections* may be raised because the job developer has failed to exhibit a business-like attitude or violated an unwritten rule of the employer. These early objections may have nothing to do with the content of the service itself, but rather the way in which the content was presented.
2. *Objections during the presentation* are usually raised as a result of the job developer failing to respond to a concern adequately or the employer misunderstanding the concept being discussed. It may also be possible that other factors are causing objections at this point, such as the conditions at the employment site (a strike may be imminent, etc.), personal conflicts of the employer (family problems are affecting work performance), or a fear of hiring persons with severe disabilities.
3. *Objections that arise late in negotiations* are probably more accurately called stalls. Objections that are raised after all the information is on the table usually indicate that there is some reason the employer does not want to go forward. Try to respond to the stated objection, while also cutting through the talk to determine the real problem.

Use the following strategies to overcome objections raised by employers: First, **do not let questions become objections,** by carefully answering all questions as completely as possible. Second, **listen carefully to the objection**—both to the words and the actions—and try to understand why it is being raised. The employer may be weighing a decision, and the objection is raised in order to obtain more information. Or, the employer has misunderstood a critical element of the presentation. Use these ideas to help you listen more effectively to objections from an employer:

- Indicate that you are interested, both with your body language and your verbal responses.
- Do not wave off an objection as if it were unimportant, or jump in and answer too quickly.
- Be patient and encourage the employer to talk.
- Focus on the *final* comments made about a problem. People often tend to leave the real issues until the end.

Third, **try to lower resistance or hostility before answering the objection**. This can be done with a statement designed to show that you understand the concern. You do not have to agree with it but it is important to understand it. *Never* respond to an objection in an angry manner, even when the situation appears to deserve it.

Fourth, **convert the objection** to a perspective with which the employer can agree, and start from there to answer it. Consider this sample conversation:

> Employer: *"With all the work we've got going on right now,* (objection) *I just don't see how we can get involved in a project like this at this time."*
>
> Job Developer: *"I can certainly understand your concern. It's not often that a restaurant is so busy.* (lowering hostility) *However, I think that I can show you how we can* (converting) *actually reduce the amount of work and confusion. Would you be interested in hearing how we might do that?"*

Fifth, **answer the objection in relation to the employer's needs**. Try to avoid falling into the trap of using pat answers. Rather, offer solutions only after careful consideration. In the example above, the job developer might have asked to observe the restaurant for a few days and agreed to meet again with the employer with a proposal that is consistent with the promised result.

Finally, **ask a closing question**. If you feel that you have answered the objection in a satisfactory manner, then ask if there are any other problems that stand in the way of an agreement. This is an attempt to close the deal. If more information is still needed, it may be necessary to set an additional meeting.

Stalls

Objections that occur late in the negotiation process may actually be an employer's way of stalling. Even the job developer feels that an objection is really a stall, it is still necessary to answer the objection as long as the status of the relationship continues to be negotiated. However, the job developer needs to assess the situation and try to determine the real reason the objection was raised. Stalls may be used by the employer for a number of reasons:

- The employer may need more time to consider a response to an objection or whether to become involved in the project.
- The employer may be covering up problems that are occurring at the company, such as an impending layoff, which is not public knowledge. In one instance, the employer was stalling because the company was about to move to another state!
- The negotiation stance of the employer may have become *Oh-No!*, and the employer is simply unable to say "No." The stall may be used in hopes that the job developer will give up.
- A stall may be used simply as a means of delaying what appears to the employer to be a complicated endeavor. This is a tactic used by many people.

Even if the employer is interested, he or she may be insufficiently confident to make the final decision. Also, the prospect may need more reassurance and confidence in you. If the company has been putting off making a decision and you have considered the points outlined above, you may decide to put the relationship on a "go/no-go" basis. Below are some common stalls and possible reactions:

Example 1

STALL: *"We don't have an opening now, but you can have the next one that is available."*

                              or

                "We have laid off workers who must be rehired before we can work with you."

RESPONSE/
ACTION: *(A strategy that works well in this case is to be understanding, then to offer this solution.) "The fact that you don't need anyone right now may work in your favor. It will give us time, without being rushed, to perform an in-depth job analysis and to get your input. Remember, there is no cost for this service, and you will be getting free labor for a few days."*

This latter strategy has proven to be quite effective, for often during the job analysis the trainer will notice a job that is available that might have been missed by your contact. Additionally, your being on site gives you high visibility and keeps your program as a high priority for the employer. Completing the job analysis and offering it to the company may strengthen its commitment to your program.

Example 2

STALL: *"I have to get together with some other people to discuss this proposal before I can make a decision."*

RESPONSE/
ACTION: *"I would be glad to meet with your management team to lay out and discuss the entire program. Can we meet early next week?"*

                              or

                "We have training scheduled for next month. The sooner you can meet, the better."

                              or

"Could I have _____ at XYZ Corporation give you a call? He had to solve some coordination problems similar to yours. He should be able to let you know what to expect."

Example 3
   STALL: *"The union will complain if you come in here with a bunch of people."*

                                   or

             "Our union doesn't usually support this type of program."

RESPONSE/
   ACTION: *"There will be only one trainer to the Job Analysis, and she will dress and perform like your other employees."*

                                   or

             "I would be glad to meet with the union steward or with the president of the local. Our experience has been that unions are supportive if they are given all the information at the outset. After all, our trainee will probably decide to join their union."

The following are additional stalls that you might encounter during follow-up negotiations:

- "The only job openings I have are at job stations that handicapped people couldn't handle."
- "I can't agree to your 'Expectations for the Employer.'"
- "Our own training department can handle any training that needs to be done."
- "All of our applicants have to take a standardized dexterity/rate-of-manipulation test."
- We can't have your trainer coming in and out of our plant at just any time."

As with the initial meeting, the stalls listed here should be studied and general answers developed to them. As you encounter new stalls during negotiations, discuss them with your colleagues for possible solutions. Keep a running record of the new stalls that you come across, and especially note down the responses that you used and their success rate.

Whatever the reasons, stalls that occur at the end of a reasonable period of negotiation tend to be frustrating and disheartening to job developers and applicants alike. For this reason, consideration should be given to "pressing" a bit and even breaking off negotiations if the stalling continues for too long. The way in which a job developer responds to a stall—after trying to answer it, of course—depends on the underlying reason the stall is being used *from the job developer's perspective.* Consider the scenarios discussed above. In the first example it would be reasonable to continue to work with the employer and allot the time necessary to work out the problems. The second example calls for the job developer to back off and observe what happens. It might also be helpful to contact knowledgeable business people to obtain access to the inside story. If the job developer is really sensing negative feelings, as in the third scenario, it is clearly time to ask the employer, "Is there a real problem here? If so, please let me know because we've got other employers to call on." If the opportunity is lost, it is better to know sooner than to wait around hoping for a change. The final stall requires some gentle but persistent pressing by the job developer. Keep referring to the need to get started and that people are anxiously waiting to work.

There is no general formula for how long negotiations should last. However, after a job developer has had an initial meeting, held one or two follow-up meetings, and toured the company, there should be no reason, except possibly with the largest employers, why a decision cannot be made. If active negotiations have been continuing for 2 months and there is no movement but only consistent stalling, it is probably time to consider thanking the employer for the time spent and to go on to another company. Remember, this is not a hard-and-fast rule. Some negotiations continue to feel positive even after several months. Nonetheless, job developers should strive to avoid the frustration and lack of confidence that often accompany long-term, dead-end negotiating.

TARGET AND DEFINE THE JOB TO BE PERFORMED

One of the most important objectives of this phase in the process of employing is to target and define a job carefully that jointly meets the needs of the employer *and* the prospective employee. The needs of the trainer must also be considered when scheduling time for training and support. Clearly, numerous elements should be included when selecting a job for a person with severe disabilities depending on the particular person targeted for the job. The following considerations generally contribute to a quality job:

- The job meets a critical need for the employer.
- The most typically performed tasks of the job have identified cycles that are repeated on a regular basis.
- Responsibilities and quality and production expectations are clearly defined.
- The job can be divided into smaller components, if necessary, to accommodate the specific needs of the employee.
- Job responsibilities and productivity can be increased gradually over a reasonable period of time.
- Prior on-the-job and educational experiences are unnecessary.
- Expectations for employees are flexible and are not based simply on production numbers.
- Work areas can be defined and organized.
- The supervisor and co-workers have good training skills.
- The job can be learned by the trainer in a reasonable period of time.
- Adaptations and modifications of the job responsibilities are both allowable and possible.
- The various work supervisors offer consistent information and assistance.
- Resulting from the employment is a marketable experience, useful to other employment sites in the community.
- Co-workers are not directly and immediately dependent on the outcomes of the work performed by the worker, such as in assembly line jobs.

Each of these considerations is important, although every job that is targeted will not have all of these components. The job developer and trainer must decide, based on the person identified for the job, which elements are necessary and which can be absent. As has been stressed throughout this book, the "personalized" approach is always preferable. Thus, agencies are encouraged to develop their own lists of components. Such a list can make a handy checklist to be used during the negotiation phase (see Chapter 10).

GAIN APPROVAL AND SET DATES FOR EMPLOYMENT

This objective is actually the keystone of the entire job development effort. At some point in the negotiation process, the job developer must seek to close the deal. The question must be asked: "When can we start?" This inquiry typically should be made by the end of the first follow-up meeting. The employer may not be ready to agree at this point, but it is necessary that the job developer asks for closure. The discussion on negotiations and stalls, presented earlier in this chapter, offers guidelines on how to arrive at the point at which the employer is ready to say "Yes."

After final approval has been obtained, the job developer should *immediately* set firm dates for the job analysis activity and for the actual date that work begins. Ideally, the job analysis should begin as soon as possible after the employer has given final approval. The sooner it starts, the less likely some unforeseen circumstance at the company will affect the process. However, if possible, try to leave a week or 10 days between the date for job analysis and the date for work to begin. This time period not only gives the trainer ample opportunity to gather all the information necessary to begin training (see Chapter 11), but it also allows the targeted employee and his or her family the opportunity to make a smooth transition from the current situation.

FINALIZE AN UNDERSTANDING WITH THE EMPLOYER

In an effort to minimize the chance of misunderstandings once employment begins, agencies should consider using some form of employment agreement. There are two types of such agreements: formal signed agreements (contracts from the employer's perspective) and a detailed summary of the expectations and duties of both parties that is not signed.

A formal signed agreement is sometimes required by funding sources. Once final approval is given to begin employment, most employers do not balk at signing such an agreement. However, expect the company's lawyers to inspect the document carefully. Appendix 11 is a sample agreement for you to consider.

The willingness of most employers to sign a formal agreement notwithstanding, any signed papers introduced at the final stages of negotiations carry with them overtones of Murphy's Law. If a signed document is *not* required for any particular purpose, then we strongly suggest that you avoid bringing up the topic. The relationship necessary to employ persons with severe disabilities successfully must be built on a stronger foundation than a signature on a document. A much more palatable alternative is to use a Summary of Expectations, which contains all the features of the formal agreement, except any need for legalese and signatures (Appendix 9).

FOLLOW-UP NEGOTIATIONS IN SUMMARY

In most instances, the decision whether or not you will obtain access to the company's job opening will likely be made as a result of follow-up negotiations; that is, *after* the initial meeting. In fact, even if a firm approval is obtained during the first meeting—an example of *Oh-Boy!* Negotiation—several follow-up meetings will probably be necessary before job analysis can begin.

Several issues involved in the follow-up negotiations phase of employing now arise for the first time:

- Because placement programs have one person to handle job development and another to do training, the issue of coordination and responsibility arises. The agency job developer/trainer must become involved in the preparatory process at this point. It must be clear, both to your agency and to the company, who is to be responsible for the continuing negotiations. If the roles of job developer and trainer are separate, there must also be well-defined lines of communication and understanding between each of these agency people.
- Some companies require a great deal of information from you before they can make a decision (*Show-Me* negotiation). Several follow-up presentations may be necessary. They may also have considerable internal coordination problems around such issues as union reaction, layoffs, and insurance.
- If a company initially seems interested in providing an opening but then stalls for a long period of time, a decision to break off negotiations might be necessary. It is extremely important to notify the company of your decision and to give the reason it was made.
- For those companies with which you wish to continue negotiations but that seem to be stalling, a set of strategies designed to close the deal needs to be developed and implemented.

**AN ALTERNATIVE APPROACH TO
EMPLOYER CONTACTS: CONSULTING INTERVIEW**

The procedures presented so far represent a time-proven business approach for contacting employers for the purpose of securing employment for persons with severe disabilities. There may be instances, however, when you feel that the traditional approaches would be ineffective. For instance, there may be a large company in your area that is generally reluctant to work with *any* government-sponsored program. Another company might have jobs for which people labeled "severely handicapped" were never given access. These companies present particularly difficult problems for job developers. Yet, you may feel that they would offer excellent employment opportunities for the people represented by your agency. It is clear to the job developer that an initial contact would yield an *Oh-No!* negotiation stance. The approach for this type of employer may be the consulting interview.

Some of the more common reasons for using the consulting interview are so that you can:

- Gain valuable information regarding the industry and the company
- Talk with the decision maker
- Bypass the personnel department and traditional application system
- Get your foot in the door
- Obtain referrals to other workplaces
- Gain the employer's confidence

The consulting interview is a strategy in which a key decision maker in a choice, but potentially difficult, company is contacted for the purposes of finding out more about the industry and the employment market in general, rather than about his or her company specifically. Advice is sought—not employment. In other words, the employer is asked to "consult" with an emerging community service regarding such topics as identifying the essential needs of employers, the liability exposure an employer faces by allowing an outside trainer into a place of business, how a certain sales pitch sounds to an employer, and so on. This strategem can be used anytime, but is most useful when an agency is just getting started.

When engaged in a consulting interview the job developer actually has two objectives in mind. The **apparent and expressed agenda** is to obtain exactly the information that is asked for—feedback, suggestions, and information. The **hidden agenda** is to make a favorable impression upon the decision maker of the company, without directly asking for an appointment to discuss the possibilities of employment opportunities. However, it is your hope that the employer will extend an offer for an appointment based on the meeting.

It is quite easy to see how this strategy could become overused or abused. The job developer should only contact such companies with real issues in mind and with a genuine interest in the subjects raised. Never overtly initiate the hidden agenda once a meeting has been secured; doing so is nothing less than lying. However, if an employer asks, "Are you really here to get a job opening?," admit your interest in the following way: "I would certainly like the opportunity to employ someone in your company, but I felt that it would be helpful first to learn some specifics about the industry as a whole."

The consulting interview approach, when used discreetly and professionally, can open doors that might never be opened to services representing persons with severe disabilities. But again—*Use it carefully.*

10

Quality Considerations in Integrated Employment Sites

There are considerable differences between the ways that non-disabled individuals find work and the ways that people with severe disabilities become employed. One of the greatest differences involves the **range of choices** available to people who are not disabled, compared to the **limited choices** available to people who are disabled. Specifically, this means a difference in the range of choices *we have* compared to the people *we represent*. Nondisabled persons may spend years in academic and experiential preparation for a career, then later change their minds, and do something totally different. Others may change jobs within their chosen field many times in an effort to find optimal working conditions, wages, and personal satisfaction.

Most people with severe disabilities are totally dependent on a service system to provide them with employment. Although there are hopeful indications that this situation is changing—for example by including families, friends and the community in the process of employing—it will probably continue to exist for some time. One by-product of being dependent upon an agency that is responsible for many other people is that the range of choices available to each individual is severely limited.

Even if agencies strive to provide an opportunity for choice for each person who is represented, certain limitations are inevitable. Therefore, job developers must be doubly careful when targeting and contacting employers. Because the employment choices may be limited, it is crucial that the opportunities that are developed be of the highest possible quality. An effective method of focusing attention on the factors that contribute to a quality job is to develop a comprehensive list of quality indicators and to utilize that list as a criterion measure when developing work sites (see Appendix 12, Quality Consideration Checklist).

The use of a Quality Consideration Checklist is an initial step in ensuring an effective match between a person and a job. This list of criteria felt to be representative of a "good job" must take into account the philosophical outlook of the employment preparation program, the job's training requirements, and most importantly, *the needs of the people to be placed.* Once an employment site has been determined to possess a sufficient number and type of quality indicators, the agency can then consider a more personalized match between the target job and the potential employee (see Chapter 12). The objectives of using a Quality Consideration Checklist are to:

- Ensure that each person placed in employment works on a job that is safe and dignity enhancing

- Identify proactively problem areas that can be solved through negotiation
- Identify "go/no go" criteria in order to save valuable time; for example, decide in advance whether the company has unsafe working conditions

Thus, a Quality Consideration Checklist should:

- Determine whether, for a person represented by the agency, an employment site represents an acceptable place to work—in relation to the philosophical perspectives developed during planning *and* in comparison to features demanded by nondisabled people
- Provide a listing of key features of quality working environments that are available in a specific employment site
- Target a list of specific deficiencies exisiting in a targeted work site that may be able to be remedied through negotiation and cooperation with the employer

When delineating the quality considerations of employment, it is critical to relate all decision making both to the *individual* and the *community*. Quality considerations are relevant to the individual because they positively affect the availability of new and enhanced opportunities, levels of independence, autonomy in decision making, personal dignity, and the ability to make personal lifestyle choices. In relation to the community, employment should provide the consumer of employment training services with enhanced opportunities to use community services, and the opportunity to establish relationships with other community members and to gain the status afforded to any other working, contributing member of society.

The quality considerations for employment considered in this chapter are intended to assist vocational training and employment personnel in evaluating their own actions in relation to individuals and the community. As our sophistication in facilitating employment increases, so too does our ability to delineate new and expanded quality considerations.

The following features are included on the **Quality Consideration Checklist**, and each is discussed in this chapter:

- Interactions with nondisabled co-workers
- Rate of wages that are typically paid and the opportunity to pay sub-minimum wages
- Available benefits, such as workmen's compensation, health insurance, vacation and other forms of leave, and employee support programs
- Working conditions of the site: safe, friendly, accessible, and comfortable
- Whether the nature of the work performed is potentially long term and in a viable company and industry
- Enhancing features, such as opportunities for increased responsibilities, raises, upward mobility, and status
- Work expectations that are clearly defined, stable, and flexible
- Effectiveness of internal controls
- Availability of in-house training and support
- Proximity and availability of transportation
- Degree to which a marketable experience is gained
- Extent to which the site has entry-level jobs
- Willingness of the employer to agree to a set of conditions necessary for employing a person with severe disabilities

- Way the company is viewed by its employees and the community
- Degree of innovation allowed and encouraged by the employer
- Proximity of the site to community resources
- Turnover rate of co-workers/supervisors and the potential for using co-workers/supervisors for support

These features are not listed in any strict priority ranking. However, certain items have a greater importance than others. Some items, such as interactions with nondisabled people, may even rate "go/no go" status. That is, the absence of such features would cause a company to be dropped from consideration as a potential employment site. The Quality Consideration Checklist (Appendix 12) specifically delineates the features we identify as "no go," should that criterion be rated as unacceptable.

The features selected for the checklist were derived after careful analysis of the following:

- Philosophical perspective of Marc Gold & Associates
- Definition of supported work in the Developmental Disabilities Act of 1984 (*Federal Register*, 1984)
- Input from agencies, professionals, parents, and consumers
- Actual experiences in developing employment sites for people with severe disabilities
- Features that nondisabled people look for in a job site

INTERACTIONS WITH NONDISABLED CO-WORKERS

This vital feature is the foundation upon which stands the concept of competitive employment. Interactions with nondisabled co-workers are possible only in integrated, regular job sites, not in segregated settings. Therefore, this feature must be viewed as a "go/no go" criterion for an employment site.

Occasionally, however, determining whether interactions with nondisabled co-workers are acceptable is not as clear as the difference between a work activity program and a regular job. Some community-based jobs are performed in settings where the employee has virtually no interactions with co-workers. For instance, a night shift janitor may not see another person for an entire shift. Such conditions as this might cause an agency to rate a site as being unacceptable, particularly if the person being represented needs interactions with others in order to be successful.

The value of interactions with nondisabled individuals, by people with severe disabilities, is well documented (e.g., Berkeley Planning Associates, 1985; Martin et al., 1982; Wehman & Moon, 1985). Brown and his colleagues (1984) feel that the opportunity for integrated employment—working alongside nondisabled co-workers—is **the** defining feature of quality employment. Agencies, however, must determine if a specifically targeted employment site offers the conditions for employees to have these interactions. A good rule of thumb is:

The more severely disabled an individual is, the more that person will require an employment opportunity that provides for interactions with nondisabled co-workers.

WAGES

The payment of wages for work performed has been a controversial issue in the human service field for several years. Brown et al. (1984) state that integrated employment should be available to all persons with disabilities, even if some would not receive direct wages if remuneration presented a barrier to employment. From an opposing perspective, Bellamy and his colleagues (1984) counter with the argument that the payment of money for work performed is a right and that money can be used to "buy" integrated opportunities—even if the site where the wages are earned is less-than-ideally integrated. This is a complex issue and we urge you to review these alternative positions, deliberate on your personal philosophy, and develop a rationale for your position.

It is not necessary to become embroiled in that controversy to assess the acceptability of a company's wages. Existing subminimum wage certificates, available through the U.S. Department of Labor, allow for the payment of wages—based upon productivity—to as little as 25% of the minimum or commensurate wage.

The wages checklist items rate two areas:

1. What are the regular wages paid to employees? Less than minimum wage = unacceptable, minimum or a bit higher = acceptable, and much higher than minimum = above average.
2. Will the employer agree to cooperate by applying for a subminimum wage certificate, if necessary?

The decision of whether a subminimum wage certificate is necessary can only be made by matching the potential employee to the targeted job. If the flexibility to use a subminimum wage certificate cannot be negotiated, the number of people who can be considered for the site is reduced. It is not necessarily a "no go" criteria, but it does affect who will be able to benefit from the opportunity.

If a company does not pay its workers at least the minimum wage in circumstances where they clearly should, then that company probably does not represent a quality employment site for people with severe disabilities—or anyone else for that matter. If, however, a company routinely pays its entry-level workers $6.00 per hour, it is above average on wages. Even with a 50% subminimum wage certificate, in that setting a worker would be making close to minimum wage.

Wages have often been perceived as the *critical* criterion of a quality job. Although the importance of remuneration should not be minimized, it should always be evaluated in relation to several factors: (1) the impact of varied earning levels upon an individual's living arrangements, i.e., will increased earnings have a negative impact upon the individual's ability to remain in a residential program *or* will they allow movement to a less restrictive setting?; (2) the degree to which increased earnings allow the individual to obtain and maintain an improved quality of life; and (3) the degree to which earnings for a particular position are comparable to the earnings of other employees in a similar position. Wages are only one indication of the importance placed upon a set of work tasks within the business context. Wages are, however, a universal pathway to increased independence and personal choice.

A final consideration relates to how well the company's salary structure compares with other local employers engaged in the same business. If the company is at the lower end of the pay scale for a particular type of work, you may want to pursue other companies first. It is important to recognize, however, that some individuals

may actually want these low-paying jobs, and every American city has service industry workers who do make it successfully on minimum wage. It is perfectly acceptable to be conservative on this issue, but not at the cost of eliminating *all* the
potential openings. A decision must be made to accept potential positions and offer
them to interested applicants or not to pursue them at all. Either decision carries a
risk: If a position is accepted, there may be no appropriate employee-applicants, and
consequently one may lose some credibility. However, by choosing not to accept
such positions, someone may be denied the opportunity to work.

BENEFITS

Along with wages and working conditions, the benefits that a company offers to its
employees provide a benchmark indicator of quality from the perspective of most
workers. For example, with the current price of health care, the availability of free or
inexpensive health insurance is often reason enough to choose one employer over
another.

Most people with severe disabilities already qualify for the governmental
benefits of Supplemental Security Income (SSI) and Medicaid *before* becoming employed. However, working on a job—even one that pays as little as minimum wage
—can jeopardize continuing access to those benefits. This loss of benefits is often
cited by parents of individuals with disabilities as a reason for their reluctance and
caution in supporting integrated employment (Elder, Conley, & Noble, 1986). Therefore, it is crucial that job developers target companies that offer some form of health
insurance to their employees. In almost every case the job developer would be doing
a disservice to potential employees by referring them to a job then fails to include a
decent benefit package, especially health insurance. An individually negotiated
health insurance policy for severely handicapped people can easily cost up to one-
half of their take-home pay.

Despite the importance of benefits, the concept of supported work can offer a
"phase-in" period for individuals who are fearful of losing their benefits and/or in
circumstances where benefits are not currently available. Job developers should
meet with the local representatives of SSI and Medicaid to obtain up-to-date information on eligibility requirements. The regulations do provide both for a gradual
phasing out of SSI benefits as earned income increases, *and* a trial work period in
which benefits can be maintained for a period of time after employment has begun.

The concept of supported work recognizes that many people with severe disabilities will require flexible working hours and wages in order to begin integrated
employment. This flexibility, combined with the flexibility in the regulations concerning governmental benefits, means that an individual could work for a significant
period of time—and possibly indefinitely—in an integrated setting that does not
offer benefits to its employees without jeopardizing his or her governmental benefits.
During this period, the agency can search for a job that does offer full benefits. This
compromise, although not an ideal circumstance, can help both job developers and
families through uncertain times.

Other benefits, in addition to health insurance, contribute to a quality job.
Workmen's compensation is a benefit that is available in virtually every employment
site. Unfortunately, some employers are reluctant to hire workers with severe disabilities because they are fearful that their insurance rates for worker's compensation

will increase. Usually, effective negotiation that focuses on the training procedures used to reduce the likelihood of injury overcomes this concern. Some agencies have sidestepped this issue by carrying worker's compensation insurance for the supported employee for a period of time until the employer's fears have eased. In such cases, the supported employee typically must remain employed by the agency.

The opportunity for leave—sick days, vacations, and other considerations by the employer for individual needs—is as important for people with severe disabilities as it is for everyone else, possibly more so. A person who is just beginning real employment and who may have difficulty letting others know their needs requires as much flexibility and support as possible. Some employers are willing to provide that flexibility, whereas others are not. Job developers must find ways to identify and negotiate for this flexibility, which is often characterized by liberal leave policies and other employee supports.

WORKING CONDITIONS

Virtually every working environment can potentially be dangerous, and employees should not be excluded from jobs that contain risk. Rather, a judgment should be made whether the employer is sincerely interested in the employee's safety. Unsafe working conditions are an absolute "no go" criterion for employment. Experienced job developers can quickly recognize indications of safety violations; some of the most blatant of these are:

- A company's disregard for its own stated procedures, e.g., employees without safety glasses in an area clearly marked for eye protection
- Unguarded machinery and equipment, and machinery on which safety systems have been bypassed
- Dangerous fumes, dust, noise, or other processing by-products without adequate personal and system safeguards
- Employees who are requested routinely to perform dangerous activities without special training
- Disorderly, potentially dangerous work stations throughout the workplace (e.g., cords, materials, old equipment) in the work area or passageways

Some safety violations may be seen during the tour and negotiations; however others may not become evident until during the job analysis and even later.

Additional considerations for working conditions are comfort, accessibility, and friendliness. If the targeted employee uses a wheelchair or has other mobility difficulties, the lack of accessibility may be a "no go" criterion unless special accommodations can be negotiated. Similarly, people with fragile health might not be able to work outdoors.

The "feeling" or atmosphere of a site is also an important working condition. Friendly settings are more likely to nurture the kinds of relationships that people with severe disabilities often need to remain employed.

LONG-TERM EMPLOYMENT

There are several reasons why the prospect for long-term employment is an important criterion for a quality job. First, once a person has lost governmental benefits or has had them reduced due to becoming employed, there is no absolute guarantee that the benefits will be reinstated. Second, it would not seem particularly sensible to offer a person who has been served all his or her life by human service agencies the dignity and freedom of full-time employment, only to have that person return—through no personal fault—to a sheltered setting after a brief work period.

The expected longevity of a job is an important determinant whether a site represents a quality place to work for people with severe disabilities. Many prospective employees must give up their SSI and Medicaid benefits after working even for a short period of time. Although Amendments 1619 (A) and (B) of the Social Security Act (1984) provide some protection for persons who become employed, each case is decided on an individual basis. Concrete commitments from local Social Security offices are often not available.

Two factors that must be considered in assessing the long-term employment potential of a job site are (1) Is the job seasonal in any way? (2) Is the company stable or in a growing industry?

Rating an employment site for its long-term employment potential does not imply that everyone with severe disabilities requires jobs that will last forever. Some persons may need or want the flexibility offered by seasonal work. Others may be willing to take the risk of working in a company with an uncertain future. However, most applicants with severe disabilities tend to benefit most from jobs that are non-seasonal and in stable, growing companies.

Seasonal/Nonseasonal Jobs

Almost every part of the country has seasonal work that must be performed. In coastal areas, fishing seasons are often only 4–6 months long. Agricultural jobs may last from 1 to 9 months, depending on the kinds of work performed. Removing snow and cutting firewood are typical winter activities, whereas grounds maintenance is primarily performed in the summer months. Businesses and other organizations that typically offer year-round employment often have seasonal hiring needs that provide short-term employment opportunities in the summer and during the winter holiday season. To make matters even more complex, many companies experience drastic swings in the volume of their business during the year. For instance, a restaurant near a college campus that barely stays open during the summer may have a 1,000% increase in business immediately after Labor Day. In some cases, applicants may specifically seek short-term employment for a trial period to see how they like it. As long as they are aware of its possible problems, short-term employment may be a perfectly acceptable option.

Job developers must work with prospective employees and their families to determine if seasonal work is appropriate. Some families may be willing for a family member to take summer work as an initial job, even though they may not support a full-time opportunity. It may be clear that others need the continuity offered by a longer-term job in order to be successful. These individual differences must be considered when rating job sites.

Stable or Growing Company/Industry

As John Naisbett (1982) clearly pointed out in *Megatrends*, significant shifts are occurring in employment in the United States and in other countries. Many large companies, such as those in the heavy manufacturing industry, that once offered life long employment to good employees, are now struggling to stay in business. In other segments of the business community, such as the service-oriented sector, business is booming and companies are barely able to keep up with demand. Additionally, within any field there are more and less successful individual companies.

These factors, considered to be important to regular workers who are not disabled, are doubly important to workers with severe disabilities. A person who loses a job because the company went bankrupt or moved to the Sun Belt may have a long wait until a new job and job trainer are available. This type of change is even more difficult to deal with than production, quality, or behavior problems because it is so difficult to anticipate. Businesses try to stay afloat until the last possible moment, and they usually do not let others know, even their own employees, about the likelihood of cutting back or closing.

ENHANCING FEATURES

In addition to the stated benefits and the working conditions of a company, there are other inherently enhancing features that make a place good to work:

- Opportunity for increased responsibilities
- Raises in pay that are available
- Opportunity for upward mobility in the company
- Status of the job in the eyes of others

Increased Responsibilities

The negotiation of initial work opportunities may involve targeting specific tasks of a larger, typically performed job that can be combined to form a "created" job for a worker with severe disabilities. This flexibility is one of the defining characteristics of supported work. However, the decision to carve out an individualized job may be based on rather incomplete information from a vocational profile (see Chapter 12). Once a person is actually on a job, the trainer may discover that the employee is capable of performing much more than the initially targeted tasks. Job sites that offer an opportunity for increased responsibilities are generally more favorable than those that restrict the employee to a preagreed set of tasks.

Even if the employee is working on a competitive job, the opportunity to perform tasks other than the entry-level position can be a key factor in longevity. For many people, a job is made bearable by its enjoyable components. Loading a dishwasher for 4 to 8 hours per day may not be an enjoyable activity. However, if the workers gets to work alongside the cook who prepares the pizza dough every day for 30 minutes, the boredom of dishwashing may be balanced with a bit of fun.

Raises

Even though many professionals would argue that the need for integrated work by people with severe disabilities far outweighs the need for a job that allows for employee wage raises, employment sites should still be rated on this dimension. Because many workers with severe disabilities may begin employment on a subminimum wage certificate at 50% of the minimum wage or lower, it is only fair to seek out employment sites that are willing to pay increased wages as productivity and other job-related skills increase. If an employer is interested only in paying a worker at 50% of the entry-level wage, transition to another job will be *mandatory* if the person wants higher wages. Job transitions are not always bad, but they are more likely to be positive when the worker wants the transition, rather than feeling forced into it as a means of receiving appropriate remuneration.

Job developers should be cautious of routinely targeting the types of jobs that systematically limit all employees to the lowest wage possible. Many fast-food service companies hire only young, part-time workers in order to reduce the likelihood of granting raises and benefits. Young, part-time workers are, of course, likely to leave for other jobs before they are employed long enough to worry about wage raises and benefits. The problem is that these are also the kinds of jobs that seem to be the most available in the community. They may also represent a good job match for some applicants with severe disabilities. Yet, job developers must ensure that they do not become locked into a fast-food portfolio of opportunities. Although these jobs are the easiest to secure, employers do not expect long-term service from their employees and may treat them accordingly. By targeting a mix of employment categories, workers will have access to jobs that routinely provide raises.

Upward Mobility

Upward mobility and wage raises are closely linked, but necessarily are different. Most new employees start in entry-level positions, which can serve a valuable purpose, e.g., provide a first employment opportunity, establish a work history, etc. Consideration must also be given, however, to the need and availability of further training services should new positions become available within the business. Try to ensure that the persons represented will have access to other, more prestigious positions once they have undergone training and have some experience. For example, if an individual is employed at a grocery store returning shopping carts to the store, what types of other job assignments may follow as skills and opportunities improve? Further, what types of training commitments can be made if additional training is required? These questions need to be given full consideration by employment training personnel.

Is upward mobility really a reasonable consideration for people with severe disabilities? If it is a concern for most nondisabled workers, then it should be a factor when rating jobs for workers with severe disabilities. The movement toward full, life long vocational integration of such workers raises interesting, yet often complex, issues. Even though many people simply **need the opportunity for a job**—any job—**now,** will they be willing to remain on that same job, doing the same thing, 10 or 20 years from now? It makes sense, as it does for virtually everyone else, that if people with severe disabilities have the chance to grow in a job, they might want to stay on that job for a long period of time. The problem facing job developers and employment trainers is figuring out how to facilitate growth in a job for people who present challenges in meeting the basic requirements of a job. There are no easy answers to this dilemma; however, attempts must be made to provide workers with severe disabilities the same opportunity for growth enjoyed by everyone else.

Status

When Marc Gold & Associates began its employment services to people labeled "unemployable" in 1979, it was a policy that no traditional service jobs would be sought. The only type of employment sought was in nontraditional settings, such as factories, offices, and small commercial concerns (Garner et al., 1985). This policy was relaxed in a few years to include nontraditional jobs in food service, such as cook and cooks' helpers, and other areas, but the concern remains valid. If one were to analyze a listing of placements made by almost any agency serving people with moderate and severe disabilities, a clear trend will almost surely emerge, with most of the jobs being offered falling into several narrow categories within the service industry. This trend has several implications: (1) the range of opportunities for work is limited; (2) job development efforts are narrowed, thereby reducing the amount of opportunity; and very importantly, (3) a perception emerges—on the part of service providers, families, and the community—that people with severe disabilities can only perform those kinds of jobs.

WORK EXPECTATIONS

Stable, clearly defined, yet flexible job expectations make success much easier to achieve for all workers, particularly those with severe disabilities. Every job, even supported work jobs, has a variety of responsibilities that must be performed. If a routine can be established for the various job tasks—a routine that can be repeated with some degree of regularity—the job will be easier to learn and to train. This is not to say that an individual cannot learn jobs with a variety of responsibilities; rather, training time and the amount of trainer supervision will be significantly increased for those jobs. Some employers may not be willing to pay for the longer time needed to reach skill acquisition levels for typical production rates.

Because every job in industry has a variety of responsibilities in its job description, the trainer must decide whether the inherent variety of work expectations creates training problems that would place the new employee's job in jeopardy. For instance, in construction work a laborer might perform 20 or 30 different tasks in one day. On the next day additional tasks may be performed, and/or a totally different sequence of the previous tasks may be required. This variability makes training very difficult and may make such a job unsuitable for some people with limitations.

Another factor of concern is the clarity of the job expectations. Can the employer concisely relate the job's requirements to the trainer and the employee? Written job descriptions are helpful, but in most instances are not available. Job developers and trainers might consider developing a job description for approval by the employer before the employee begins work.

Flexibility by the employer contributes to success on the job. Within clear and stable work requirements, an employer can offer the degree of flexibility needed to focus on a particular training problem, to deal with an uncertain behavior, or to allow for endurance and stamina to increase.

INTERNAL CONTROLS

Occasionally, employees become trapped between conflicting points of view in a company. Co-workers say one thing, and the supervisor says another. One manager does a job one way while another prefers a different method. A job performed acceptably one day is considered unacceptable the next. These problems are usually caused by poor internal controls in the company; they affect directly and with great force the worker with disabilities. Job developers should try to get a feel for the effectiveness of the internal controls of a targeted company. The following are indicators of appropriately tight internal controls:

- Written job descriptions
- Established standards for productivity
- Clear quality expectations
- Consistent information from various managers
- Open channels of communication
- Regular performance feedback given to employees
- A clear company policy concerning work, which is understood by all employees

The problem of dealing with a company that lacks effective internal controls is that an employee can be negatively affected, regardless of his or her quality of performance. This criterion may be difficult to assess, but it is important to search for indicators of it both before *and* during training.

IN-HOUSE TRAINING AND SUPPORT

This criterion is emerging as perhaps the most critical factor for long-term success on a job site. Even though the concept of supported work incorporates ongoing support from a human service agency to assist new employees to remain employed, it makes much more sense for the employer to provide training and intervention whenever possible. Employment sites with established training procedures may be able to respond to the training needs of workers with severe disabilities, rather than routinely calling on the support agency. Job developers should look for indications of systematic procedures for training procedures and for a general willingness of the employer to provide direct supervision and training to an employee with disabilities.

TRANSPORTATION AVAILABILITY

A vital concern for most employers is that their employees arrive at work reliably and on time. Many businesses are beginning to take a proactive role in this area by assisting employees to form carpools, providing information on bus schedules, and positioning companies close to bus lines and easy-access thoroughfares. A prospective employer should be rated concerning the ease of access for the applicants who are represented. Employment sites that require a long drive in a car may be less desirable than those on city bus lines or those located on typically traveled routes (see Chapter 15).

MARKETABLE EXPERIENCE GAINED

We all seek jobs in which we can grow and learn—jobs that offer experience, opportunities for increased pay, and likely improvements in the future. Job developers should look for similar circumstances for those we represent.

Specifically, we should seek positions in companies that have growth potential, and jobs that will continue in the future. With the increasing development of robotics in industry and other automation techniques, this may prove to be a difficult assignment. But because straightforwardness is appreciated, consider asking the employer direct questions about the long-range and short-range plans for the jobs that you are seeking.

Workers with severe disabilities may require several jobs before they finally discover a good match for their needs, skills, and preferences. During the initial period of employment, it can be argued that learning general work skills outweighs the importance of acquiring specific skills that may be of use in other jobs. However, once a person begins to enjoy stable employment, job developers should seek positions in those job categories for which a number of employers in a community need workers. This strategy can allow people to change jobs in a planned, positive way, rather than only in a negative, mandated manner.

ENTRY-LEVEL POSITIONS AVAILABLE

Some companies do not offer unskilled, entry-level employment to any employee and prefer to hire only experienced workers. Although the supported work concept of job creation can provide access to these work settings for people with severe disabilities, the opportunity for a full-time job may be restricted by company policy. Entry-level positions need not be open at the time of development, but ideally the potential for such work should exist in an employment site.

AGREEMENT BY EMPLOYER TO "PROCEDURAL EXPECTATIONS"

The implications of this consideration are clearly evident. If an employer is unwilling to agree to some or all of the conditions that the job developer/trainer feels are necessary for employment (see Appendix 9, Summary of Expectations), three courses of action are available.

1. Reconsider the conditions of the agreement, and attempt to reach a compromise through negotiation.
2. Turn down the job completely. But, do so graciously, making clear to the employer the reasons for this decision.
3. Turn down the job in terms of agency involvement. Inform prospective applicants and their families of the potential for employment with the employer. Also, detail the points of disagreement and carefully describe the extent of services that applicants can expect from the agency.

The relationship between training personnel and employers is based upon the mutual meeting of needs. Employer needs focus upon quality, quantity, and cost effectiveness. Employee needs focus upon the benefits that are derived from meeting established criteria in a timely fashion. Effective negotiations are directed toward bridging the gap between employer and employee needs. Thus, employment training personnel must work to meet employer standards while protecting the philosophical and programmatic integrity of the human service agency and the employee.

COMPANY VIEWED FAVORABLY

In order for a company to be used as an employment site for people with severe disabilities, it should be viewed favorably by both its employees and the community. This is a crucial concern for several reasons. First, it makes no sense to employ a person in an environment filled with unrest and tension. Companies that are having labor problems, experiencing a strike, or that treat employees as commodities should be avoided. Second, companies that are controversial or are "last chance" places of work tend to do little to enhance the status and general employability of people with disabilities. For example, we suggest that if a nuclear power plant is being bitterly opposed by a neighboring community, the development of a job at that facility would be a mistake.

In addition to the image problems of working in undervalued work settings, there are undoubtedly a multitude of other problems that could negatively affect employment. If the employees and the community as a whole dislike a place of business, there is certainly something wrong with it. We suggest that you try to avoid controversial worksites.

EMPLOYER OPEN TO INNOVATION

Successful employment for people with severe disabilities almost always requires an employer who is willing to try new and different ways of accomplishing tasks. This willingness is available more often than not from employers. However, a good rule of thumb is that the smaller and less "bureaucratized" a setting is, the more likely the employer will be to try out new approaches. This is not to say that large concerns will not try to do so, but the levels of bureaucracy make it much more difficult.

PROXIMITY TO COMMUNITY RESOURCES

People who have limited mobility because of their inability to drive or their need for assistance and support should ideally work in settings in close proximity to the community resources that they need for the nonwork areas of their lives. Too seldom are nonvocational needs considered when targeting potential job sites for people with severe disabilities. Efforts should routinely be made to identify employment in areas close to stores, governmental offices, the employee's home, and other typically used services.

CO-WORKERS AND MANAGERS

The co-workers and managers of a worksite should be rated from two perspectives: their turnover rate and their potential for providing support. In a manner similar to the issue of in-house training and support, co-workers and managers play a vital role in the longevity potential of a worksite for those workers who will need more assistance than usual to learn new tasks.

Companies that have a high personnel turnover rate present structural problems for the possibility of long-term employment—even with the agency training provided by supported work. As soon as the co-workers and supervisors develop ways to interact successfully with a worker with severe disabilities, they leave, and the process must begin again. This is inevitable to some degree, but the problem can be minimized through careful targeting of sites that have stable employment patterns.

The potential for co-worker support is difficult to assess before training begins at a site. The job developer can, however, get a feel for the way employees and supervisors might react through conversation with workers during the negotiation phase and by discussing the issue with the contact person.

CONCLUSION

This chapter reviewed and defined quality considerations for employment in integrated settings. The task for employment training personnel now becomes one of analyzing and operationalizing these considerations with reference to specific individuals. This task requires continual discussion, critical review, and debate as the field of employment training grows in sophistication and importance. As changes occur within society, the quality consideration of employment likewise will be refined and grow in importance. In any event, employment training personnel must always strive to ensure the highest quality of life for the people they represent.

III

EMPLOYMENT TRAINING

11

Employee Profiles, Matching, and Selection

The information discussed in the **Employment Training** section is an outgrowth of Marc Gold's *Try Another Way* system (Callahan, 1986; Garner et al., 1985; Gold, 1980a, 1980b) for facilitating employment in integrated sites for people traditionally considered unemployable. This powerful training methodology provides an in-depth introduction to basic training and task-analysis technologies used in industrial placements. The latest perspectives of leading researchers and practitioners in the field are also incorporated into this section to provide a sound base for facilitating successful employment for persons with severe disabilities.

Whereas the last section on **Job Development** dealt with activities necessary to secure a quality, integrated employment site for a person with severe disabilities, this section, **Employment Training,** focuses on strategies which can be used to ensure that the new employee has the best possible chance to experience success at the job site. Even though discussion of these major activities has been separated, there is considerable overlap between them, especially in the phase of making a successful match of an employee with a job site.

First, however, there are a few issues to consider that relate more to the heritage of the profession's historical orientation toward work than to systems for capturing a match between employee and employer. The issues concerning the selection of applicants are among the most difficult facing any placement program. There can be little disagreement that employment offers a major life change for individuals served by agencies throughout their lives. Because of this, the process used for determining *who* will be selected for employment opportunities must be well planned and be as close to the normal practice of business as possible.

Before applicants are considered for jobs, it is imperative to determine whether they want to work. This can be quite a difficult task because many of them have learned to respond in ways that they imagine we want and expect— irrespective of their true motivation. Others may not be able to express a desire to work unless represented by a parent/guardian or other advocate. Too often we neglect simply to ask them if they want to work. Also, the workshop employee who prefers one kind of job over others should have the option to apply only for the preferred employment. It seems that this right has often been overlooked in the drive to get someone placed.

A large component of people's desire for work comes from their expectations about the workplace and the people who will readily offer them suport. If all human service agencies routinely had gainful employment as the anticipated outcome for those in their programs, then this desire to work would not be an issue. Influences are also exerted by parents, family, and significant others, which can affect an individual's desire for employment. Without the support of parents or staff, successful, long-term employment is almost impossible. Only rarely will a person who has been through our traditional service system be willing to go against the wishes of significant others. In all instances, it is critical for vocational training personnel to establish and maintain relationships and communication with all interested parties.

PROMOTING COMPATIBILITY BETWEEN WORKER AND WORKPLACE

Job developers, parents, and guardians were asked to consider factors of compatibility between the needs, skills, and preferences of both the individual and the potential job sites during the job development planning and prospecting phases. Ideally, these considerations result in a "glove-fit" match between a developed job and a prospective employee. However, it is more often the case that additional planning must be done once an employment site has actually been secured to ensure that the site offers the conditions necessary for successful employment. The issue, as discussed earlier, is then raised of whether a job site should be developed specifically for a targeted individual or if a site can be developed using some general set of criteria—Appendix 12, Quality Consideration Checklist, for instance—with a number of potential employees being considered. In practice, comprehensive job development services need to include both approaches.

Although employers should be approached with the prospect of developing "customized" jobs for specific employees, job development should not be so narrowly focused that opportunities become restricted or in other ways minimized. Quality employment sites that offer good working conditions, flexibility, and opportunities to develop relationships with co-workers might be appropriate for any of a number of persons with severe disabilities. In either situation, it is still necessary to consider information about the prospective employee—related specifically to considerations about the employment site—in order to finalize the decision of who will actually get the job.

The objectives of this phase—employee profiles, matching, and selection—are to:

- Develop and refine further the vocational profiles of prospective employees
- Use the profiles in combination with information about the developed job site to consider potential employee/employer matches
- Decide on the *processes* to be used in contacting potential employees; the manner of responding to the employer's typical application, interview, and orientation procedures; the degree of applicant involvement; and processes for selecting an application for a developed job

PROFILES

A vocational profile is a composite picture of a potential employee's skills, experiences, available supports, preferences, needs, and living situation. These factors are considered when determining the kinds of employment situations that might best be suited to a particular individual. Information contained in the vocational profile differs from that obtained through more formalized vocational assessments in several important ways:

- The vocational profile consists of already existing information, rather than information developed solely for the purposes of evaluation.
- The profile is used only as a guide for matching an individual to an appropriate job and is *not* intended to exclude systematically a person from a certain job.
- The profile seeks to have ecological validity, rather than predictive validity. It is more important that a match makes sense in relation to a person's life than to attempt to predict success. Predictive measures almost invariably predict failure for persons with severe disabilities (Brown et al., 1986).
- The use of the profile frees the applicant from the necessity of taking standardized or norm-referenced tests as a means of proving his or her readiness. Readiness to begin work is assumed for all applicants.
- Selection of a particular job for a person is based on information obtained from the person's entire life and not from one or more brief samples of "work" performance.
- The use of a profile indicates a belief that a person's skills, experiences, available supports, preferences, needs, and living situation are not captured accurately or comprehensively on a standardized checklist. A format composed of open-ended categories allows each person to be described in a unique manner. Implicit in these statements is a belief that there is a danger lurking in any effort to determine systematically the "best job" for an individual. Many researchers and practitioners (Bates, 1986; Brown et al., 1986; Gold, 1980a, 1980b) have noted that traditional standardized assessment/matching procedures simply do not work for persons with severe disabilities. Even when more individualized approaches are instituted in a systematic manner, they can prove to be unsatisfactory. Consider this comment about Vermont employment projects.

> Although a complex system was developed to identify the best candidate for each position by matching the results of job skill inventories with individual skill inventories, decisions are usually made based upon transportation, agency and parent support, and perceived interest in a given position. (Vogelsburg, 1986, p. 38)

Martin (1986) makes the case that effective matching is both an objective and a subjective process. The use of a vocational profile provides sufficient information for objectivity while allowing the job developer, trainer, or parent to make a match based on factors that "feel" right and make sense.

Factors to be Considered

A suggested format for a vocational profile and sample profile on an applicant with severe disabilities is provided in Appendices 13 and 14. The following categories of information were developed from a review of the current literature and best practices (Bates, 1986; Brown et al., 1986; Vogelsberg, 1986) and should be included on a Vocational Profile Outline.

1. **Identification Information**
   a. Name
   b. Date of birth

    c. Social Security number

    d. Address & phone number

    e. Marital status

    f. Current occupation/status

2. **Residential/Domestic Information**
   a. Family (parent/guardian, spouse, children, siblings)
   b. Extended family
   c. Names and ages of persons living in same home/residence
   d. Residential history
   e. Family support available
   f. Description of typical routines
   g. Friends and social group(s)
   h. Description of neighborhood
   i. Location of neighborhood
   j. Services near home
   k. Employment near home
   l. Transportation availability

3. **Educational Information**
   a. History and general performance (from school records, interview data, observations)
   b. Vocational programming/performance
   c. Community functioning programming/performance
   d. Recreation/leisure programming/performance

4. **Work Experience Information**
   a. Information work performed at home
   b. Formal chores at home
   c. Informal jobs performed for others
   d. Sheltered employment
   e. Paid work

5. **Summary of Present Level of Performance**
   a. Domestic skills
   b. Community functioning skills
   c. Recreation/leisure skills
   d. Academic skills (reading, math, time, money)
   e. Motor/mobility skills
   f. Sensory skills
   g. Communication skills
   h. Social interaction skills
   i. Physical-/health-related skills and information
   j. Vocational skills

6. **Learning and Performance Characteristics**

7. **Preferences**
   a. Type of work that applicant wants to do
   b. Type of work that the parent/guardian feels is appropriate
   c. What the applicant enjoys doing at home
   d. Observations of the kinds of work that the applicant likes to do best
   e. Observations of social situations that the applicant likes best

8. **Connections**
   a. Potential employers in family

   b.   Potential employers among friends
   c.   Potential employment sites in neighborhood
   d.   Business/employer contacts for leads
9.   **Flexibility/Accommodations that May Be Required in the Workplace**
   a.   Habits, idiosyncrasies, routines
   b.   Physical/health restrictions
   c.   Behavioral challenges
10.   **Description of an "Ideal" Employment Situation**
   This is based on input by applicant, parents/guardians, service agency staff, and data from profile.

The Vocational Profile Outline can be an effective substitute for traditional standardized and checklist-type approaches to gathering data on applicants for employment services. The profile also adds a degree of ecological validity to the common-sense decision making identified by Vogelsberg (1986). The manner in which this form is filled out and the items selected for inclusion are determined by personalized, local decisions. However, we urge service providers to adhere to an ecological perspective, rather than criterion or norm-referenced approaches. If evaluative information is needed for purposes other than facilitating a successful match between a person and a potential worksite *after* a person is on a job, readers are referred to work by Bates (1986) and by Brown and his colleagues (1986).

When Profiles Should Be Developed

In order to target potential employers, job developers must have access to as much ecologically valid information as possible on each person represented. The development of vocational profiles, therefore, should begin with the intake process of the service agency. The composite picture of an ideal type of job that results from the profile is used by the job developer in compiling the Working List and the Call List for making employer contacts (see Chapter 6).

It may not be possible to gather all the information required to complete the profile in a single intake meeting with a potential employee and his or her parent/ guardian or advocate. It is vital, however, to obtain sufficient information to make a reasonable guess about a potential worksite *before* attempting to develop a job. It is also necessary to have a completed profile *before* attempting to match an applicant with a developed job. Although we do not propose that the process of completing a profile should stand in the way of a person getting a job, nonetheless, information contained on the profile can be crucial to facilitating employment opportunity. In every case it is the agency's responsibility to ensure that the process is completed efficiently.

MATCHING AN APPLICANT WITH A JOB SITE

It might seem logical that if an agency develops comprehensive vocational profiles on every applicant and then uses the profiles as guides to develop employment sites, then the need for further matching would be unnecessary. However, it is seldom that easy. First, identifying an ideal type of job on the profile only guides job development efforts, it never ensures that the ideal job **will** be located. Alternatively, there may be many jobs that a person could do well, and it may not be possible to develop a specific, targeted job. In addition, employers vary a great deal even within the same job category. A person for whom an office job seems appropriate may do better in one office than in another. Therefore, the conditions of individual sites must be considered. Occasionally, jobs are developed that were not targeted specifically for a particular person. Finally, it remains to be determined if the applicant likes the developed job. All these factors make matching applicants and potential job sites a multistep, rather than single-step, process. The following steps describe a typical matching process:

1. Develop a vocational profile of each applicant.
2. Target several employers who roughly fit the composite of an ideal job in the profile.
3. Target other employers that might represent quality employment sites for any employee who was well matched to the site.
4. Develop the job site; assess the requirements demanded by the employer; negotiate for accommodations needed by applicants; and complete the Quality Checklist.
5. If the site represents the type described in Step 2:
    a. Compare the conditions and requirements of the job site with the information in the applicant's profile to determine if there are large discrepancies.
    b. If the match seems compatible, contact the applicant and have the employee begin work at the site.
    c. If discrepancies exist that might turn out to be problematic, consider negotiating with the employer, discussing options with the applicant (and parents/guardian), and determining what accommodations are available by the agency to delimit or in some way reduce the importance of the identified discrepancies.
    d. If it is not possible to reconcile the discrepancies, look for another job site for the targeted applicant (but don't forget to consider other applicants for the job!).
6. If the job site represents the type in Step 3, or in Step 5 (d):
    a. Review the profiles of other applicants and select one or more who seem to be consistent with the conditions and requirements of the employer.
    b. Narrow the list to one applicant by using a set of considerations that make sense locally; for instance, choosing persons with the most family support, those who have been waiting the longest, etc.

As clearly indicated by this sequence of steps, matching is usually an imprecise process. However, agencies should strive to refine continually the profiles on each applicant so that the most current and accurate facts are available. Yet, matching is only a process for ensuring a good start on the job. Even with the most sophisticated matching process, success on the job site of persons with severe disabilities is affected by other factors, including:

- Flexibility and accommodations of the employer
- Compromises and agreements made by the agency on behalf of the employee

- Quality of training, facilitation, and support offered to the employee *and* the employer
- Whether the applicant actually likes the job that was developed
- Support available from the family or residential program

Agencies should not focus solely on either matching processes or on training/facilitation/support processes. Rather, *both* components should be considered. When matching is viewed as the key ingredient for success, an agency tends to utilize more standardized, predictive approaches and may neglect the importance of services delivered after placement. When matching is ignored in favor of powerful training and facilitation strategies, it is likely that people will be forced to fit into jobs they may not want and for which they are not suited. A balance of matching and facilitation services offers the best opportunity for long-term success on job sites.

INDIVIDUALIZED ALTERNATIVES FOR RECRUITMENT, APPLICANT INVOLVEMENT, AND INTERVIEWING

In addition to developing profiles and matching applicants with job sites, decisions must be made on the degree to which the typical hiring procedures of individual employers will be followed. A review of recent publications that describe employment services for persons labeled "severely disabled" might lead you to conclude that an agency must choose between either conforming to the hiring and selection procedures that employers currently use *or* develop a set of procedures that relate to the needs of the applicants and then attempt to negotiate those conditions. In fact, everyone would be better served if a range of choices, rather than these polarized options, were available to each individual applicant and employment site. The decision to follow existing practices or to create acceptable alternatives should be an individualized one, based on the needs of the people who are represented and the flexibility provided by a given employer. A number of areas are affected by this decision:

- Whether single or multiple applicants are represented to the employer
- Degree of applicant involvement
- Manner in which applicants are recruited
- Interview process
- Selection of the employee

Single or Multiple Applicants

Single Applicant Approach The single applicant strategy has some counterparts in typical employment in that some employers utilize employment services that represent individuals who are seeking work. In this approach, the job developer seeks employment situations for targeted persons based on the information available from the vocational profile. During negotiations with employers, the targeted applicant is referred to as the person for whom the job is intended. Once the job is developed, more specific factors are considered to ensure that the match is a good one.

This approach is particularly useful for representing applicants who have identified needs that require negotiation with an employer and for persons who would not typically do well in competition with other applicants—even with other applicants who have disabilities.

Multiple Applicant Approach   This strategy is modeled after the application system used by most businesses. The job developer targets employers who are felt to offer working conditions that would enhance success for any employee. A job is secured with the understanding that one of a number of potential applicants will be selected based on an agreement between the employer and the job developer. The main difference between this approach and that typically used by employers is that the pool of potential applicants is limited to an identified group of persons represented by the agency.

This approach is attractive because of its similarity to natural hiring practices. However, agencies should *not* consider using such an approach with persons who would be continuously denied opportunity for employment because of their difficulty in competing with others. Indeed, careful consideration should be given to providing individualized representation to anyone who has applied for more than a couple of jobs, each time to be overlooked in favor of another applicant.

Applicant Involvement

Employment services often either require no applicant involvement, handling virtually everything for the applicant, or they require applicants to have a level of skill sufficient to conduct the application and interview process without assistance. The desired balance is to encourage the greatest amount of involvement possible but not so much that an applicant is systematically denied opportunities for employment. Because many persons with severe disabilities find it difficult to communicate effectively with others, frequently opportunities for applicant involvement are overlooked. Suggestions for increasing the amount of applicant involvement in seeking employment are to:

- Require applicants who can speak to make the call or have an appointment with agency personnel to indicate their degree of interest in working
- Give information, directions, and instructions directly to the applicant—then later give it to parents or caregivers, if necessary
- Include the applicant in *all* meetings and discussions that concern his or her employment, except for the negotiations with employers
- Consider encouraging a traditional interview between the employer and applicant; also consider asking the applicant and employer to hold the interview without assistance from the agency
- Treat each applicant in a manner similar to any nondisabled applicant for employment

Remember, however, that your desire to encourage applicant involvement should not endanger an individual's chances for employment. For instance, if holding a traditional interview with an employer might lead to doubts that the applicant could do the job because of an inability to communicate, the job developer or trainer should negotiate an alternative to the interview. Many people with severe disabilities have not had sufficient practice or opportunity to speak for themselves. An employment agency in a large city in the Midwest was baffled that more applicants with severe disabilities were not applying for their services. When asked how they recruited applicants, they responded, "Through word-of-mouth. Employees just tell their friends." One wonders just how many real friends that many persons with severe disabilities have and whether they are all able to talk regularly to others. In this example, the procedures being used to encourage applicant involvement were actually denying opportunity to people with severe communication difficulties.

Recruitment

The example cited above indicates the care that agencies must take in designing strategies to increase the applicant's involvement in active recruitment. However, regardless of the attention given to the needs of individuals, agencies often find the issue of recruitment to be a pervasive problem. Recruitment involves the targeting, encouragement, and selection of potential applicants to be represented by an employment service. Because so many persons with severe disabilities have not had the chance for integrated employment, the number of applicants applying often exceeds the capability of the agency to provide timely services. Typically, agencies respond to this problem by instituting procedures that are self-selective, such as the example where word-of-mouth recruitment was used.

Unfortunately, current levels of commitment and funding for supported and competitive employment services for persons with severe disabilities are rather limited. Agencies are forced to target one group of people to the exclusion of others. There is no easy answer to this dilemma. We hope, however, that agencies will be as fair as possible when targeting potential applicants for their services and that traditional exclusionary factors, such as the assumed functioning level of an applicant or the perceived or observed ability to respond to natural hiring procedures, will be eliminated from consideration.

Once the targeted group of potential applicants has been identified, the agency must also deal with such issues as who receives the first job that is developed (if it was not developed for a specific person) and for whom are job development efforts targeted? As with decisions concerning the composition of the group of people to be served, there are no easy answers. So local factors, which it is hoped are not discriminatory for persons with more severe disabilities, must be considered. One approach that simulates regular business practices and encourages applicant involvement is to use a Job Posting. The posting is an information sheet that is made available to a number of potential applicants for whom the developed job is appropriate. See Appendix 15 for a Sample Job Posting.

A Job Posting includes the following components:

- Job title
- Company name & location
- Job summary
- Eligibility requirements (if any)
- Training and support offered
- Job responsibilities
- Salary and benefits
- Hours of work
- Information on how to apply

Of course, agencies must make a commitment to assist applicants who may not understand the meaning or purpose or the posting and those who are not able to read the posting. It is a good idea to send an extra copy to the parents/guardians of each applicant and to follow up the posting with a telephone call to ensure that families/caregivers understand the importance of the information.

Interviewing

The interview is typically an integral part of the hiring process. Therefore, as a general rule, interviews should be a part of the hiring procedures designed for persons with severe disabilities. This can be the initial step in forging a relationship between employer and employee—a feature that may be critically necessary for long-term success on job sites. However, for some persons, the traditional interview may be the worst way to introduce an employer to them. If the job developer/trainer feels that either the employee's prospects would not be enhanced or that the employer would be affected negatively by a traditional interview, some other method of introduction should be used.

By the time of the interview, the job developer should have a good understanding of an important issue:

Is the employer hiring an employee, or is the employer hiring a relationship—which includes *an employee?*

Again, this does not have to be an either/or choice. Yet, those jobs that were developed on the basis of a relationship between the employer and the agency usually offer more room for flexibility in a variety of areas including the interview. The decision of which approach to pursue is a job development issue that must be dealt with much earlier during the planning phase (see Chapter 5).

Alternatives to the traditional interview include the following:

- Assist the employer in conducting the interview by suggesting the form of the questions that the employer needs to ask, helping the employee understand and respond to the questions, and, when appropriate, responding for the applicant.
- Negotiate an opportunity to provide the conditions that the employer expects as a part of the agency's relationship with the employer. In this case there is no traditional interview. The job developer/trainer conducts a meeting with the applicant and his or her parents/guardians or residential providers before the commencement of employment.
- Negotiate for a training-based interview in which the applicant would perform actual work for a period of time, say 1 to 4 hours, in lieu of an interview. The employer could observe the training and meet the applicant in the context of work.
- In the event that more than one applicant is applying for a job, the agency may negotiate for a training-based interview to be used in conjunction with the traditional interview to give the employer a criterion basis for selecting an employee.

The interview process provides an excellent opportunity for the agency to support a number of naturally occurring procedures without negatively affecting applicants with more severe disabilities. The following is a listing of items that should be facilitated for all applicants:

- A Social Security Card
- An open file at the local Job Service office

- A typed application form and brief resume
- Initial means of transportation to work (this is a concern of nearly all employers)
- Assistance with the proper dress to wear to the interview
- Assistance in getting to and from the interview
- Practice on answering the expected questions from the employer, e.g., "Why do you want to work here?", "What kind of work have you done in the past?", etc.

Employee Selection

The last section of this chapter considers the actual selection of the employee. It may seem that this is a moot point if the employer has essentially hired a relationship that includes the agency, the trainer, and the employee. However, the employer always has the final word in approving a worker's continued access to an employment site. If an agency is able to convey to employers the sense that they have an active role in selecting applicants, even those represented individually, the chances are infinitely stronger that a true employer-worker bond will develop and grow.

At times, it may seem in the best interests of both the employer and the applicants to negotiate for a true selection process to determine the actual employee at a job site. If this is the case, the agency may choose to simply have the employer interview a number of applicants and make a decision. If this subjective approach of selection is viewed as potentially problematic for the people represented, the job developer/trainer can negotiate a training-based interview to be conducted along with the traditional interview. A sequence for using a training-based interview for selecting job applicants follows.

1. The trainer selects a Core Work Routine (see Chapter 12). The length of the cycle of the routine should not be more than about 5 minutes.
2. A task analysis containing the steps of the routine instructional strategies and data sheet is developed.
3. Applicants are given scheduled times approximately 1 hour apart. When each applicant arrives for the interview, the trainer meets the applicant, explains the process, and accompanies him or her to the job.
4. The trainer assists the applicant to prepare to perform the routine as if it was the first day of work.
5. The trainer demonstrates the routine to the applicant for one or two cycles.
6. The applicant is then asked to perform the task with instructional assistance from the trainer for a specific period of time (usually 20 or 25 minutes).
7. A data collector, either a co-worker in the company or another trainer, records the number of steps performed correctly, the number of cycles completed, and the time per cycle. Observational comments are also made on the session.
8. After the training-based interview is over, the applicant is accompanied to the regular interview with the employer (this can take place on another day).
9. When all the applicants have completed both interviews, the trainer interprets the data from the training-based interview.

10. Based on all the information available, the employer, possibly with assistance from the trainer, selects an applicant for employment.

This same procedure can be used if only one applicant is represented for a job if the employer wants additional information about the applicant and/or the agency wants to ensure that the applicant likes the type of work that he or she is expected to perform.

Job developers and trainers have numerous other responsibilities relating to the process of selecting an employee for a job. For example, although it is too often overlooked in human services, it is standard business practice to respond to applicants and employees by letter. Agencies should therefore attempt to provide the people who are represented with updates and decisions in writing. This paperwork is necessary to keep applicants abreast of the information and decisions made concerning the jobs that are being developed.

12

Job Analysis

Job analysis is the plan used by employment trainers or "job coaches" to ensure that employees are able to perform their jobs to the standards agreed to when negotiating with employers.

Before trainers can begin to facilitate the acquisition of a job's routines for workers with severe disabilities, they must be completely aware of all the job's components. An effective way for the trainer to gain this awareness is to invest time in the company *before* the new employee begins work. By doing this, the trainer can observe the procedures of the company, participate in typical work routines, learn from co-workers and supervisors, perform the job expected of the new employee and, most importantly, plan for the most effective strategies for training the job.

The job analysis process suggested in this chapter is based on procedures utilized by Marc Gold & Associates during 5 years of employment facilitation for persons with severe disabilities in the early 1980s (Callahan et al., 1981; Callahan, 1986; Garner et al., 1985). This approach, although different in form and specific content, should prove compatible with other suggested ways for capturing the information necessary to begin training on work sites (See Belmore & Brown, 1978; Martin, 1986; Moon, Goodall, Barcus, & Brooke, 1985).

Job analysis serves three major purposes:

1. It serves as the training plan for facilitating successful employment for the new employee.
2. It can be used as an accountability measure to help agencies ensure that the trainer's work is of the highest quality possible.
3. It can be offered as a resource to the company providing the job.

An integral component of job analysis is the trainer's commitment to spend time in the company before the employee begins work. This is a necessary prerequisite component of employment success for persons with severe disabilities. There may be a few instances in which an agency might consider this activity to be unnecessary or counterproductive, but those cases are rare. Too often, a rationale for not having a trainer visit a work site before a worker is employed is merely an excuse for a less-than-ideal approach to training or a lack of resources. Lack of resources is always difficult to deal with, yet agencies should be careful not to couch the real reason for not visiting the site as misleading strategies for training.

We certainly agree with the concerns of many in the field that agencies should recognize and develop the role of natural co-workers and supervisors when training and supporting employees with severe disabilities (see Shafer, 1986). However, the trainer's presence at the job site before employment in no way hinders the role of co-workers and supervisor: In fact, before the employee begins work is probably the most effective time to form the relationships that are helpful in gaining co-worker support.

The on-site trainer's job analysis objectives are to:

- Develop an effective format for capturing all the components of the job that need to be trained
- Decide on a sequential process for performing the job analysis
- Perform the component steps of the job analysis process including:
    - Finalizing a comprehensive training plan based on all the information collected in the job analysis
    - Developing the relationships and lines of communication with co-workers, supervisors, and the employer, which are necessary for the new employee to begin work
- Submitting a completed job analysis to the employer

JOB ANALYSIS FORMAT

There are countless ways of organizing the information on training requirements of job sites. Virtually every employment project described in the professional literature has its own format for capturing the tasks, requirements, and other features of the jobs for which training is needed. The purpose of our discussion is not to suggest another "ideal format," but rather to propose a way of looking at jobs that can be adapted to meet the needs of local employment services. A sample format and a completed Job Analysis are provided in Appendices 16 and 17.

One of the first challenges confronting an employment trainer is how to organize the large number and type of routines that an employee must perform—even when working supported jobs. Trainers need a strategy that can easily categorize routines into groupings. The use of groupings also ensures that nonwork tasks, which so often affect evaluations of work performance, are both identified and facilitated. Four useful categories when analyzing a job site are (Meyer-Voeltz & Lynch, 1983):

1. Core work routines
2. Episodic work routines
3. Job-related routines
4. Accommodations to the worksite "culture"

These categories are not listed in order of priority.

Virtually all the requirements for almost any job can be divided into one of these four categories. Workers may experience problems in any one category or in any combination of categories. For example, a worker can lose a job just as easily for not coming to work (Category 4) as for making consistent errors on the routine performed most frequently during the day (Category 1). Take particular note that the term "routine" is used to describe the job responsibilities of an employee, rather than the terms "tasks" or "skills," to encourage you to include all the steps required to perform a component of the job in the analysis and training plan. Too often, the initial steps of a sequence—the linking steps to other sequences—and end-of-sequence steps are omitted from training plans. The concept of "routines" includes these vital steps (Callahan, 1986; Center for Applied Urban Research, 1986).

Core Work Routines

Core work routines are job routines made up of cycles that are naturally repeating, without significant interruption between the cycles. The cycle of a task begins with the first step of a job sequence and ends with the step that precedes the initial step of the next sequence. Core routines are those tasks that are likely to be the most frequently performed by the employee; for example:

- Laundry in a hotel: sorting items to be washed, loading the washer
- Grocery: stocking shelves, picking up carts from parking lot
- Factory: operating press machine, assembling circuit breakers

Organizational Tool Task analysis is the name typically given to the organization of the above routines into teachable, sequential steps. A sample and abbreviated task analysis for the 14 steps in operating a machine that automatically tapes box corners might be:

1. **Locate** unstayed boxes from supply pallet.
2. **Select** a stack of boxes approximately 12 inches deep.
3. **Place** stack on working pallet.
4. **Move to** operating position (seated in front of machine).
5. **Turn** machine on at switch under front of machine.
6. **Select** a small stack of boxes (2″–3″ deep).
7. **Place** stack on lap.
8. **Select** one flat box.
9. **Fold** two corners to form a 90 degree angle.
10. **Place** corner of box on angled rest with fingers away from corners.
11. **Depress** foot pedal to activate tape dispenser.
12. **Repeat** steps 9 to 11 until all four corners are taped.
13. **Push** punch counter on machine.
14. **Place** stayed box on pallet.

Facilitation Strategies For most core routines, the job trainer chooses to provide direct systematic training to the employee. Because the core routine's cycles are naturally repeating, the trainer can utilize informing and fading strategies that are so effective with massed-trial training situations. The trainer may also decide to modify the sequence of steps or in some other way devise an adaptation to assist the employee to perform the task. Another strategy is to use job creation or restructuring to define more narrowly the parameters of the job. In the sequence just described, a worker might only load the pallet while another worker stays the boxes. Any job restructuring, adaptation, or significant modification of a routine should always be approved by the employer *before* it is implemented.

Evaluation of the Worker Evaluation of worker performance on core routines occurs during training. The trainer should collect sufficient data to make training decisions and to account for the worker's performance during acquisition and production of the routines.

Episodic Work Routines

Episodic work routines are required routines that are made up of cycles that occur infrequently; for example, two or three times per shift, once a day, or possibly even a few times per week. These routines are often more difficult to train for because of the time lapse between the cycles. They do not easily lend themselves to the types of systematic instructional strategies developed for massed trial training. Examples of episodic work routines include:

- Restaurant: cleaning the dishwasher at the end of the shift, taking out the garbage
- Grocery: punching a time clock, assisting a co-worker to unload a truck
- Factory: Filling out production forms, getting supplies for work station, lubricating a machine

Organizational Tool   The organizational strategy for ordering the skills of an episodic routine is often referred to as an *inventory* (Belmore & Brown, 1978; Sweet et al., 1982). An inventory is compiled by observing the way in which typical workers perform various work routines. The concept of breaking a routine into component steps in an inventory is essentially the same as for a task analysis. The different terms are used simply to reflect the difference in the way in which the routines are facilitated.

An example of an episodic work routine might be cleaning the water filter on the dishwasher at the end of the shift. A sample inventory would be as follows:

1. Fifteen minutes before the shift is over, **turn off** the dishwasher.
2. **Open** drain valve at bottom of washer.
3. **Wait** approximately 3 minutes for washer to drain.
4. **Press** backwash switch to "On" position (red light comes on).
5. **Watch** switch until the light turns off.
6. **Turn** backwash switch to "Off" position.
7. **Close** drain valve at bottom of washer.
8. **Open** fill valve on side of washer.
9. **Wait** until water stops filling. (Shutoff is automatic—listen for sound of rushing water to stop).
10. **Close** fill valve.
11. **Mark** maintenance card for correct date, and initial.

Evaluation Strategies   Evaluation strategies are considered **before** facilitation strategies for episodic work routines because they naturally occur before training in the work setting. Because the cycles of these routines do not naturally repeat on the job, traditional systematic instructional and fading strategies will probably not be as effective as for core work routines. The trainer, however, can reduce the number of skills to be trained by performing a *job-referenced evaluation* based on the skills identified in the inventory. After the trainer or a co-worker has demonstrated the routine to the new employee a few times—preferably during the typical time for the performance of the routine—the trainer asks the employee to perform the routine. For each skill, the trainer notes the actual performance of the worker. If the worker is uncertain what to do or if an error is made, the trainer gives enough information to keep the routine progressing correctly. By carefully considering each step of the evaluation, the trainer can plan how to teach most effectively the steps of the routine.

Facilitation Strategies   In training the task of cleaning the dishwasher's filter which is only done once per day, the trainer can consider several strategies to ensure the routine's successful performance. Let us consider, for instance, that the employee has difficulty on the initial step of the routine—stop dishwashing duties

15 minutes before the shift's end. Let us also imagine that during the job-referenced evaluation the worker did not recognize 2.15 P.M. as the time to stop washing dishes, and he simply kept right on working. The trainer could intervene by following this decision-making sequence for training.

1. **Facilitate** the performance of the routine, without focusing on systematic instruction.
2. **Train** the skill (1) in the regular sequence, (2) by increasing the frequency at which the sequence occurs, or (3) by "mass trials" of the skills.
3. **Modify** the way in which the routine is performed.
4. **Introduce** an adaptation to provide additional information or assistance.
5. **Arrange** for partial or co-performance of the skill by other workers, as initiated by the trainer.

If the trainer knows, for example, that the worker had received instruction in telling time in school for several years and was still having difficulty with it, it would not make much sense to continue to provide more time-telling instruction during the regular performance of the routine at the end of the day. A better decision might be to introduce an *adaptation*—say a large photograph of the kitchen's clock with 2:20 on it—taped alongside the clock; this adaptation is just as feasible whether a digital or analog clock is used at the workplace. The photograph would serve as a sample for the worker to match to the actual clock. If that procedure did not work over time, then the trainer might negotiate with a co-worker or the restaurant manager to remind the worker when it was 2:20 P.M.

Other skills in the routine are much easier to train; for instance, step 5, Watch switch until light goes off. The trainer could give consistent instructions during each routine, referring to natural cues, such as "Watch this light" or "Is the light off now?," and possibly using a gesture and verbal emphasis as well.

The referencing of natural cues and the consequences of not attending to those cues are vital considerations for teaching episodic work routines and job-related routines. Chapter 13 provides an in-depth discussion on the use of natural cues and consequences in employment training.

Job-Related Routines

Job-related routines involve tasks that are not explicitly required by the employer for the job, but which are vital for successful performance of the job. These routines may occur either on-site or off the job. Poor performance on these routines by workers with severe disabilities is more likely to occur than on core work routines. Reasons for this poor performance vary, but it is a regularly stated lament of job trainers that "He/she could do the work just fine, it was _____ (here fill in the blank with any of countless reasons) that caused him or her to be fired." Probably the most usual reason for difficulty on these particular routines is that trainers routinely ignore the importance of teaching them. There seems to be an expectation that anyone "ready" for work should already be able to perform such skills as appropriately using the restroom and arriving at work on time. However, many workers with disabilities lose their jobs when assistance is not offered to facilitate acceptable performance on job-related routines. Consider these job-related routines.

- Restaurant: getting ready to work, washing hands after taking out garbage
- Grocery: taking the bus to work, bringing one's lunch to work
- Factory: using the soda machine in the workers' break area, getting back from break on time

Organizational Tool   The inventory is used for organizing information on job-related skills/routines in the same way as for episodic work routines. A sample inventory for the job-related routines of getting ready to work in a pizza restaurant might be:

1. **Get off** bus in front of restaurant.
2. **Walk** to employee's entrance.
3. **Enter** door into foyer.
4. **Walk** through kitchen area to employee's lounge.
5. **Locate** and open personal locker.
6. **Remove** coat and other items.
7. **Place** all personal items in locker.
8. **Take** apron from locker and put it on.
9. **Close** and lock locker.
10. **Visit** lavatory: Wash hands, comb hair, check clothes.
11. **Go to** timeclock to punch in to begin work day.

Evaluation and Facilitation Strategies   Strategies for evaluating and facilitating successful performance of job-related routines are much the same as for episodic work routines. The important concept to remember is that the trainer may need to provide direct assistance to ensure that job-related routines are performed satisfactorily.

Accommodating to the "Culture" of the Company

This category deals with the expectations that an employer has for employees and the degree of flexibility that is allowed in a workplace. Trainers often make the dangerous assumption that all employers have the same expectations; thus, their approach to different companies varies only to a small degree. The fact is, however, that worksites differ widely in the way in which employers view employee behavior. In some work settings it is permissible for a worker to sit down once a job is completed or a particular component task has been reached. In others, the worker may be fired for sitting. Some employers expect workers to deal with personal differences away from the workplace, whereas others tolerate occasional disagreements between workers. It is in this category that the success of effective job matches is achieved. Consider these examples of behavior problems:

- Restaurant: drooling while serving customers, talking to customers while bussing tables
- Grocery: touching customers walking by in the aisle, opening and eating a box of cookies while stocking shelves
- Factory: forgetting to return to work after break, throwing parts when angry

An example of an actual situation might clarify the importance of this category:

Ted is a 21-year-old man working on a supported work job of operating a dishwasher in a pizza restaurant. Ted does not speak, he is described as being severely disabled, and he also demonstrates the inappropriate behaviors of screaming and hitting others at his residential setting. Ted has learned over time to operate the dishwasher with only minimal assistance; his trainer feels that soon the assistance can be faded altogether.

A problem occurs, however, after the noontime rush is over when the manager turns down the piped-in music by using the control over the counter next to the dishwasher. Ted likes loud music, and he becomes disturbed when the music is turned down. Occasionally, he will even climb up on the table to turn the music louder. This is unacceptable to the employer.

One way to look at this situation is to say that Ted has not accommodated to one of the components of the culture of that restaurant: The music gets turned down when the lunch crowd leaves.

Organizational Tool   The most reliable way to capture all the important components of this category is through observation at the worksite and discussions with the employer. Often, the trainer may not know that a behavior or lack of a certain behavior is a problem that has actually happened. The trainer's job is to be aware of as many cultural demands, taboos, and unacceptable behaviors as possible. It is also difficult to assess exactly what an employer's reaction to a breach of typical practices will be. It is safe to say, however, that the degree of flexibility is dependent on the strength of the existing relationship between the employer and the employee, and the employer and the trainer. Extensive latitude is not typically found early in an employment experience.

Evaluation of the Worker   The employer, and, possibly, trusted co-workers are the best source of information about whether the employee is conforming appropriately to the culture of the particular worksite. A trainer should never automatically assume that a worker must behave a certain way. Many times trainers impose behavioral standards on workers with disabilities that are far more strict than those typically set for other workers.

Before a trainer can decide how to facilitate a successful accommodation to a company's culture, a vital evaluative decision must be made:

> *Is the targeted problem best perceived as a skill to be learned by the employee* (in which case it is handled like a job-related routine), *or is it a behavior that requires some form of intervention or accommodation?*

The following two scenarios of actual job-site problems may help clarify the distinction between these points.

On Donna's first day of work, she gave her trainer the sign for toilet. She had to go quickly! The trainer pointed to the door of the women's room and said, "It's through that door." Donna got up from her work station in the factory, walked to the door, opened it and walked in. She then proceeded to use the toilet with the door open onto the production floor. Her trainer walked quickly to the door and closed it. The trainer knew that Donna's behavior was unacceptable in the company, and it would be necessary to devise a plan to ensure that it would not happen again.

Ken was employed at a restaurant in a medium-size motel. His trainer had been told that Ken had severe emotional disturbance and that he would exhibit bizarre behaviors in public places. During the first several weeks of employment, Ken was a model worker. His productivity was high, and he learned skills rapidly. Additionally, he did not demonstrate any of the behaviors for which we were warned. However, one afternoon Ken's job coach had an appointment immediately after Ken's shift. The trainer usually waited with Ken until the bus arrived. On this day, the bus was about

30 minutes late. With nothing to do, Ken went into the men's room and smeared feces over himself and the walls. He then went out to the front of the motel to wait for his bus. The manager of the motel called the project office in a panic to say something had to be done to keep this from happening again.

Both of these situations involved problems relating to the level of acceptable behavior at a workplace. In both instances the trainer knew that the behaviors would not be tolerated on a repeated basis. Do they require similar or different interventions? In Donna's case, her trainer decided that using the restroom correctly was a skill to be learned. She then implemented procedures as if using the restroom was a job-related routine. In Ken's case, on the other hand, his trainer knew that he was capable of using the restroom without assistance. More teaching on toileting skills would probably be a waste of time. Ken's trainer had to commit to an intervention of providing supervision until the bus arrived. Either the trainer or someone in the restaurant needed to make sure that Ken had some meaningful activity to engage in while he waited for his bus. In this case, the intervention did not eliminate the problem behavior, but it did keep Ken on the job.

Facilitation Strategies   Trainers must be ready to implement any of a variety of training strategies, behavioral interventions, and environmental manipulations to ensure that the worker is able to meet the employer's essential requirements. The trainer must use his or her best judgment to choose a particular strategy. In Ted's situation, his trainer saw several co-workers wearing "Walkman"-like headphones while working. She asked the manager if Ted could wear a portable cassette player similar to the other workers. The employer said that this would be fine. The trainer bought an inexpensive unit that evening and showed Ted how to use it the next day. It was immediately apparent that he enjoyed the headphones. Ted never again complained when the music was turned down. The trainer had succeeded in implementing an intervention that resulted in Ted not being fired.

If job site developers more closely considered creative ways to intervene to solve problems arising in this category, many more persons with severe disabilities could be employed. Even persons with a significant degree of excess behaviors could be matched to particular job settings by creative and committed job developers and trainers.

Summary of Job Analysis Format

Using this framework of the four categories of routines enables the trainer to plan more easily for how to handle all the job site information. Some trainers rely solely on their memory to store all the data. Unfortunately, most people are not able to organize, store, and retrieve easily the vast amount of information on training for a job. Furthermore, the more difficulty the worker has in acquiring and performing the routines, the more vital it is to have accurate and easily accessible information about the various methods, component skills, and specific requirements of all the routines. Therefore, most trainers rely on a structured format (see Appendices 16 and 17).

The particular format chosen by an agency is less important than whether the trainers have sufficient information to train the job successfully. In fact, the printed format probably best serves as a guide or reminder to the trainer that all the important factors have been considered. Many trainers simply use a note pad or looseleaf binder to store task analyses, inventories, and other job-related information. Most trainers keep their data sheets apart from the job analysis form.

However, if a number of job trainers are providing assistance on a given job, the standardized format can make communication much easier among them. Additionally, if employment project managers are unsure of the organizational skills of new trainers, having them fill out a complete job analysis form can provide a degree of assurance that all components of the job are being considered.

A useful distinction can be made for practitioners concerned about the value of the more and the less formalized approaches to job analysis. The formal, structured document can be perceived as the job analysis, and the information contained in informal notebooks and on data sheets can be thought of as the training plan. The training plan is the organizational tool that the trainer actually uses for capturing information for training, whereas the job analysis describes comprehensively the components of the entire job.

JOB ANALYSIS PROCESS

Job trainers need to understand the sequence of activities necessary to obtain the information for the job analysis. The following sequence has proven to be effective over 5 years of use.

1. **Visit** the job site to begin a detailed job analysis of the tasks/routines identified in Step # 5.
2. **Observe** the way in which current employees perform the various routines.
3. **Participate** in the typical orientation procedures of the company, if at all possible.
4. **Meet** and get to know co-workers and supervisors. Remember the names of employees so that you can facilitate introductions when the new employee starts work.
5. Have someone at the job site **teach you** the routines. Notice the procedures, cues, amount of supervision provided, and complexity of the routines.
6. **Perform** the routines that are novel to you until you have a feel for the job.
7. **Decide** on the need for detailed job analysis and inventories for the various tasks/routines of the job.
8. **Write** task analyses and inventories for the tasks/routines that you feel will require the most intervention.
9. **Obtain approval** from the employer on the methods chosen for the tasks/routines to be trained and any modifications/adaptations that you have devised.
10. **Identify** natural cues and consequences in the work routines of the employee.
11. Based on Step # 10 and your knowledge of the needs and skills of the employee, **select** potential training strategies, motivating strategies, possible adaptations, opportunities for job restructuring, and partial participation of other workers.
12. **Write** a comprehensive training plan based on Step 11.
13. **Complete** the job analysis form, if required.
14. **Set** a starting date, **communicate** with the employee and his or her family, and **begin training**.

Performing the Job Analysis Process

Visit the Job Site   The importance of having the job trainer visit the worksite before the new employee begins employment was discussed earlier in this chapter. We recommend that agencies make a policy that trainers *must* visit worksites *before* placing workers there.

Observe the Job Site   Perhaps the most critical skill of the trainer during job analysis is observation. The trainer needs to be able to see or visualize the way in which the routines to be performed by the new employee are performed by others in the workplace. This observation forms the basis for determining the methods of the jobs to be trained. Simply stated, the method of a routine is the way that routine is typically performed in the natural setting. In employment settings, the employer usually has a method or procedure in mind for most of the core routines and many of the episodic routines. If the employer does not recommend a method to employees, workers themselves usually devise typical ways for performing most jobs. These natural methods provide the trainer the most logical starting point for methods for training. Only if natural methods prove to be ineffective for teaching should the trainer introduce modifications.

Participate in Orientation   Although this activity is not mandatory for trainers, participating in the usual orientation procedures of a worksite can be extremely beneficial for several reasons. First, the trainer is exposed to the same information system that would be available to the employee with disabilities if the employer was to provide the training. Not only is there a likelihood that the employer will do some initial training of the new employee, it is the method of choice. The sooner the trainer can facilitate a comfortable training relationship between the employer and the new employee, the better. Second, attending orientation procedures creates an expectation that the new employee will also be provided with an orientation. Too often, trainers and employers ignore the typical procedures offered to all new employees in favor of "getting down to business." No wonder it takes so long for some workers with disabilities to know where the break room is or to learn some other job-related routines covered during orientation. The trainer should also find out about company policies, acceptable dress codes, and other components of the company's culture.

Meet Co-Workers and Supervisors   To a large degree, the trainer is lending competence to the new employee until the worker is able to learn the job and to fit in. It is often necessary for the trainer to get to know the people in the company in order to have competence to lend. A trainer who comes in for a brief period, doing some observation and writing but not saying much to the co-workers, is likely to lend a problem, *not competence,* to the new worker with disabilities. In contrast, a trainer who seeks to become introduced to as many co-workers as possible and who shows interest in their work is laying a strong foundation for the new worker.

Learn the Job from a Co-Worker or Supervisor   An excellent way to meet co-workers and form relationships on the job is to ask to be trained by someone at the site. Job developers should request this opportunity during the negotiation phase. This training also provides an opportunity to assess the procedures used by an employer to teach skills to new employees. The availability and sophistication of the employer's in-house training capabilities dictate the speed and success that the trainer will have in transferring the responsibility for training and supervision to the company and in fading from the site.

Perform the Job   If for no other reason, the trainer should perform the job so as to have empathy with the new employee. It is difficult to observe such factors as rhythm, fatigue, judgment, and speed; they must be experienced. Moreover, because the trainer needs to impart information to the employee on these components of jobs, it is necessary to have some idea of the difficulty inherent in each job routine.

The question most often asked by new trainers is, "How long should a trainer work at a job site for purposes of job analysis?" As with virtually everything else in the process of employing, there is no firm answer. The best advice is to try to work the job long enough to get a feel for each core routine and until fatigue sets in. For most jobs, this means at least one-half day of work at the site.

Determine the Need for Detailed Analyses   Some tasks may be especially important to the employer; others may correspond to identified skill deficit areas for the prospective employee. Job coaches typically choose to analyze and train the most *critical* routines and may work with co-workers and supervisors to train less critical and more infrequently performed routines.

Write Rough Drafts of Analyses and Inventories   An analysis and inventory that reflects the needs of a typical employee of the company should be written first, for the following reasons:

- They provide a logical starting point for all analyses and inventories. Additional steps can be added as needed.
- If the employee can learn from the steps typically used by regular employees, it is a more natural process of training and should help contribute to longevity on the job.
- The resulting analyses and inventories have potential use to the employer without modification.

Choosing the methods for the various tasks/routines should first reflect the natural methods used in the company and second, if necessary, the particular needs of the employee.

Gain Approval for Methods Used   After writing the initial drafts of the routines of the job, check with the employer to ensure that the methods that were observed are acceptable. Occasionally, workers will perform tasks in a manner unacceptable to the supervisors. Significant training problems can result from teaching the wrong method of a routine, only to be told that another method must be used. This small investment of time can guard against wasting time and inadvertently teaching incorrect procedures.

Identify Natural Cues and Consequences   For example, in one business the natural cue to take a break might be that the clock shows 10.00 A.M., and the consequence of not responding to the natural cue is that you miss your break! In another company, the natural cue for break may be a buzzer that cues everyone to leave their work stations. And the consequence of not responding in that situation may be that the supervisor comes by and says, "It's time for a break!"

The trainer must use natural cues and natural consequences to aid in teaching and maintaining the successful performance of the routine.

Identify Considerations for Training   At this point in the sequence, the trainer must pull together all the information about both the company and the new employee when considering how to train each targeted routine. The decision-making sequence for training is a helpful resource. The trainer also needs to plan how the instructional cues that will be used for the worker can relate to the relevant natural cues for each routine (Ford & Miranda, 1984). Consider the following training factors at this time:

- Where to stand while training and sit while observing
- Noise problems: can verbal instructions be understood?
- Safety considerations and rules
- Whether or not to teach judgment on a routine or to create an adaptation
- Type of assistance, interventions and demonstration to be used for training

Write a Comprehensive Training Plan This is the informal, personalized tool that the trainer uses for training all the routines of the job. Most trainers find it sufficient to develop data sheets to reflect the number of steps the employee is expected to need to perform the task/routine, rather than rewriting the task analyses and inventories. The data sheets should be based on the methods identified in the analyses and routines developed in Step 9. Also included in the training plan are the decisions reached in Step 11. It is important to put these training decisions in writing for several reasons:

- To assist the trainer in recalling all the decisions that were made
- To provide co-trainers with a written source of information about the training plan
- To provide accountability so that trainers/agency supervisors are assured that all necessary components for training have been considered

Complete the Written Job Analysis Form This step is necessary only if it was promised to the employer or if the agency supervisor needs additional documentation of the job analysis activity. A standardized form can also be useful if the agency has chosen a group-based form of supported work, as in an enclave. In this situation, the general information contained in the job analysis form would be useful in training several employees.

Get Started The time has finally arrived for employment to begin. The trainer needs to talk to the employer to set a firm start date for employment and to communicate to the new employee and his or her family all the information needed to begin work. Double-check the means of transportation to be used, and consider having backup plans for getting the employee to work in case of initial confusion.

Time Required for the Job Analysis Process

Even though the time needed for each job site is different, it would be hard to perform all the activities of a quality job analysis in much less than a week. That is to say, the job developer needs to negotiate for *at least* 7 workdays from the date the employer agrees to provide employment until the new employee begins work. Many situations require an even longer period to prepare for the very important first day of work. The 7 day period is recommended, even though we fully understand that employers often push for employment to begin in several days or, at times, the day after the job is developed. Agencies must balance the needs of employers with the training needs of the people who are being represented. It may be better to turn down a job or at least to send a trainer to the workplace to maintain production until the job analysis can be completed, rather than rush onto a job site unprepared.

Tips for Performing the Job Analysis Process

Not surprisingly, because the trainer enters a company as an outsider, current employees might wonder what is happening, who the trainer is, and how they may be affected. The trainer's presence at the worksite may also cause production to drop by distracting the employee's attention from their jobs. Therefore, it is necessary for the trainer to consider how he or she wishes to be introduced, how to dress and behave, and what to say when questioned about the project's procedures and the new employee. Keep the following points in mind before reporting to the worksite to perform the job analysis:

- Dress in the same manner as the other employees—not the supervisors.
- Come on the shift at the same time as the other employees and leave only at a logical break time, such as lunch.
- Answer questions honestly, although not necessarily in complete detail. Remember the need to respect the new worker's privacy. Stress the concept that the new worker will produce at the quality level expected of others. Do not use labels.
- Ask questions of co-workers and show interest in their opinions.
- Take notes, but not at the expense of doing the job you are supposed to do.
- If you wish to observe someone, ask for their permission, tell them what you want to do, and show them your analysis or inventory of their work.
- Do not be too familiar with supervisors or the employer while in the work area.
- If in doubt, do not sit down on the job.
- Wear comfortable shoes and, if requested, wear the uniform or other specialized clothing common to the site.
- Write down *everything* of importance.

Lines of Communication

Before the job analysis is completed, the trainer must develop with the employer a clear process for communication. Who should the trainer call if he or she cannot make it to work? Who should the employee or his or her family call if he or she is unable to work? What should be done about problems that may arise with a co-worker? Should the employer give information to the employee or the trainer, or both? Can visitors observe the job site? Is it permissible to take pictures? These, of course, are only a sample of the issues that will come to mind when you actually sample the job and the culture of the workplace. Certainly, every contingency cannot be planned for and solved, but every effort must be made to cover the most critical and common problems of communication.

13

Training and Assessment
The Acquisition of Job Skills

This chapter describes a variety of specific training and assessment strategies for facilitating skill acquisition in the workplace. In this phase of the process of employing, the new worker is introduced to the job site and provided with the training and other supports necessary to perform the routines agreed to with the employer. The ultimate goal of the acquisition phase of employment is for the worker to be able to perform the targeted routines without the assistance of an outside trainer. For some individuals this will be achieved easily in 1 or 2 weeks of intensive training. For others, the goal will be attained through arduous effort and only by persistent and systematic training, the use of adaptations, co-worker supports, and job creation strategies (Rusch, 1986).

The employment trainer is confronted with a difficult challenge: to facilitate successful performance of the job routines, to fade out of the worksite to the greatest degree possible, *and* to be available to provide support as needed. Although these outcomes are often at odds with each other, the trainer must discover a way to make each happen.

All the planning, effort, and aspirations of both trainer and agency will be tested at this point. Systematic training can make a significant difference in the work performance of persons with severe disabilities. It can, most importantly, help bring about significant life changes. These changes often result in stress and uncertainty that, on occasions, can compromise the success of the person on the job. It is important that the trainer be prepared to handle both the foreseeable training challenges and the unforeseen situations that arise during the first weeks of training.

The training system referred to in this chapter is based on an application of Marc Gold's *Try Another Way* system (1980a) in integrated work settings. This approach provides structure for capturing the information to be trained; instructional and reinforcement strategies useful for training skills, especially to workers who find it difficult to learn; and a value perspective governing the use of the strategies. It is a structured, effective, data-based, and generic approach for meeting the needs of workers with severe disabilities.

Many new and complex issues arise during the initial training on a job site. Some relate to training, and an equal number of others concern nonwork factors. The trainer must be aware of *all* the factors that influence the new employee's success on the job. Thus, this chapter describes a variety of these nonwork concerns, as well as issues relating directly to training and evaluation.

The objectives of the acquisition phase of employment training are to:

- Ensure that the new employee is introduced to co-workers and supervisor(s) at the job site and becomes oriented to the company's procedures
- Perform job-referenced evaluations on all episodic work routines and job-related routines; additionally, perform systematic training on core work routines in a manner that provides ongoing assessment during training
- Implement training and facilitation strategies on all routines of the job so that the employee can perform the routines as independently as possible
- Keep detailed training, production, and quality data to use for decision making, measuring progress, and as accountability criteria
- Facilitate the development of relationships between the new employee and others in the workplace for purposes of support, training, and friendship
- Deal with the work-related and nonwork issues involving the new employee that might affect his or her acquisition of work skills

It is important to remember that most jobs have routines that do not involve production, but that are required components of the job. Depending upon the trainee, many of these tasks require training, as well as the production routines. Examples of tasks related to production are:

- Production reports—filling out the paperwork; this may involve using a calculator or counter, writing letters or numbers, and counting
- Moving supplies
- Using a time clock
- Using tools for adjusting and repairing a machine
- Informing the supervisor when supplies are getting low
- Handling finished goods

ORIENTATION OF THE NEW WORKER

If at all possible, the new worker should participate in the routine orientation provided by the company for all beginning employees. The trainer can provide assistance as needed, and modifications can be made to suit the needs of each worker. If the trainer was able to participate in the orientation during the job analysis phase (See Chapter 12), sufficient information should be available to decide whether to personalize the orientation or to allow the worker to participate in the typical procedures.

The sophistication of employee orientation usually varies, depending upon the size of the company, the type of business, and the management philosophy of the employer. Regardless of the approach used to orient new workers, the trainer should ensure that the worker:

- Receives assistance in completing all necessary insurance, withholding, and personnel forms
- Is given a tour of the workplace
- Is introduced to all direct supervisors and co-workers
- Knows the location of lunch and break areas, restrooms, and employee lockers
- Is shown the location of the time clock and informed of procedures for starting work
- Knows what to do when ill and unable to report to work

- Is informed of company policies on work behavior
- Is informed of his or her initial work schedule

Some of the items on this list will be covered during orientation, and the others can be discussed by the trainer with the worker. Some may require systematic instruction. In any case, it is important for the trainer to inform the employee's parents or caregivers of the information communicated during orientation. The only exception to this would be for the worker who is living independently who prefers handling work-related matters personally.

Even though it should be the responsibility of the employer to provide all new employees with this orientation information, the trainer must ensure that the worker with severe disabilities is included in this process. If the employer does not provide a formal orientation or if it does not seem appropriate for a new worker to participate in the typical procedures, the trainer must assume responsibility to gather all the necessary information for the employee.

If the employer does offer an orientation, the trainer should not automatically assume that he or she should attend with the new worker. It may be possible to assist the employer in communicating information to the worker and to remain apart from the interaction between employer and employee. This decision should be made on a case-by-case basis. The primary outcome of the trainer's responsibilities during orientation is that the new employee is fully prepared to begin work and has been provided with all the necessary information. Communication with all those concerned is the vital element needed to accomplish this goal.

EVALUATIONS

You may already have noted that it is not traditional rehabilitation practice to have the evaluation of an employee occur *after* the person begins work. However, in our approach to employing, one's readiness to work is routinely assumed. What remains for the trainer to assess is how best to facilitate successful performance of job routines by the new worker as negotiated with the employer. Gold (1980b) offered these thoughts on evaluation:

> The most effective demonstration of a learner's ability . . . will naturally occur when he is actively engaged in learning. Because the trainer is constantly adjusting to changes in the learner's behavior, he is continually evaluating while teaching. (p. 4)

From the information learned in Chapter 12, you will already recognize the three distinct types of evaluation that occur on job sites:

1. Evaluation during the training of the massed-trials of core routines
2. Job-referenced evaluations of episodic work routines and job-related routines
3. Observational evaluations of how well the new employee is accommodating to the culture of the workplace

Evaluation During Training

When training core work routines—*those routines that have naturally repeating cycles*—the most accurate evaluation occurs during the actual teaching of the routine. The vocational profile (see Chapter 11) provides the trainer with sufficient information to plan for the most appropriate instructional cues and the need for adaptations

and modifications. On the first day of work, the trainer should begin systematic instruction on targeted core routines based on the plans made during the job analysis.
Necessary adjustments to the planned training approaches can only be made once
training has actually begun.

The role of evaluation in this approach to employing is solely for the purpose
of facilitating successful performance on the job. Because core routines are naturally
repeating, they offer the trainer an opportunity to assess the effectiveness of cues and
adaptations, the extent and rate of learning, and the speed of performance each time
a cycle is performed. It makes sense, therefore, to evaluate core routines continually
while training, rather than to set aside a special time for evaluation.

Job-Referenced Evaluations of Episodic and Job-Related Routines

Episodic and job-related routines do not have the naturally repeating cycles of core
routines. These routines may be performed several times per day, once a day, or even
less often. Because of this, the systematic instructional strategies that are so effective
when teaching core routines must be modified to reflect the time gap that occurs
between the performance of various episodic and job-related routines. The opportunity to use training as an ongoing evaluation is also adversely affected. The power
of structured informing and fading strategies can also be compromised by the infre-
quency of the routines. For this reason, job-referenced evaluations are performed on
targeted routines based on the inventories developed during job analysis.

The sequence and the steps of the inventory are used as a benchmark for determining any discrepancies between the way the worker with disabilities performs
a targeted routine and the way in which nondisabled co-workers typically perform
the same routine. The trainer can also target specific skills/steps that the employee
does not currently perform.

To conduct a job-referenced evaluation the trainer must do the following:

1. First, compile an inventory on each targeted routine that the worker with
    disabilities needs to perform.
2. The trainer or a co-worker then demonstrates the routine several times
    during the naturally occurring time for the routine.
3. The trainer then asks the worker to perform the targeted routine. For
    each step of the inventory, the trainer gives enough information to keep
    the routine going, but does not offer direct instruction unless an error is
    made.
4. The worker's actions are noted on the inventory form alongside each
    step/skill. The trainer should also note the manner in which the employee
    attends to and benefits from the natural cues and consequences that are
    available in the setting.
5. The discrepancy between the way the worker performs the routine and
    the way a typical employee correctly performs the task, together with the
    way the targeted worker responds to the available natural cues and deals
    with their natural consequences, combine to provide the basis for the
    training/facilitation plan used by the trainer.

This evaluation allows the trainer to target specific steps/skills of the routine
for intervention. Options for intervention, which we have modified from the work of
Luanna Meyer, as reported in Ford et al. (1986), are as follows:

- **Provide no direct intervention; facilitate the occurrence of the routine using only the natural cues found in the workplace.** This decision allows the learner to acquire the skills of a task/routine merely by regular participation, the manner by which most people acquire information about routines.
- **Provide systematic training.**
  Train the step each time that it occurs in the natural sequence.
  Break the step into smaller, more teachable steps. Then teach as above.
  When the step occurs in the natural sequence, halt the sequence, teach the step using a number of massed trials, and then continue the sequence.
  Pull the step out of the natural sequence and teach it in massed trials until criterion is met. Then plug it back into the natural sequence.
- **Modify the natural method.** Change the natural method typically used to perform the task to one that better matches the needs of the learner.
- **Provide an adaptation.** Add an assisting device or other aid to the method to assist the learner to perform the task.
- **Arrange for partial assistance from co-workers.** If you find that the above strategies did not facilitate successful performance, provide ongoing assistance on targeted steps of the task that enables the worker to participate in the routine. The assistance can initially come from the trainer, but eventually must be provided by someone in the work environment.

Observation of Employees

This evaluation is the least structured of the three presented here, but is perhaps the most important. The trainer must be keenly aware of the degree to which the new employee conforms to the employer's expectations. The worker with severe disabilities may not have to meet all expectations that a company has for its employees, but the trainer must be aware of problems in this area. If the trainer is able to anticipate problem areas or observe them soon after they occur, interventions can be initiated and/or accommodations from the employer can be negotiated. However, if no one identifies potential problems early, the employee's job may be in jeopardy regardless of his or her performance on the work routines.

The best way to evaluate the new employee's success in accommodating to the culture of the company is through close observation, open communication with the employee, and review of accurate data on targeted behaviors. This data can be kept in the form of plus/minus or other counting codes and recorded on a data sheet. Or, it can consist of a narrative log of descriptions of the behavior. Evaluation of the worker's success in performing within acceptable limits is especially crucial early in the training phase until a strong relationship has been developed with the employer.

TRAINING AND FACILITATION STRATEGIES

Many considerations affect the effectiveness of training and the success of the new employee. This section describes the most critical considerations for systematic training. It is important to remember that the main objective of this phase of employing is to enable the worker to perform the negotiated requirements of the job at an acceptable quality level, with continually decreasing amounts of assistance from the trainer. A listing of the most critical considerations and a brief discussion of each follow:

1. Instructional cues
2. Natural cues and consequences
3. Power of assists
4. Fading
5. Criterion
6. Cycle constancy
7. Formats
8. Quality
9. Pace and speed
10. Judgment

Instructional Cues

Instructional cues are the avenues through which the trainer communicates information to the worker about the job. The most common instructional cues are verbal, physical, gestural, demonstration, and modeling. Adaptations, color cues, photographs, and drawings can also be used by the trainer to provide information. Assists may be given by the trainer before the worker starts an action, during the action (e.g., timing), or after an action has resulted in an error. Instructional cues are essential when referring to the natural cues to which the worker must attend if the trainer is ever to fade from the work site.

A challenge for both the trainer and the new employee is to separate information from conversation. The typical workplace is filled with distractions, conflicting messages, and confusion. When instructional cues are planned in advance, the information will be communicated to the worker. A description of the most commonly used instructional cues shown in Table 13.1 follows.

Assists for individual workers should be chosen based on the degree of effectiveness each assist has for the worker. This can be determined from the vocational profile and past experience. Adherence to a predetermined "assist hierarchy" or a "cookbook" protocol is not recommended. Rather, the trainer should increase power and fade information, using a variety of assists.

Verbal Information   Verbal assists are particularly useful for teaching order and discrimination steps, but are not typically effective in teaching manipulation skills. The trainer can distinguish verbal information from routine conversation by the tone used to convey the information and by the amount of information included in a verbal interaction.

Gestures/Modeling   Gestures/modeling assists can effectively communicate information without the use of language or touching. Trainers can simply point to an object or in the direction that represents the correct action. Gestures are also useful for referring to natural cues.

Physical Assists   Physical assists are often useful on manipulation steps of tasks and when safety is an issue. Even though physical guidance is not commonly used in integrated work settings, it is appropriate if used correctly. Trainers should use physical assists only when necessary. Be gentle and responsive to the learner's needs and reactions. Trainers can never teach against resistance—only

Table 13.1.   Types of instructional assists

	Early in training	Close to acquisition
Verbal information	Information-packed short phrases Concise description of desired action Instructional tone References to correct actions	More conversational use of open-ended questions Conversational tone References to natural cues
Gestures/modeling	Exact simulation of the desired action Pointing directly at the next action	Use of a questioning gesture Gesture in the direction of the next action
Physical assists	Manipulating the worker's fingers Placing the trainer's hand over the worker's, e.g., while operating a meat-slicer	Softly touching the worker's hand to move it to the next action Nudging the worker toward the next step
Demonstration	Trainer performs routines and points out natural cues while worker observes	Trainer works alongside worker performing the same routine

with cooperation from the learner. Never force the learner. Fade by requiring the learner to do more and more of the step.

Demonstration   Demonstration is not usually thought of as an effective way of giving specific information to a worker, but it is very effective in informing the worker of what is expected, what a routine looks like, and how "fast" looks. Demonstrating routines before training also shows respect for workers who have no idea what is about to happen next.

Natural Cues and Consequences

Every work routine contains a variety of cues that assist persons to perform the required tasks and routines. Some work settings provide a great deal of information; others contain many fewer cues. Natural cues are important to trainers because they can be utilized to enhance the acquisition and maintenance of vital job routines.

Natural cues are the prompts that are generally available in work settings that cue employees to perform the correct action. For instance, a restaurant may place a sign over the lavatory reminding the employees to wash their hands after using the restroom. Some factories mark dangerous areas with red paint. Most fast-food places use a buzzer to indicate when the french fries are done. These forms of information exist already and do not need to be faded during training.

Virtually every step/skill of an inventory of a work routine has a number of natural cues that can be referenced by the trainer to help teach and maintain the skill. It is critical that, during the development of an inventory *and* when conducting the job-referenced evaluation, the trainer identify all relevant natural cues and observe how the learner attends to those cues (Ford & Miranda, 1984).

When a worker who does not know how to perform a particular task fails to observe a natural cue, one of several things might occur:

1. The routine may be interrupted or perhaps terminated
2. The person may receive negative consequences
3. The person may receive assistance or additional information.

It is the responsibility of the trainer to ensure that the likelihood of consequences (1) and (2) occurring is slight and that consequence (3) be used in teaching the targeted routine.

The most negative consequence of not attending to natural or instructional cues is injury to the worker. If this is a possibility, the trainer must be doubly careful in providing effective instructional cues during training and assessing the degree to which the worker is attending to the natural cues. Natural cues and consequences should be identified by the trainer during the development of the inventory and utilized, as appropriate, during training.

Instructional Power

Instructional power is the amount of intervention, direction, or assistance required for the worker to acquire the skill. Today, this definition, originally created by Marc Gold in 1980, also includes the level of support offered by the trainer. With all the examples of effective systematic instructional approaches in the professional literature, the trainer can virtually ensure the acquisition of core work routines. However, these approaches may be distinctly different from those typically used in the work setting. Trainers must balance the availability of powerful training strategies with the realities of the setting. Consider these points when deciding upon the necessary power to use for instructional assists.

- Use as little power as necessary to accomplish the step.
- Begin with the most natural assists and increase power only as necessary.
- Modify the selection of assists according to environmental conditions, such as noise, space, safety considerations, etc.
- Use physical assists only when necessary and fade them as soon as possible.
- Try to follow the company's procedures for communicating information and training as much as possible.

Fading

Because instructional cues originate from the trainer, the trainer is responsible for developing and fading those cues. Fading of instructional cues is essential for the independent performance of a task. Some instructional cues, such as adaptations, may become natural cues, if used over a long period of time and if their use is supported by others in the work setting. In these cases the trainer must ensure that the assist remains a permanent part of the work environment.

Fading involves purposefully diminishing the power of instructional assists as the learner acquires more and more information about the task and the relevant natural cues. A trainer has successfully faded once the learner no longer depends on the trainer to perform at an acceptable level in a task/routine. Successful fading *can* involve the continuing partial assistance by a person in the natural setting if such assistance is critical to a person with disabilities performing a task/routine.

The strength or power of an assist is an important consideration in fading. The relative strength of the various instructional assists differs from person to person. Some people respond well to verbal assists, and others need constant demonstration. However, within each type of assist, the trainer can give less and less specific information as the learner approaches criterion.

The fading of instructional assists can be accomplished by starting training with assists that require little of the worker and much of the trainer and later moving to assists that require much of the worker and little of the trainer.

Criterion

Criterion is the predetermined, arbitrary point at which the trainer and/or the employer feels that learning has taken place on a given routine. This point of assumed acquisition is specific to each job and may be expressed either as a number of correct trials performed without trainer assistance or as an amount of time of successful production without assistance. Keep the following points in mind when considering the criterion for work routines.

- Set criterion at a level commensurate with the employer's standards.
- Maintain criterion over a number of days.
- Assume criterion only on those tasks trained in the work setting. If tasks are taught apart from the work setting for some reason, criterion must be verified on the job.

Even though the level at which criterion should be set varies depending upon the routine and the needs of the worker, there are some general considerations to follow. These are discussed under the next consideration of cycle constancy.

Cycle Constancy

Cycle constancy is the topographically correct performance of all the steps of a routine, cycle after cycle. Topographical correctness occurs when the steps of the method are performed in the manner *taught by the trainer* and result in the task being completed with acceptable quality. Cycle constancy may be the single most important factor in the acquisition and production of core work routines. If the trainer is able to teach the specific set of movements that comprise the correct way to perform the routine—that is, the natural method—and ensures that the employee maintains those actions throughout the acquisition of the routine, then acquisition time should sharply decrease and production should increase.

In order to assess cycle constancy the trainer needs to be able to see or visualize the correct action, as though on a videotape that can be played back in the mind. There are times on each job when the trainer must be especially concerned with maintaining cycle constancy. Typically, these are also instances when criterion should be set high. We suggest that you set criterion especially high and closely monitor topographical correctness and cycle constancy when:

- Safety is a concern
- Quality is an issue
- Productivity requirements are high
- The task is a core work routine
- The cycle is short
- The cost of materials and/or errors is high

Formats

Formats refer to the *amount* of information that a trainer presents to the new employee when training a routine. The trainer can use a number of formats. However, we suggest that such formats as total task, clusters, and mixed formats are much more similar to natural ways of providing information and should always be tried first. A brief description of each of these natural formats follows.

Total Task Presentation   This involves the performance of all the steps/components of the task by the employee each time that the cycle naturally occurs. By modifying the job, it is possible to use an easy-to-harder sequence within a total task presentation.

Clustering   This is the presentation of naturally grouped portions of the task that are later chained together to form the total task.

Forward Chaining   This is the process of presenting the clusters of the task for training purposes in a typical, first-to-last sequential manner.

Backward Chaining   This is the process of presenting the clusters of the task for training purposes starting with the typically occurring final cluster first and then proceeding backward toward the first cluster.

Mixed Formats   These involve training situations that begin using total task or cluster formats and then require that a step or cluster of steps be pulled-out and taught using massed trials. The steps/cluster are later plugged back into the initial format at criterion.

Massed-Trial   This presentation of selected steps, or clusters of steps, of a task involves repeating the same step/cluster again and again. Although for episodic and job-related routines, this approach is artificial, it can be effective in focusing attention on a targeted problem area. Massed-trial training of tasks without naturally repeating cycles usually must be negotiated in employment settings and may be too artificial or unacceptable to use in some work settings.

Quality

Quality performance of the targeted routines is perhaps the most important outcome of the acquisition phase of employment training. The description and ultimate evaluation of quality are determined by the company and vary from setting to setting. The trainer should strive for each product or outcome of acquisition to meet the quality guidelines of the employer by having a strategy that reduces the likelihood that errors will occur.

The generic application of powerful systematic training approaches, such as Gold's *Try Another Way* system (1980a), provides the trainer with the ability to ensure that quality can be established and maintained throughout the acquisition phase. When training episodic and job-related routines, the trainer may accept occasional errors as part of the learning process. But, with the repeated opportunities for assistance and correction offered by core routines, quality performance can be ensured for the most frequently performed tasks. We recommend the following procedures to ensure quality performance:

1. Use a systematic instructional approach that encourages the trainer to monitor worker performance closely during acquisition.
2. Obtain a visual standard of quality from the employer, if at all possible, to help you "eyeball" the work quality.

3. Ask for written specification of quality.
4. Set criterion high, and monitor cycle constancy.
5. Strive for a quality level *at least* as high as the company's during acquisition.
6. Try to make sure that the various supervisors have similar concepts of quality for the targeted routines.
7. Refer to the natural features of "correctness" when giving information and correcting an error.
8. Quality and safety are directly related. Train for one, and you usually obtain the other.

Pace and Speed

These two considerations are usually thought of as being more related to production than acquisition. However, it is essential to establish a smooth pace during acquisition so as to have a foundation from which you can encourage an increase in speed. Pace and speed are related in that pace precedes speed (see Chapter 14). Pace involves performing the component movements of the routines, especially core routines, at an efficient, fluid, regular rate. Once a comfortable pace is established, the rate of production (speed) can be increased by increasing the pace. If the trainer attempts to increase speed before the employee has established a smooth pace, errors and "jerky" inefficient performance usually result. When training pace, try to do the following:

1. Try to eliminate very fast and very slow movements within the routine.
2. Watch for well-paced work during acquisition, and communicate this to the worker.
3. Model well-paced demonstrations of routines, and/or have the worker observe or work beside another efficient worker.
4. Try to increase speed slowly and evenly during the acquisition phase.
5. Allow for a period of time for a smooth pace to develop, and do not try to rush the worker too quickly.
6. Encourage increasingly rapid, well-paced movements as the worker is able to perform them.

Pressure on the new employee to produce at a given rate is likely to affect his or her acquisition of routines. The rate of a routine's acquisition may be progressing smoothly, even though the rate of productivity is problematic. In this case, the trainer often must perform the work to maintain an adequate level of productivity to meet the employer's needs. When the trainer is doing this, training is difficult. Depending on the level of assistance required by the employee, the trainer has several options in this situation.

- Ask the employee to observe while the trainer catches up.
- Assign the employee to a routine at which he or she has already reached criterion while the trainer catches up.
- Assign a portion of the job to the employee and co-work the job with the trainee.
- The trainer can attempt to make up the difference while training the employee.

- The trainer can negotiate for more flexibility from the employer, possibly through the addition of a co-worker in production.

Judgment

Judgment is necessary on any step of a routine where there is a "range of correctness" and is often more difficult to train than steps with discrete information. Therefore, trainers often reduce the need for judgment by dividing a step into smaller, discrete components or by introducing adaptations. However, some movements simply cannot be broken down into discrete steps. Other movements may not be performed smoothly or rapidly enough using an adaptation. For instance, any adaptation to help a driver learn the "friction point" on a manual clutch would probably result in a jerky ride. The use of an automatic transmission is a modification of the method of shifting. At times, it is necessary to modify the method of the routine in order for the worker to perform the job successfully. The key to teaching judgment is to allow sufficient time for *consistent practice* of the entire routine.

Many jobs involve not one, but a number of, tasks that the trainee will be responsible for performing. If this is the case, be aware of these areas of concern.

- The trainee should reach criterion level on a given task *before* beginning another. If this dictum is not acceptable to the company, this is a major problem and may possibly be a reason not to place a person with that company. Train the most difficult task first; another option is to train the primary routine first that the employee will initially perform most of the day.
- A separate job analysis needs to be completed for each task.
- Training time is inevitably longer than for a job with only one or two component tasks.
- The company may have to assume training responsibility for tasks that are not performed when the trainer is there.

The length of time required for acquisition varies depending upon the trainee and the complexity of the job. Many jobs can be trained to acquisition in 1 or 2 weeks, whereas others may require many weeks. Remember, the successful completion of a number of trials does not mean that the job is thoroughly learned. Accurate performance, without trainer assistance, over a number of days is a far more accurate indication of learning.

TRAINING AND PRODUCTION DATA

During acquisition, it is essential that the trainer use some method of data collection to measure the employee's progress in each targeted routine. These data also highlight problem areas and offer a measure of accountability that training was performed. Data collection is vital for establishing criterion performance, which is particularly important on potentially hazardous routines.

The simplest form of data collection that provides the necessary information is usually the best. Most trainers begin a job using coded data sheets and move on to narrative logs as the employee acquires more and more skills. The following data collection approach can be used for core routines. Episodic and job-related routines can be handled in a similar manner.

1. Get to know the task being trained.
2. Develop a sequential analysis of the task.
3. Make initial data collection decisions; for example, type of coding system, number of steps/skills to be included on data sheet, how the data will be used.
4. Compile and become familiar with a data sheet for the task.
5. Start the training routine without taking data for 15–30 minutes; keep in mind the steps/skills done without an assist.
6. Stop training momentarily, and chart from memory on the data sheet the approximate number of cycles and steps done *without* an assist.
7. Resume training, and do not collect data for 20–40 minutes; again keep in mind steps/skills done *without* an assist.
8. Repeat step 6.
9. Resume training, without collecting data for 30–45 minutes; target those steps/skills requiring the *most* assistance.
10. Stop training momentarily, chart from memory the approximate number of cycles and those steps/skills requiring the *most* assistance (if possible, record the type of assist used).
11. Resume training, and for the first several days keep data on a cycle-by-cycle basis on the steps/skills requiring the most assistance.
12. During the remainder of the acquisition phase, conduct probes by taking data on all the steps/skills of a selected cycle on a regularly scheduled basis: two times per hour, once per hour, four times per day, to a minimum of about twice a day. Begin keeping narrative data on general performance and areas of difficulty.

Bear in mind these additional considerations related to data collection.

- During the first few trials, do not try to keep data on every step. Identify trends and glaring problem areas when you have a chance to write.
- Keep a production log to record impressions, changes, and other related information.
- Use a quality control data collector, if one is available, during the initial trials or for the entire first day of each new task.
- Decide what you will record—the symbols you will use—on the data sheet in advance.
- Be sure to record the date, time, and the process or product involved.
- Time data can either be time-per-trial or time to produce a specified number of units. Use both types at different times for different purposes.
- During the acquisition stage, training data also serves as production data, although the trainer might have to complete a separate production report beginning with the first day.
- Study each day's data sheets to check for trends or problems, and make adjustments, if necessary, during the next day's training.
- Keep data sheets organized and as clean as possible. A clipboard with a clear plastic flap keeps data sheets clean and organized on the production floor.
- File the reports for easy referral.

FACILITATION OF RELATIONSHIPS

The trainer is both a vital link and a potential barrier to the establishment of relationships between the new employee and others on the job site. If the trainer acts as a conduit through which all information concerning the job must flow, the employer and co-workers will feel that the trainer is the *only* person at the job site who can successfully interact with the employee. This perspective inevitably lays the groundwork for future problems.

If on the other hand, the trainer seeks out every possible opportunity to link the worker with other people at the company, co-workers and supervisors can learn how to communicate, teach, and relate to an employee with severe disabilities. This linking must begin during the acquisition phase. Initially, all nontraining communication should come directly to the employee from someone in the company. The trainer's role is to facilitate the communication apart from the employer/employee link, rather than take a position between the two.

Difficult steps on episodic and job-related routines, as identified through the job-referenced evaluation, that require co-worker assistance to perform, can provide an ideal vehicle through which to develop relationships on the job. Similarly, the trainer should be sensitive to any overtures of assistance offered to the employee by co-workers on core work routines. Some co-workers naturally assume an assisting role on the job. These workers need to be identified and supported as they attempt to assist the new employee with disabilities (Shafer, 1986).

Employers often sponsor recreational and social activities for their employees. Company picnics, bowling leagues, social gatherings, and other nonwork functions can bring co-workers together with the new employee. The trainer needs to become sufficiently socialized into the relationships of the worksite so as to be aware of all the opportunities for interactions and relationship building.

ISSUES THAT AFFECT ACQUISITION

Worksite Issues

One of the most frustrating things that can happen during acquisition training is for the trainee to be progressing on schedule and then a factor not directly related to his or her ability to learn the task begins to cause trouble. These problems can be particularly frustrating because they can be much more difficult to solve than training problems. A brief discussion of some common problems that may affect training follows.

Lines of Communication   Problems concerning lines of communication arise when more than one person gives the employee or the trainer conflicting information about the job. Mixed messages and expectations can affect job performance. Often, the only solution is to try to bring all the people together and ask for a decision that can be put in writing. Quality concerns can be the most frustrating as they usually have a range of correctness that allows several people to feel differently about what is acceptable.

Fatigue   Most of the people you place on jobs will come from work activity centers or schools that may offer only a few hours of work each day. New employees will have to adjust to working during the agreed time frame. Fatigue can affect the trainee's acquisition of skills, especially later in the shift. Trainers should realize that there will be an adjustment period for all new employees and should remind them to get plenty of sleep during the first few weeks of training. This is even more important for employees working on the evening or night shift. It is helpful to chart hourly production data to see if performance drops late in the shift or before breaks or lunch. Ideally, a schedule of gradually increasing hours will have been negotiated for the worker during job development. If fatigue or endurance continues to be a problem on the job, the trainer might consider negotiating a more flexible work schedule.

Trainer/Employee Relationship Often, during the latter stages of acquisition training, the worker may begin to resent the trainer's presence. This is a natural and even positive occurrence. The employee, sensing his or her growing competence, wants to work without having the trainer always around. It is the trainer's responsibility to realize this and to discuss the reasons for his or her presence with the employee before a problem arises. The trainer might also change training positions so as to be less noticeable.

Relationship with Other Employees The feelings of the new employee's co-workers can affect training in subtle ways. Employees with severe disabilities can sense feelings of resentment, uncertainty, or "coolness" if they remain apart from co-workers. The trainer can consider the following steps to assist the new employee to develop positive relationships with other employees:

- Learn the names of co-workers and introduce them to the trainee.
- Consider fading trainer presence at lunch and break times.
- If the employee wants to know some information, have him or her ask others. If possible, do not always talk for the worker.
- If you have routine questions about the job during training, ask a fellow employee for advice.
- Encourage the new employee to sit with others and talk to them at break, lunch, and after work.
- Encourage the employee to get involved in company-sponsored activities: softball team, carpool, company party, and the like.

Employer's Noncompliance with Agreed-Upon Expectations This can cause major training problems. The most common situation occurs when the worker is asked to work on a new core routine before criterion has been reached on the current one. Other problems that might be encountered include:

- Shortened probation period for reaching production
- Increased responsibilities for the job
- Unsafe working conditions or lack of safety equipment
- Failure of the employer to provide time for training nonproduction tasks, if agreed upon

These and other problems can occur after training begins. Negotiations with a company decision maker are crucial because these problems can compromise the success of the training. If the problems are not solvable, a decision may have to be made to resign your position as a trainer. The employee would then have the choice to stay on without training or to resign.

Unacceptable Behavior/Mannerisms of the Employee Occasionally, a new employee exhibits behaviors or mannerisms learned in another environment that bring unwanted attention or disrupt the production of fellow employees.

"Do's and Don'ts" established for the employee should clearly follow company policies. If such a behavior as shaking hands with everyone in sight is not against company policy but is bringing negative attention from employees, then discuss the problem with the employee without forcing your opinion on him or her. If the behavior is against company policy, have the supervisor discuss both the problem and possible outcomes with the trainee.

   Shift Work, Evening or Night   In many companies, in order to obtain a job on the day shift, all employees must first work the evenings or night shift until a position is open during the day. Shift work causes problems for all employees, so the trainer should be prepared to deal with any factors that may affect the trainee's production. Not surprisingly, the trainer must also be willing to work evenings or nights!

   The most common problems for shift workers are problems with obtaining enough sleep and not having the same time off as family and friends. The trainer should carefully weigh the pros and cons of shift work before deciding to accept a job for training and should inform all the applicants of the possible problems of shift work.

TRANSFER OF SUPERVISION

Because the trainer eventually fades out of the job, the best time to begin this process is during acquisition training. An orderly transition of supervision is critical; what follows are some hints to accomplish the transfer of supervision smoothly:

- When the employee asks questions about the company or needs other information not directly related to training, refer him or her to the supervisor.
- When the supervisor has information affecting the job or the trainee but that is not related to training, ask that the supervisor tell the employee, not the trainer.
- If the machine or process breaks down, have the employee report it to the supervisor.
- Ask the supervisor to observe training as much as possible.

CONVEYING THE PHILOSOPHY OF COMPETENT WORKERS

If you expect the employees of a company to treat the employee like any other worker, you must be careful not to revert to labeling, gossip, and the lack of confidentiality so common in most human service agencies. We suggest that you keep the following points in mind during training:

- The trainer's attitude and professionalism influence how others perceive the new employee.
- Do not discuss the employee's personal problems in front of others.
- Do not revert to labels or speak in terms of "handicapped," "disabled," or "retarded."
- Talk with the employee as you would with anyone else.

- If co-workers have a question about the employee, help them and then direct them to the employee for answers.
- Explain that the reason you are needed on the job is that the worker has been unemployed and needs extra training to be able to perform his or her job like everyone else.
- Remind co-workers how they felt on the first days of their first job. This is an example of empathy, not sympathy.

CROSS-TRAINING TRAINERS—OR WHAT TO DO IF THE TRAINER CANNOT MAKE IT TO WORK

During the job analysis or before the new employee is hired, it is advisable to train another trainer on the job. Because the trainer needs to be with the new employee during acquisition, a substitute trainer may be necessary should the trainer get sick or is detained in any way from getting to work. The substitute trainer may be an agency staff member with knowledge of the job.

If the trainer must be out during acquisition and no other trainer is available, the trainee should be assigned to some other task that does not require trainer assistance. The trainer should have plans worked out with the supervisior before training begins regarding this assignment.

DO'S AND DON'TS—AN A-TO-Z COMPENDIUM OF SUGGESTIONS FOR TRAINERS

A. Get plenty of sleep during training.
B. Initially, arrive at work *before* the trainee.
C. Collect data on tasks that need to be trained, and keep a training log.
D. Do not leave the employee during acquisition of critical routines if he or she is still making consistent errors.
E. Begin training episodic and job-related routines immediately and at the time they naturally occur.
F. Do not become involved in attempting to change industry's problems. Train employees to function effectively in the current situation or negotiate for reasonable accommodations for the employee.
G. Remember Murphy's Law: *Anything that can go wrong—will.* This is especially true on the first day of training.
H. Establish cycle constancy immediately on core routines.
I. Set acquisition (criterion) levels high.
J. Obtain everything in writing.
K. Dress like the other employees.
L. If you have to train several routines, then train the hardest job first.
M. If the company does not have an orientation, arrange for the new employee to meet other workers at the site.
N. Do not use the most powerful instructional assists first; try to use natural assists whenever possible.
O. Be flexible and adaptive.
P. Ask questions.

Q. Keep the new employee informed.

R. Do not use labels.

S. Do not make decisions for the employee, rather, offer suggestions.

T. Do not offer unlimited help "in any way I can." Rather, provide the employee with a system that delineates who will be asked for assistance in specific instances, e.g., supervisor, co-worker, trainer.

U. Deal with training problems only; assist supervisors to deal with all other problems, including training.

V. Keep management informed.

W. Inform the employee when he or she has met criterion on a routine—and that you won't be around as much afterwards.

X. Be organized.

Y. Do not try to keep what you are doing a secret, but do maintain confidentiality.

Z. When possible, offer to help the company if there is a rush period or if the employee is sick or unavailable.

By now you should surely feel ready to get out and train!

14

Increasing Production Rate

This chapter focuses upon strategies for improving and maintaining an adequate rate of production, and methods of collecting and analyzing production data in natural work environments, and strategies for the transfer of supervision and training responsibilities from the trainer to the company.

The interactions between the trainer and the worker are in transition during production rate training. The relationship between the trainer and company supervisors is also changing. A smooth transition ensures that the new worker will be able to perform effectively for the company and that in turn the company will be able to train and supervise the employee effectively.

Training for speed begins in the acquisition phase and continues throughout the production phase. At this point, the worker should be able to perform the job with little or no trainer assistance. The trainer's efforts are now geared to increase the rate of production necessary to meet the standards agreed upon with the employer. The trainer is no longer required to be with the worker all of the time and should have an established schedule to monitor the employee's progress. Invariably, this schedule involves decreasing amounts of observation and supervision of the worker by the trainer and increasing amounts by company supervisors.

The objectives of the production phase are to:

- Train the worker to perform the job and related work at the production and quality rates agreed to with the employer, with decreasing assistance from the trainer
- Identify and implement systematic strategies to attain and maintain targeted productivity levels
- Continue to keep detailed production and quality data for use in measuring progress
- Implement a schedule for fading the trainer's presence
- Request an employee evaluation by the supervisor
- Meet with supervisors, as a consultant, to assist them in their interactions with the employee
- Complete the transfer of responsibilities for supervision and training of the worker from the trainer to the company
- Implement follow-up services for the employer and the employee

STRATEGIES FOR INCREASING THE PRODUCTION RATE

Because it is typical business practice only to hire those employees who can make a profit for the company, production at the established rate is essential for the new worker, even for workers on supported work jobs. However, enabling people to work rapidly and efficiently is often more difficult than training them how to do a job. Before a trainer implements strategies for increasing production, the following principles should be considered.

The best strategies are natural ones, found in the work environment.

- Naturally occurring incentives imply that "normal people are engaged in normal activities."
- Natural incentives do not focus negative attention on the worker.
- Natural incentives remain even after the trainer leaves.
- The trainer should always exhaust the inventory of natural strategies before implementing artificial strategies.

Artificial strategies are those not used by or with other employees in the work environment.

- Artificial incentive strategies must be temporary.
- The more artificial incentives that a trainer uses, the more that will later need to be eliminated.
- If artificial incentives are or have been used, a systematic plan must be developed to lead from the artificial to natural strategies.

Strategies should be implemented in the following sequence: (1) strategies involving the method, work environment, and company not directly relating to the worker, and (2) strategies directly related to the way the worker performs the job.

Strategies Relating to the Job

The trainer needs to ensure that the job has been designed and trained as efficiently as possible. If this is the case, most people will increase their production according to a learning curve unique to the task and the individual. Some companies have established learning curves for each task, and others have an established period for the production rate to be met.

If the employee has completed the acquisition stage and he or she is experiencing difficulty in increasing production, then the trainer should consider the following steps (roughly in this sequence):

1. Provide time for the employee to get the *feel* of the task, especially if the task involves use of judgment.
2. Check the features of the job station for efficiency, particularly lighting, comfort (temperature, standing versus sitting), arrangement of materials, and cleanliness. Report any problems seen to the supervisor.
3. Reduce or remove distractions: talking among employees, the direction in which the worker is facing, amount of off-task responsibility, all can cause problems.
4. Assess materials handling; try to reduce the distance to carry materials, and the number of times supplies and finished goods must be moved.
5. Is the employee too exact? The employee may be taking more time to ensure quality than is absolutely necessary or required.
6. Double-check production standards. Occasionally the standards you are given by the company are not used in the same way on the production floor.

7. If meeting production standards is a problem, resume training and increase the power of training strategies until cycle constancy is established. Let the new employee know what is going on and why. Consider negotiating for more flexible standards if training is not effective.
8. Review the components of the work activity, making sure it is as efficient as possible. Recast the activity, if necessary, with permission from the company.

Strategies Related to the Worker

Once the trainer has assessed the job and related issues and made required adjustments, he or she should then focus on strategies that directly affect the employee. It is a good idea to rely on strategies initially that the company uses for all employees. Other strategies, developed by the trainer, can be implemented if necessary. Activities and incentives implemented by the trainer should be as close to usual business practices as possible. Artificial incentives should be temporary and used only as a last resort.

Typical company strategies used to increase production are:

- A company performance chart showing the new employee's weekly production rate is posted in the job area.
- Incentive bonus pay is given for any work beyond the production quota.
- Commendations for "Operator of the Week/Month" are awarded to the worker with the highest productivity and quality.
- Pay raises and/or promotions are given once production rates are met or exceeded.
- The new employee's daily counts are turned in to the supervisor, and the supervisor meets with the worker to discuss productivity.
- The supervisor discusses production problems with the employee and offers possible solutions for increasing rate.

STRATEGIES THE TRAINER CAN USE TO INCREASE PRODUCTION

The trainer can use several strategies to increase productivity based on these three principles: (1) Make sure an efficient pace was established during the acquisition stage, (2) set appropriate goals for productivity, and (3) use artificial methods and incentives only as a last resort.

Efficient Pace

First, make sure an *efficient pace* was established during the acquisition stage. Increase speed by increasing the pace of the entire task, rather than speeding up certain steps. Use the following strategies to increase the pace:

- Demonstrate proper pace and speed—modeling.
- Place the worker alongside a fast producer for purposes of modeling skills and general workplace manner.
- Provide continuing encouragement while staying near the worker.
- Use a pacing device, such as a machine, metronome, music or other sound, or flashing light as appropriate. Clearly, these are last-resort solutions.

Goals for Productivity

These goals may be set by the company, the trainer, or the new employee. The company's goals are usually related only to the established production rate, whereas trainer and employee goals are set as increments of the targeted production rate and cover short periods of time. Meeting the company's goals, however, is the bottom line. We suggest you implement the following steps to help increase the employee's production rate:

- *Consider having the new employee contribute to setting his or her own goals.* This requires the trainer to explain to the employee at what level he or she is currently producing and how much more productivity is involved in a rate increase. For workers with severe disabilities, concrete examples of productivity are always more effective than numbers and percentages.
- *Set quantity goals.* A plan is developed systematically to increase the amount of work produced within the same time period—from 200 units/hour to 225 units/hour, then to 235 units/hour, etc.—until the employee meets the expected production rate.
- *Set time goals.* A plan is developed to decrease the time needed to produce the same amount of work—200 units produced in 1 hour, fading to 200 units/45 minutes, 200 units/30 minutes, etc.—until the employee meets the expected production rate.
- *Set speed goals.* The trainer can time each trial and make comparisons with the time allowed for each trial according to the company's time study. The trainer can inform the worker during production of how he or she is performing in relation to the established standard or to the day's goal for speed by saying, "You are right on target" or "Try to work a little faster." Or, during production, as the employee is working, the trainer may say "Time" at the end of the standard cycle or goal. The worker can then increase speed as necessary to meet the "time."
- *Set goals based on past production.* Use time, amount of work, or speed as comparisons, for example, by saying, "You did four boxes last hour—try to do one more this hour."

Artificial Methods and Incentives

These should be used only as a last resort. The trainer may have the supervisor drop by hourly to offer encouragement or ask fellow workers to compliment the new employee at break or lunch. If an artificial pacing device is used, make sure it does not bring negative attention from co-workers. Artificial strategies should be used to establish production and then be removed from the work area. Be sure to first clear the use of artificial incentives with the employer.

KEEPING PRODUCTION DATA

There are clear differences in data collection between the acquisition and production phases. Acquisition data are concerned with skill acquisition; production rate data indicate progress toward meeting the agreed-on production rate negotiated with the company. Nonproduction information should be recorded in the general log kept by the trainer.

Many companies have a standardized process for recording and collecting production data. Often, production is recorded at the end of the day on a standard form by the employee. This form is turned into the supervisor and then may or may not be available to the trainer. Some companies have sophisticated computer printouts of production data, others plot the performance on a chart, and some merely file these reports.

The trainer needs to keep production data for decision making, and the company's methods may not be sufficient for this purpose. Visual data are usually more meaningful than numbers on a list. The frequency of collecting data is also important. For example, a trainer may wish to collect data hourly during the early days of production rate training, but only weekly at the end of the training.

Consider the following methods of data collection:

- Keep your own production data, especially early in production rate training.
- Use daily listings of performance, charts, and narrative formats.
- Collect hourly data early in production rate training.
- Express production data as a percentage of the targeted and established standard.
- Share production data with the new employee.
- Base decisions to implement strategies for increasing production on your data and discuss them with the supervisor.

FADING TRAINER ASSISTANCE

During production rate training, the trainer spends less and less time with the new employee. The total length of time required for production rate training involvement varies greatly, depending upon the complexity of the job. Employees may require weeks, months, or even years to reach the expected production rate on all tasks of the job. A sample training schedule for a 6-week period might be:

Shift	Trainer supervision/ observation schedule
7:00 A.M.–3:30 P.M.	
Weeks 1 and 2	*Time at company: 8 hours* *Check on employee: On the hour and at beginning and end of shift* *Available: All day*
Weeks 3 and 4	*Time at company: 4 hours* *Check on employee: At beginning of shift and 2 hours later—at end of shift and 2 hours before* *Available: 7:00–9:00 A.M.* *1:30–3:30 P.M.*
Week 5	*Time at company: 2 hours* *Check on employee: At beginning of shift and 1 hour later—at end of shift and 1 hour earlier* *Available: 7:00–8:00 A.M.* *2:30–3:30 P.M.*

Week 6   *Time at company: One hour*
                                      Check on employee: At beginning and end of last
                                      hour on shift
                                      Available: 2:30–3:30 P.M.

For supported work jobs, the trainer may spend fewer hours per day with the employee; therefore, the total length of training time may be substantially increased. It is not unusual for workers to continue to increase production rates on supported work jobs over a period of 18 months to 2 years.

SOME FINAL ISSUES FOR PRODUCTION RATE TRAINING

Employee Evaluation

Seek an overall evaluation of the employee during production training. It is important to obtain the company's evaluation of the worker in writing. This evaluation should be conducted in the same manner as for any other employee.

Changing Roles

The trainer's role, as perceived by the company, will change from the task trainer to "trouble shooter" during production training. The trainer should become increasingly reluctant to communicate information about the job directly to the employee. Rather, you should assist the supervisor in communicating with the worker.

The employee may also notice a change in the relationship compared to the skill acquisition stage. The trainer will not be in the company nearly as often and will not be giving information directly to the worker, except as it relates to increasing production rates.

Follow-up Training

Many workers require long-term assistance to meet production goals, especially for those on supported work jobs. However, in subsidized programs, such as JTPA, the company often agrees to hire an employee only when they reach a certain production level—usually not as high as 100%. Thus, the acquisition, production, and follow-up training phases might have these outcomes:

- Acquisition: perform job, without assistance, at the quality level acceptable to the company
- Production rate: 50% production at the quality level acceptable to the company, employee then hired by company
- Follow-up: 80% to 100% production at the quality level acceptable to the company; training over

The services offered during follow-up training are directed as much as possible toward the employer, and much less to the employee. These services should last for a specified length of time that is agreed upon in advance by all parties. A reasonable length of time for follow-up training would be about 6 months. Possible services to be offered to a company during this form of follow-up training include:

- Assistance to line supervisors on production-related matters that concern the employee
- Consultation with the supervisor on methods to train the employee on new jobs in the future
- Information on planned follow-up responsibilities, if any
- Interpretation of the job analysis used for training
- Conducting a final discussion with the employee to explain "the breaking of ties" that occurs once training is over

Follow-up training and related issues for workers receiving long-term supported work services are discussed in Chapter 15.

15

Final Considerations in Developing a Successful Worker

During the final phase in the process of employing, follow-up services offered to the employee differ greatly, depending on the agency's rationale for placement and training efforts. One approach, competitive employment through the business consultant or the employee representative approaches, trains the labor force to perform jobs competently and then allows employer and employee to function without input or assistance once training is over. This approach is based on the philosophy that people with handicaps in the work force can learn and produce effectively on full- or part-time jobs and should therefore be treated as any other employee except during the specified training period required to learn the job.

In contrast, the supported work approach provides job development and employment training services to people labeled "severely handicapped" and continues providing these services for as long as they are needed. This approach is based on the perspective that, although these individuals can produce effectively, it is the training program's responsibility to ensure they they continue to have the opportunities to do so. Both perspectives have potential advantages and disadvantages. You will need to decide which viewpoint or hybrid of both will guide your program.

The objectives of the follow-up phase are to:

- Determine the approach/viewpoint to be used regarding follow-up
- Carry out follow-up responsibilities as dictated by the follow-up approach
- Fulfill the legal and accountability responsibilities required by funding sources
- Deal with employee terminations in accordance with your chosen follow-up approach

ASSUMPTIONS AND RESPONSIBILITIES OF ALTERNATIVE EMPLOYMENT MODELS

Some implicit assumptions and responsibilities underlying the alternative employment models are described below.

Preagreed, Specified Duration of
Services to Employee: Business Consultant Model

Assumptions

- Effective training during acquisition and production rate training will offer all the assistance necessary for a person to do the job. Further training, after these stages of acquisition and production rate training, serves only as a "band aid" for problem solving.
- The company is responsible for problem solving with the former trainee, as with all other employees.
- The people placed should have the dignity of not being "checked up on" for long periods of time by human service agencies.
- The purpose of the placement/training program is to provide people with the skills necessary to perform effectively on a full- or part-time job—not to provide them a lifetime of services.

Responsibilities

- The agency should train employees and offer the company assistance for an agreed-upon period of time.
- The agency should offer assistance after the agreed-upon time on a case-by-case basis and *only* to the company—not to the employee.
- The program is *not* responsible for finding new jobs for former trainees if they lose their present jobs.
- Legal responsibilities—see the section below on Responsibilities in Open-Ended Services.

Open-Ended Duration of Services
to Employee: Employee Representative Model

Assumptions

- People labeled "severely handicapped" can perform meaningful work on a full- or part-time basis with effective training. However, they do not necessarily learn to find new jobs if they are fired or laid off. Therefore, they will probably require continued assistance to remain employed.
- Those to be assisted in employment are the responsibility of the agency that places them—until they have held jobs for a long period of time or have demonstrated the ability to find their own jobs.
- People benefit from having jobs developed expressly for their individual needs, preference, or skills. Employee's needs are considered *before* employer's needs.
- The placement program is willing to offer assistance to the employer to help an employee remain employed for an indefinite period of time. Assistance will be offered only to supervisors; retraining, except on new jobs, will not be offered to the former trainee.

Responsibilities

- Provide services to employees through production rate training and offer the company assistance for as long as the former workers are employed.

- Contact the employer and/or the employee on a regular basis (weekly, monthly, etc.) to ensure that the person is still employed; these contacts may continue for a specified number of years or even indefinitely.
- Offer to provide job development and employment training to former employees if they lose their jobs and wish to return to work.
- Legal responsibilities: no matter which approach you choose for follow-up, the funding source that pays for your services will probably require a certain amount of accountability through contact. Make sure you are aware of required follow-up procedures in advance so as not to compromise the agency's philosophical viewpoint. The employee should also be aware of follow-up calls necessary once production rate training is completed.

Specified Commitment to Long-Term Services: Supported Work

Assumptions

- Persons labeled "severely handicapped" can learn to perform meaningful work in integrated settings if they receive systematic preparation. However, for some individuals, the agency may need to make a lifelong commitment to training, follow-up, and support.
- The people placed in jobs are the responsibility of the agency that placed them into work. This commitment is for long-term services, perhaps throughout the individual's entire working life.
- This assumption of responsibility is a serious commitment of resources to promoting the dignity and value of the individual and his or her right to work in an integrated setting.
- The placement program is willing to offer ongoing support to the employer as needed and to support the employee. This support may include the assignment of personnel to provide additional training and assistance for an *extended* period of time.
- Because the people we represent typically have difficulty seeking their own jobs, we will either have to teach them the skills necessary for finding jobs or be willing to continue to represent them for as long as they need.

Responsibilities

- Provide services to employees throughout their working career
- Maintain ongoing contact with the employer and allocate those required resources that support the needs of the employee/employer.

WHEN A MATCH DISINTEGRATES: EMPLOYEE TERMINATION

An employee can become dissociated from an employer as a result of an employer initiative, an employee initiative, or sundry miscellaneous factors that are tangential yet implicate both parties, such as a company takeover or economic downturn. Several of these features and the implications they create are now considered, with greatest emphasis placed on the employee who foregoes a developed employment opportunity.

Dehiring or termination is a natural and usual workplace experience for non-handicapped people, and it will be no less so for those workers with handicaps. The issue of employee termination is one of the most important and surely the most confusing aspects of placement. Traditionally, job placement activities for people labeled "severely handicapped" have been evaluated simply on duration—success for those who work a long time and failure for those who stay on the job only a short period. *Those,* in this usage, refers both to the employees and to the programs that placed them.

Duration of employment will, and probably should, remain an important criterion in evaluating success of placement activities. However, many factors related to the individual, to the training offered them (see Appendix 18), and to the company in which they are employed affect long-term employment. In order to become long-term, employees must:

- Receive quality representation and training
- Perceive an intrinsic value in work, and develop a perception of themselves as being producers
- Gain job-seeking skills or have someone else represent them whenever they need a job
- Gain work experience and longevity in employment
- Choose the job best suited to them—this may only be possible following exposure to a variety of jobs
- Be personally satisfied with the work they do
- Have the support of their families and significant others
- As soon as possible, return to integrated employment settings if they lose a job

When an employee is terminated either during or soon after the training preparation, most employment preparation programs must decide whether to try to re-employ the individual on another job. Ask yourself the following questions when considering employee terminations:

- How long do most *non*handicapped people stay on their first job?
- How much time and energy were invested in your preparation for employment?
- What is the philosophical viewpoint of your program concerning re-employment?
- Did the employee quit? Why? Does the person really want to work?
- Was the employee laid off or fired? What were the reasons?
- Were the problems work-related or non-work-related?
- Does the person have the skills to find another job on his or her own?
- If there were training problems, did you identify and attempt to correct them?

Take a moment or two to think about the aspirations, expectations, investment, and experience that have been required for you, the reader, to reach your current productivity level. For most of us, productivity is a result of our upbringing in a family and society that always has expected productivity. Typically, it takes a professional at least 16 full years of formal education and experience—summer jobs, part-time jobs, internship/practicum experiences, etc.—to prepare for the first job. All of these preparations contribute cumulatively to eventual productivity.

If we remain cognizant of these phenomena, then we see employee dissatisfaction as a natural occurrence. A conditioning of sorts, getting in physical and mental "shape" to work, will probably be required. This conditioning may be compared to running. Even a runner who jogs 2 to 3 miles every day is not automatically ready to enter a marathon. A number of longer running experiences are necessary. Similarly, the fact that a person has worked for years in a sheltered workshop does not ensure that he or she will keep the first job for a long period of time. Keep in mind the number of "conditioning experiences" most nondisabled people have in the world of work. We must be careful therefore not to place a label of failure on every individual who needs more experience.

Most persons with severe handicaps obtain employment by responding to the rather narrow range of job possibilities identified by agencies. The options most often available have been, *"Do you or don't you want to work?"* It follows, then, that individuals with severe disabilities may exercise their choice and preference in job selection by regularly being a "job placement failure" on a whole variety of jobs, until the very job they really like comes along. This may be a bit hard to accept for job trainers and developers and their funding agencies. Yet, recall again the variety of experiences you have had. How many of us are on our first job? How long did that first job last? Would you *really* be happy if you were still working at it?

Personal Satisfaction

An issue closely related to job choice is personal satisfaction. Does the job offer the employee sufficient psychological and material payoffs to keep him or her working? The novelty of work can wear thin pretty quickly and must then be replaced by something stronger. If the employee's job does not offer personal satisfaction, then likely responses are work avoidance, problems with co-workers, a drop in production output and quality, or simply quitting.

These are problems that are, for many human services personnel, particularly difficult to handle. As a job trainer, you may try counseling the employee—and encourage work supervisors, co-workers, friends, and parents to do the same. If, finally, you decide that the employee is simply dissatisfied with the job or with the company, then the only appropriate solution may be to assist the person to find another job.

Problems of personal satisfaction create a real dilemma. If we feel that we have developed a quality job, informed prospective applicants of what the job entails, and offered effective training, it would seem to follow that the employee should be happy to have the job and should be willing to persevere at it for a reasonable time. When this does not happen your response will depend largely on your agency's objectives and philosophy. One usually helpful strategy is to consider how a nondisabled individual would deal with a lack of satisfaction on the job.

In the process of employing people who have never had an opportunity to work gainfully in an integrated setting, the employment trainer will find that factors other than the ability of the employee and effective training can compromise the success of long-term placement. Depending upon their objectives and philosophy, some programs attempt to influence these factors in favor of successful employment. Whether the programs currently serving potential applicants are involved in training-related issues or not, we must realize that these issues may have a significant impact on success.

Two issues having the greatest impact on employment success are pre-employment preparation of prospective employees, including features that affect the employee's level of independence, and practical concerns, such as transportation, living arrangements, parental support, and company factors.

Employees' perceptions of themselves as producers and specifically their attitudes about the "worth" of work can be critical prerequisites for eventual success. Most of the people who apply for developed jobs come from programs and environments that have cared for them and made all their decisions throughout their lives. Even the very best vocational workshops represent a sheltered environment quite different from integrated employment. Parents, teachers, and some agency staff all too rarely have helped instill the perception, values, and expectation of being productive and independent.

It is hard to say just how and when the realization that one is a productive individual occurs. Possibly, only a number of job experiences bring about this attitude. We need also to accept that, indeed, some individuals may *never* feel that way. If the employee feels that "it's better to receive than to produce," he or she may want to return to the lower-pressure world of the agency workshop. This decision may be made regardless of the effectiveness of the preparation program or the productive capacity of the employee. Nevertheless, a person's perception of the value of productivity can be enhanced by all who have contact with him or her.

Practical Concerns for Maintaining Employment

Transportation   It is particularly important to remember that many employers require a dependable plan for transportation from the applicant *before* they can seriously consider a firm offer to hire. There are several transportation options to consider, each of which has a different set of advantages and disadvantages.

Car Pools   In this approach, the employee checks with supervisors and others and handles details, with the trainer providing behind-the-scenes assistance. A fair charge should be paid for participation in the carpool. Make sure that the ride is available every day, morning and evening.

Family or Agency Transportation   This should preferably be a short-term approach until other methods can be arranged. The system must bring employees to work on time.

Public Transportation   The public bus service is an excellent option if company and employee are near a bus line. Taxis are expensive, and are usually best used exclusively for emergencies.

Personal Transportation   The bicycle is fine in good weather and for short distances. Walking is also an option if the employment site is not too far away from the employee's residence. Hitchhiking is potentially dangerous and is certainly not a dependable method of transportation.

Employer-Provided   This is available from some very large employers.

Community Service Agency Van   Use of this option may pose philosophical contradictions. Such vans are often not very punctual.

Living Arrangements   These issues, which concern the individual's residence, may affect employment success.

- It may be necessary for an individual to move in order to get a job. However, the worker may not yet have learned to cook, manage a home, and manage money, and supervised living arrangements simply may not be available. Too, individuals who move away from home for the first time may get homesick and quit their job.

- The closer an individual lives to a job, the easier it will be to arrange transportation.
- If the employee is working on a shift, expecially the night shift, noise and other distractions during the day may hinder his or her sleeping.
- Living in a publicly subsidized residential facility poses unique problems. The worker may not have the opportunity to spend his or her money as desired, and restrictions imposed by the residential facility may dilute the impact of the dignity earned through integrated employment. Income received from the job may jeopardize residential arrangements. Not all publicly subsidized residential facilities are designed to meet the needs for consistency, punctuality and shift working demanded by employers in integrated, community-based settings.

Parental Support   Most of the individuals you represent will not choose to go against the wishes of their parents or guardians when deciding whether to take a job. Or, we may feel that the individual has not been given the option of choosing, because choice requires options. Thus, we strongly advise that parents be kept continually informed of prospective options for employment, the methods of training, and relevant information about potential employers, such as wages, benefits, and working conditions. However, parents should be discouraged from attending interviews with applicants, touring the work area to check out the job station, and receiving the employee's paychecks. Parents can choose to arrange a tour for themselves with the employer, to observe training, if done in a discreet manner.

Company Factors   There is a good possibility that an employee may quit or be fired because of factors beyond the control of the trainer or the employee. If you see problems forming or become aware of them after they occur, you should attempt to negotiate a solution with the people responsible.

Company-related problems that can affect the duration of an employee's job include the following:

- The company did not fulfill agreements made in the Employment Contract or in the previously negotiated Summary of Expectations.
- The employee has a personal conflict with the supervisor or co-workers.
- The employee was required to perform routines or tasks other than those previously trained, without adequate additional on-site training.
- The employee was required to work longer hours or on different shifts than previously negotiated.
- The company has a lay-off, strike, etc.
- The employee has a dispute with the company over pay, time off, benefits, etc.
- The employee is dissatisfied with the assigned job.
- The employee is unable to meet production and/or other job requirements of the employer.

QUALITY OF REPRESENTATION AND TRAINING

Simply stated, employment training personnel and the agencies they represent must make a commitment to facilitate the provision of all the components necessary for a person to obtain, learn, and maintain jobs that developers negotiate. Both off-the-job and on-the-job activities must be facilitated. However, even the most thorough planning may not be sufficient to ensure long-term employment. People may quit or be fired from jobs on which they can perform at industrial standards. In many of these cases, neither the employee nor the placement program has necessarily failed. Rather, the value of the employment experience should be assessed through reviewing the process used, the training decisions that were made, and similar factors.

If an employee quits or he is fired and you have considered and eliminated personal factors, consider whether a training problem was at fault. It is essential for the trainer to assess the entire training relationship to determine whether the training was adequate and to ensure that a similar problem will not occur with other employees in training.

A thorough reassessment of all the pertinent factors should be undertaken, preferably with other staff input to ensure objectivity. Training-related problems are varied but some commonly encountered situations include insufficient practice for developing judgment, training not being offered for all of the job's responsibilities, a personality conflict between trainer and employee, the trainer's lack of effectiveness in giving necessary information, or the trainer's lack of enthusiasm or dissatisfaction with the job being trained.

Two questions have been posed throughout this book: What are the skills and competencies being taught to persons labeled "severely handicapped," and for what types of environments are they being prepared? Answers to these questions must be forthcoming if we are to prevent a new generation of sheltered workers. To help provide these answers, we now review several important issues relating to preparation for employment in integrated, competitive work environments. These issues include the instructional content of employment preparation enterprises, the environments in which employment training should take place, and some of the perceived logistical problems that may arise in the process of preparing for employment.

The primary assumption underlying all employment training is that participants are being prepared for some type of employment. What appears to be at issue is the **nature of the employment preparation setting and eventual employment site**, which traditionally has included a range of options from adult day care to private sector employment. The professional literature reflects this diversity of definition and purpose. For example, in 1980, Gold and Pomerantz contended that employment training skills can only be "those which enable an individual to earn a living and other normative reinforcers associated with working" (p. 432). Others also emphasized competitive employment, but acknowledged a continued role for sheltered work environments (e.g., DuRand & Neufeldt, 1980). Perhaps the most concise definition, from a perspective of delineating meaningful work (by that we mean skill outcomes), was developed by Brown, Ford, Nisbet, Shiraga et al. (1983). It reads as follows:

> *Meaningful work* refers to a series of actions that, if not performed by a severely handicapped person, must be performed by a nonhandicapped person for money. Assume that a severely handicapped student is asked to put a nut on a bolt, assemble an electronic circuit board, package and unpackage pink fuzz, sort colored pipe cleaners, and make piles of popsicle sticks, but did not. If it is now necessary to pay a nonhandicapped person to perform these actions, by definition, they can be considered meaningful work. If not, they can be called simulated work tasks, prerequisite work skills,

work attitude builders, artificial work, putting a nut on a bolt, etc., but by definition *they cannot be called meaningful work.* (p. 4)

For the purpose of our discussion, what follows is a composite definition of those employment activities for which we think persons labelled "severely handicapped" should be prepared:

Involvement in meaningful work in integrated environments that enables the individual to earn a living wage, and receive all the other typical benefits associated with working, such as interactions with nonhandicapped co-workers, greater degrees of independence and decision-making power, benefits, etc.

Acceptance of this definition has potent implications for the instructional content of employment training programs. That content traditionally has focused on *simulated work experiences* (Brown, Ford, Nisbet, Shiraga et al., 1983), such as sorting various objects by color, shape, and texture; having one group of individuals assemble nuts and bolts so that another group can disassemble them later; folding and collating the same materials day after day; assembling three-piece puzzles; and making macrame plant hangers for sale at meetings of a parent's organization. All of these activities have been repeatedly justified on the grounds that they help develop "good work habits, stamina, positive attitudes toward task completion, eye-hand coordination, and appropriate responses to criticism and supervision."

Unfortunately, evidence to support the most relevant justification—that individuals exposed to this training have been able to secure employment—has been markedly lacking. We contend that the goal of all employment preparation programs *must* be to select and use those instructional strategies that have an empirically documented relationship to successful employment. This type of curricular selection process requires that employment training personnel move beyond sheltered workshops and actively determine what really goes on in the worlds of business and industry. Unfortunately, as has been adequately documented elsewhere, relatively few human service personnel have had direct experience in the environments for which they are preparing persons with severe handicaps (e.g., Gold, 1980a; Gold & Pomerantz, 1980; Pomerantz & Marholin, 1977; Wehman & Pentecost, 1983).

The practice of training skills that are not functional, relevant, chronologically age appropriate, or ecologically valid can no longer be tolerated if employment training personnel are to take seriously their responsibility to prepare persons with severe handicaps for employment. In relation to the curricular content issue, Gold and Pomerantz (1980) cogently observed:

Obviously, any work setting involves communication skills, daily living and self-help skills, transportation skills, etc. as well as the specific tasks peculiar to a particular job. All socially appropriate behaviors in the work world are just as much "vocational" as they are any other arbitrary classification. There can be no topographic definition of a vocational task. (p. 431)

Fredericks (1983) further clarified this position when he described the following rationale for the selection of instructional content:

Associated work skills are those behaviors essential for survival in a working environment. Many of these behaviors, such as appropriate dressing, hygiene, and communication and social interaction, are covered in other curricular areas. But they are also included in this domain to stress their importance in the world of work. We believe that associated work skills are the most important in vocational programs at the secondary level. For these are the skills that can generalize to other work settings and have been found by numerous researchers to be skills for survival in the work world. (p. 2)

A relatively recent study by Rusch et al. (1982) illustrates this curricular selection and validation process. These researchers analyzed the entry-level survival skills in various service operations jobs, such as food service and janitorial, through a 47-question survey that was sent to 120 potential employers in those industries. The respondents indicated that 70 skills were considered necessary for initial employment. Five skills were unanimously agreed upon by this sample of employers: reciting one's full name and address; demonstrating the ability to do basic addition; keeping one's hair combed; following one instruction at a time; and, completing repetitive tasks previously learned at a proficiency level within 25% of the average rate.

An analysis of the Rusch et al. data indicates that as many as 53% of the skills could be taught and learned across a number of curricular domains, such as domestic, recreation/leisure, community. These skills included reciting one's home address, communicating such basic needs as toileting necessities, using deodorant, recognizing the importance of punctuality, and moving about safely in the environment. Based upon the results of their survey process, Rusch and associates concluded that opportunities for employment can be greatly enhanced by emphasizing instruction on the skills perceived as important by potential employers.

A word of caution is needed here regarding the data just presented. The fact that the skills were identified—and undeniably they *are* important to potential employers—should **never** be considered as pass/fail criteria for employment. Some people may view this listing of skills as *prerequisites* to employment, and thereby, certain individuals may be seen as "unready for" employment. As a counterpoint, we propose that, if a learner does not demonstrate proficiency on a selected skill, then employment training personnel have a responsibility to facilitate skill acquisition through systematic training. Another possibility would be to develop adaptations that minimize the relative importance of the particular skill. For example, if the learner is nonvocal and cannot recite his or her address upon request, then the trainer could prepare a name card that can be presented in response to the verbal cue, "What is your name?" Or, a set of sequenced language cards could be used to facilitate the following of a specific set of directions for task completion and the use of a calculator could eliminate the need to perform calculations. The limits of available prosthetic learning aids are defined only by the trainer's creativity.

ENVIRONMENTAL CONTEXTS FOR EMPLOYMENT PREPARATION

Given the premise that one of the primary goals of employment training is to prepare all learners for integrated employment, a critical question becomes: In what types of environments should employment preparation occur? Traditionally, employment training experiences have been provided in nonwork environments exclusively, alongside persons with handicaps, such as in special school classrooms and simulated work adjustment programs, with the assumption that acquired skills can be easily transferred to the workplace. There is, however, a fast-growing body of research to validate employment preparation in *natural environments*—the varied locations in which specified skills and competencies ultimately are to be performed (e.g., Brown, Branston, Hamre-Nietupski, Pumpian et al., 1979). In the employment preparation domain, adoption of this practice invariably necessitates training in actual work locations as opposed to simulated environments.

There are several reasons why training in natural environments is preferred. First, many learners have difficulties in generalizing acquired skills across environments, instructional materials, persons, language cues, and correction procedures. This finding, although frequently ignored or minimized during training, has been validated through numerous research studies (Drabman, Hammer, & Rosenbaum, 1979; Freagon & Rotatori, 1982; Panyan & Hall, 1978; Reichle, Williams, Vogelsberg, & O'Connor-Williams, 1980; Stokes & Baer, 1977; Walker & Buckley, 1972). Traditional vocational training practices for persons labeled "severely handicapped," however, are tantamount to "train-and-hope" (Stokes & Baer, 1977). This practice discounts the need for generalization training and assumes that skills taught in one environment will, automatically and magically, be performed spontaneously in other instances and environments.

As a counterpoint to the train-and-hope pitfall, several authors have outlined the critical training rules that have greatest implication for employment training programs. Gold (1980a, 1980b), for example, discussed the inherent differences between "learning" environments and "doing" environments, i.e., locations in which training is conducted, locations in which learners ultimately perform specified skills. Brown, Nietupski, and Hamre-Nietupski (1976) proposed that a trainer cannot reasonably be assured that a learner has acquired a skill unless it can be performed in at least three different places, for at least three different people, with at least three different sets of instructional materials, resulting from at least three different sets of language cues. Falvey, Brown, Lyon, Baumgart, and Schroeder (1980) encouraged trainers to use *natural cues and correction procedures*—those available in natural environments—during the training process.

The consequences of not accepting the necessity for generalization can be tragic to the future opportunities afforded to persons labeled "severely handicapped." Performance in a classroom or workshop setting is simply not enough—learners must be given the opportunity to perform selected skills and routines within the ultimate environments, the community, and the workplace.

A second, and probably the most important reason for training in natural environments, is the opportunity to engage in longitudinal interactions with nonhandicapped persons. Clearly, sheltered environments do not provide such opportunities. Full integration into the community requires that persons labeled "severely handicapped" acquire the skills necessary to interact with a wide variety of individuals, both known and unknown. For many persons so labeled, these skills must be systematically trained and practiced. Natural environments offer an excellent opportunity for employment trainers to conduct specific training related to interpersonal interactions with nonhandicapped persons.

A third advantage to training in natural environments involves the interrelated variables of expediency and cost effectiveness. By selecting natural environments as the primary location for training, the wise trainer has automatically reduced the need for extensive generalization training. Such an approach can be translated into reduced training time, reduced staff requirements, a reduced need for large simulated training facilities, and ultimately, cost savings.

A final consideration, discussed earlier but from a differing perspective, centers upon the employment trainer's expectations for learner performance. Gold (1980b) defined *expectancy* as follows:

> Whether or not the learner will be able to learn a task for which he/she has the entering behaviors and for which the trainer thinks he/she has sufficient power and teaching time available. The trainer must try to see the learner as he/she really can be, for what he/she sees as inadequacies may be inadequacies—but of the environment, not of the learner. (p. 7)

PERCEIVED LOGISTICAL PROBLEMS IN PREPARING FOR EMPLOYMENT

In segregated environments, there is a common tendency to have lowered expectations for learner performance. Wehman and Pentecost (1983) described this phenomenon in the following way:

> It may be all too easy to modify or eliminate an objective which all members of a special population find difficult, when they are the only ones in the program. If, however, they are trained alongside workers who do succeed, for example, at using a time clock, there is increased motivation . . . to find a way to adapt, or practice the skill until it is learned. (p. 126)

Pomerantz and Marholin (1977) expanded upon this point with the following observations:

> Programs using the sheltered workshop as a model are in danger of incorporating its habilitation deficiencies. The problem of low expectations exists . . . as indicated by reliance on simple tasks for training purposes. *By accepting the challenging goals of providing . . . job-related skills . . . these programs can create significant change.* (Emphases added, p. 134)

As an illustration of expectancies or, perhaps more aptly, a lack of appropriate expectancies, consider the following incident that occurred in a sheltered work environment. One of us observed a work evaluator interviewing several young men about their aspirations in the world of work. When asked this question, one responded, "Sing, dance, and make King Kong movies," and another, "Be a night show host." Tragically, these young men had no concept of work and why should they, having attended a segregated school for 16 years, followed by their move across a parking lot to the sheltered workshop. At the age of 25, these two young men had no experiences in actual work environments. Certainly, these practices must be challenged and changed if persons labeled "severely handicapped" are to gain full access to employment opportunities—not just based on affirmative action, but based upon competencies.

Another critical component of the job training and placement process is the involvement of parents. This variable is so important that it can literally "make or break" the entire employment preparation process. Wehman, Hill, and Koehler (1979) identified several practical issues that have a fundamental impact upon employment opportunities for persons labeled "severely handicapped." They included loss of Supplemental Security Income (SSI) benefits, parental fears regarding the unknown pitfalls of employment, the effects of job schedules on family routines, transportation problems, and parental concerns regarding potential job loss through layoffs and firings. Too often, these problems have been exacerbated by professionals who neglected to discuss employment with parents until just prior to placement in a work setting. Furthermore, parents' reservations regarding their son's or daughter's entrance into the work world are often viewed solely, and most probably incorrectly, as a reflection of overprotection.

Employment trainers can overcome most parents' concerns through discussion and exploration regarding employment preparation early in the employment process. Through their discussions with parents, professionals can validate the expectation that every young child with handicaps will someday be entering the work world and that education and training processes are directed toward that end. Such a prediction, although feared by some professionals, encourages accountability and serves later to reduce many disagreements and hardships. The process of working with parents, finding answers to their questions, and soliciting their involvement should certainly culminate with employment.

At this point we hope that you feel equipped to begin the process of providing effective employment preparation services for persons with severe handicaps. You will find a multitude of additional ways that complement the ideas offered in this book for working creatively with the people you serve and the employers with whom you establish ongoing relationships. All these tactics will be valuable.

Most importantly, however, is your own commitment to finding meaningful, competitive employment within integrated settings. Successes in establishing a foothold on gainful employment in a regular work setting provide the motivation and rewards to carry you over the rough spots. Your commitment is your most powerful tool. Keep your commitment protected—but be prepared to use it often!

References

Albin, T. J., Stark, J. A., & Keith, K. D. (1979). Vocational training and placement: Behavior analysis in the natural environment. In G. T. Bellamy, G. O. O'Connor, & O. C. Karan (Eds.), *Vocational rehabilitation of severely handicapped persons: Contemporary service strategies* (pp. 161–180). Baltimore: University Park Press.

The Association for Persons with Severe Handicaps. (1983). *Position statement on employment for persons with severe handicaps.* Seattle, WA: Author.

Baer, D. A. (1981). A hung jury and a Scottish verdict: "Not proven." *Analysis and Intervention in Developmental Disabilities, 1,* 91–97.

Bass, B. M., & Barrett, G. V. (1981). *People, work, and organizations.* Newton, MA: Allyn & Bacon.

Bates, P. E. (1986). Competitive employment in southern Illinois: A transitional service delivery model for enhancing competitive employment outcomes for public school students. In F. R. Rusch (Ed.), *Competitive employment issues and strategies* (pp. 51–63). Baltimore: Paul H. Brookes Publishing Co.

Bellamy, G. T., Bourbeau, P. E., & Sowers, J. A. (1983). Work and work-related services: Postschool options. In M. Snell (Ed.), *Systematic instruction of the moderately and severely handicapped* (2nd ed.) (pp. 490–502). Columbus, OH: Charles E. Merrill.

Bellamy, G. T., Peterson, L., & Close, D. (1975). Habilitation of the severely and profoundly retarded: Illustrations of competence. *Education and Training of the Mentally Retarded, 10,* 174–187.

Bellamy, G. T., Rhodes, L. E., & Albin, T. J. (1986). Supported employment. In W. E. Kiernan & J. A. Stark (Eds.), *Pathways to employment for adults with developmental disabilities* (pp. 129–138). Baltimore: Paul H. Brookes Publishing Co.

Bellamy, G. T., Rhodes, L., Bourbeau, F., & Mank, D. D. (1980). Community programs for severely handicapped adults: An analysis. *Journal of the Association for the Severely Handicapped, 5,* 307–324.

Bellamy, G. T., Rhodes, L. E., Bourbeau, P. E., & Mank, D. M. (1986). Mental retardation services in sheltered workshops and day activity programs: Consumer benefits and policy alternatives. In F. R. Rusch (Ed.), *Competitive employment issues and strategies* (pp. 257–271). Baltimore: Paul H. Brookes Publishing Co.

Bellamy, G. T., Rhodes, L. E., Wilcox, B., Albin, J., Mank, D. M., Boles, S. M., Horner, R. H., Collins, M., & Turner, J. (1984). *Quality and equality in employment services for adults with severe disabilities.* Eugene, OR: Specialized Training Program.

Bellamy, G. T., Sheehan, M. R., Horner, R. H., & Boles, S. M. (1980). Community programs for severely handicapped adults: An analysis of vocational opportunities. *Journal of The Association for the Severely Handicapped, 5,* 307–359.

Belmore, K., & Brown, L. (1978). A job skill inventory strategy for severely handicapped potential workers. In N. Haring & D. Bricker (Eds.), *Teaching the severely handicapped* (Vol. 3, pp. 223–262). Seattle, WA: American Association for the Education of the Severely and Profoundly Handicapped.

Berkeley Planning Associates. (1985). *Development of performance measures for supported employment programs. Report to the U.S. Department of Education, Office of Special Education and Rehabilitation Services.* Berkeley, CA: Author.

Boles, S. M., Bellamy, G. T., Horner, R. H., & Mank, D. M. (1984). Specialized training program: The structured employment model. In S. C. Paine, G. T. Bellamy, & B. Wilcox (Eds.), *Human services that work: From innovation to standard practice* (pp. 181–205). Baltimore: Paul H. Brookes Publishing Co.

Bourbeau, P. E. (1985). Mobile work crews: An integrated approach to achieve long-term supported employment. In P. McCarthy, J. Everson, S. Moon, & M. Barcus (Eds.), *School to work transition for youth with severe disabilities* (pp. 151–166). Richmond: Project Transition-into-Employment, Virginia Commonwealth University.

Bricker, W. A. (1977). Alternative perspectives on assessment and intervention. In N. G. Haring (Ed.), *Developing effective individualized education programs for severely handicapped children and youth* (pp. 269–293). Washington, DC: Bureau of Education for the Handicapped.

Brickey, M., Browning, L., & Campbell, K. (1982). Vocational histories of sheltered workshop employees placed in Projects with Industry and competitive jobs. *Mental Retardation, 19,* 113–116.

Brown, L., Branston, M., Hamre-Nietupski, S., Johnson, B., Wilcox, B., & Grunewald, L. (1979). A rationale for comprehensive longitudinal interaction between severely handicapped students and non-handicapped students and other citizens. *AAESPH Review, 4,* 3–14.

Brown, L., Branston, M. B., Hamre-Nietupski, S., Pumpian, I., Certo, N., & Grunewald, L. A. (1979). A strategy for developing chronological-age-appropriate and functional curricular content for severely handicapped adolescents and young adults. *Journal of Special Education, 13*(1), 81–90.

Brown, L., Falvey, M., Vincent, V., Kaye, N., Johnson, F., Ferrara-Parrish, P., & Grunewald, L. (1980). Strategies for generating comprehensive, longitudinal, and chronological age-appropriate individualized education programs for adolescent and young-adult severely handicapped students. *Journal of Special Education, 14*, 199–216.

Brown, L., Ford, A., Nisbet, J., Shiraga, B., VanDeventer, P., Sweet, M., & Loomis, R. (1983). *Teaching severely handicapped students to perform meaningful work in nonsheltered vocational environments.* Draft paper, University of Wisconsin and Madison Metropolitan School District.

Brown, L., Ford, A., Nisbet, J., Sweet, M., Donnelan, A., & Grunewald L. (1983). Opportunities available when severely handicapped students attend chronological age-appropriate regular schools. *Journal of the Association for the Severely Handicapped, 8*, 16–24.

Brown, L., Nietupski, J., & Hamre-Nietupski, S. (1976). The criterion of ultimate functioning. In M. A. Thomas (Ed.), *Hey! Don't forget about me* (pp. 2–15). Reston, VA: Council for Exceptional Children.

Brown, L., Shiraga, B., Ford, A., VanDeventer, P., Nisbet, J., Loomis, R., & Sweet, M. (1986). Teaching severely handicapped students to perform meaningful work in nonsheltered vocational environments. In R. Morris & B. Blatt (Eds.), *Special education: Research and trends* (pp. 131–189). Elmsford, NY: Pergamon.

Brown, L., Shiraga, B., York, J., Kessler, K., Strohm, B., Sweet, M., Zanella, K., VanDeventer, P., & Loomis, R. (1984). *The direct pay waiver for severely intellectually handicapped workers.* Unpublished manuscript, University of Wisconsin, Madison.

Brown, L., Shiraga, B., York, J., Kessler, K., Strohm, B., Sweet, M., Zanella, K., VanDeventer, P., & Loomis, R. (1985). Integrated work opportunities for adults with severe handicaps: The extended training option. *Journal of The Association for Persons with Severe Handicaps, 9*(4), 262–269.

Brown, R., Hibbard, M., & Waters, B. (1985). The transition of people with mental retardation from school to work: The implication of structural unemployment. In M. S. Gould & T. G. Bellamy (Eds.), *Transition from school to work and adult life.* Eugene, OR: Specialized Training Program.

Burton, T. A., & Hirshoren, A. (1979). The education of severely and profoundly retarded children: Are we sacrificing the child to the concept? *Exceptional Children, 45*, 598–602.

Callahan, M. (1986). Systematic training strategies for integrated, supported workplaces. In *Job match— Together: For good business (a multi-media training kit for employers and employing agencies).* Omaha, NE: Center for Applied Urban Research.

Callahan, M., Balicki, P., Guardanapo, E., McBride, H., Pelmonter, C., & Rutherford, K. (1981). *The Mississippi project: The process of employing.* Urbana, IL: Marc Gold and Associates.

Center for Applied Urban Research. (1986). *Job match—Together: For good business.* Omaha: Center for Applied Urban Research.

Certo, N., Brown, L., Belmore, K., & Crowner, T. A. (1977). A review of secondary-level educational service delivery models for severely handicapped students in the Madison Public Schools. In E. Sontag, J. Smith, & N. Certo (Eds.), *Educational programming for the severely and profoundly handicapped* (pp. 111–128). Reston, VA: The Council for Exceptional Children.

Crosson, J. E., & Pine, A. L. (1979). The application of experimental behavior analysis in vocational training for the severely handicapped. In G. T. Bellamy, G. O. O'Connor, & O. C. Karan (Eds.), *Vocational rehabilitation of severely handicapped persons: Contemporary service strategies.* Baltimore: University Park Press.

Cruickshank, W. M. (1960). Planning for the severely retarded child. In *Report of the governor's committee for the mentally retarded.* Columbus: Ohio Department of Education.

DeFazio, N., & Flexer, R. W. (1983). Organizational barriers to productivity, wages, and normalized work opportunity for mentally retarded persons. *Mental Retardation, 21*, 157–163.

Donnellan, A. M., LaVigna, G. W., Zambito, J., & Thvedt, J. (1985). A time-limited intensive intervention program model to support community placement for persons with severe behavior problems. *Journal of The Association for Persons with Severe Handicaps, 10*(3), 123–132.

Drabman, R. S., Hammer, D., & Rosenbaum, M. S. (1979). Assessing generalization in behavior modification of children: The generalization map. *Behavioral Assessment, 1*, 203–219.

DuRand, J., & Neufeldt, A. H. (1980). Comprehensive vocational services. In R. Flynn & K. E. Nitsch (Eds.), *Normalization, social integration, and community services* (pp. 283–298). Baltimore: University Park Press.

Elder, J. K. (1984). Job opportunities for developmentally disabled people. *American Rehabilitation, 10*(2), 26–30.

Elder, J. K., Conley, R. W., & Noble, J. H. (1986). The service system. In W. E. Kiernan & J. A. Stark (Eds.), *Pathways to employment for adults with developmental disabilities* (pp. 53–66). Baltimore: Paul H. Brookes Publishing Co.

Falvey, M., Brown, L., Lyon, S., Baumgart, D., & Schroeder, J. (1980). Strategies for using cues and correction procedures. In W. Sailor, B. Wilcox, & L. Brown (Eds.), *Methods of instruction for severely handicapped students* (pp. 109–133). Baltimore: Paul H. Brookes Publishing Co.

Farber, B. (1968). *Mental retardation: Its social contexts and social consequences.* Boston: Houghton Mifflin.

Federal Register. (1974). Employment of handicapped clients in sheltered workshops. Chapter V, Part 525, May 17, 1974, 17509.

Federal Register. (1984). Supported employment, September 25, 1984, 15025.

Flexer, R. W. (1983). Habilitation services for developmentally disabled persons. *Journal of Applied Rehabilitation Counseling, 14,* 6–11.

Flexer, R. W., & Martin, A. S. (1978). Sheltered workshops and community vocational training settings for the moderately and severely handicapped. In M. Snell (Ed.), *Systematic instruction for the moderately and severely handicapped* (pp. 414–430). Columbus, OH: Charles E. Merrill.

Ford, A., Dempsey, P., Black, J., Davern, L., Schnorr, R., & Meyer, L. (Eds.). (1986). *The Syracuse community-referenced curriculum guide for students with moderate and severe handicaps.* Syracuse: Syracuse City School District.

Ford, A., & Miranda, P. (1984). Community instruction: A natural cues and corrections decision model. *Journal of The Association for Persons with Severe Handicaps, 9,* 79–87.

Freagon, S., & Rotatori, A. F. (1982). Comparing natural and artificial environments in training self-care skills to group home residents. *Journal of The Association for the Severely Handicapped, 7,* 73–86.

Fredericks, H. (1983). Vocational services for students with severe handicaps. *Newsletter of The Association for the Severely Handicapped, 11,* 2, 6.

Galloway, C. (1982). *Employers as partners.* Sonoma, CA: Times-Mirror Publishing Group.

Garner, J. B. (1985). The young handicapped child: Philosophical beliefs and pragmatic actions. In C. S. Mcloughlin & D. Gullo (Eds.), *Young children in context* (pp. 111–133). Springfield, IL: Charles C Thomas.

Garner, J. B., Zider, S. & Rhoads, N. (1985). *Training and employment for persons labeled mentally retarded: A project with private industry.* Ocean Springs, MS: Marc Gold & Associates.

Gilbreth, F. B., & Gilbreth, L. M. (1924). Classifying the elements of work. *Management and Administration, 8*(2), 151.

Gold, M. W. (1972). Stimulus factors in skill training of retarded adolescents on a complex assembly task: Acquisition, transfer, and retention. *American Journal of Mental Deficiency, 76,* 517–526.

Gold, M. W. (1980a). *Did I say that?: Articles and commentary on the Try Another Way System.* Champaign, IL: Research Press.

Gold, M. W. (1980b). Research on the vocational habilitation of the retarded: The present, the future. In M. W. Gold (Ed.), *Did I say that?: Articles and commentary on the Try Another Way System* (pp. 61–104). Champaign, IL: Research Press.

Gold, M. W. (1980c). *Try another way: Training manual.* Champaign, IL: Research Press.

Gold, M. W., & Pomerantz, D. J. (1980). Issues in prevocational training. In M. W. Gold (Ed.), *Did I say that?: Articles and commentary on the Try Another Way System* (pp. 287–300). Champaign, IL: Research Press.

Gold, M. W., & Ryan, K. M. (1980). Vocational training of the mentally retarded. In M. W. Gold (Ed.), *Did I say that?: Articles and commentary on the Try Another Way System* (pp. 207–224). Champaign, IL: Research Press.

Goldberg, I., & Cruickshank, W. (1959). The trainable but noneducable: Whose responsibility? *National Education Association Journal, 47,* 622–623.

Goldstein, H. (1960). Report to the governor's committee for the mentally retarded. In *Report to the governor's committee for the mentally retarded.* Columbus: Ohio Department of Education.

Greenleigh Associates, Inc. (1975). *The role of the sheltered workshop in the rehabilitation of the severely handicapped.* Report to the Department of Health, Education, and Welfare, Rehabilitation Services Commission. New York: Author.

Hill, M., & Wehman, P. (1981). Cost benefit analysis of placing moderately and severely handicapped individuals into competitive employment. *Journal of The Association for the Severely Handicapped, 8,* 30–38.

Hobbs, N. (1975). *Issues in the classification of children* (Vol. II). San Francisco: Jossey-Bass.

Hunter, J., & Bellamy, G. T. (1976). Cable harness construction for severely retarded adults: A demonstration of training technique. *American Association for the Education of the Severely/Profoundly Handicapped Review, 1,* 2–13.

Karan, R. L., Eisner, M., & Endres, R. W. (1974). Behavior modification in a sheltered workshop for severely retarded students. *American Journal of Mental Deficiency, 79,* 338–347.

Kiernan, W. E., & Stark, J. A. (Eds.). (1986). *Pathways to employment for adults with developmental disabilities.* Baltimore: Paul H. Brookes Publishing Co.

Lecours, R. G., & Garner, J. B. (1982). *The great unemployability hoax.* Unpublished manuscript. Akron, OH: Mid-Eastern Ohio Special Education Regional Resource Center.

Manchetti, B. M., Rusch, F. R., & Lamson, D. S. (1981). Social validation of behavioral training techniques: Assessing the normalizing qualities of competitive employment training procedures. *Journal of The Association for the Severely Handicapped, 6,* 6–16.

Mank, D. M., Rhodes, L. E., & Bellamy, G. T. (1985). *Four supported employment alternatives.* Eugene, OR: Specialized Training Program.

Martin, J. E. (1986). Identifying potential jobs. In F. R. Rusch (Ed.), *Competitive employment issues and strategies* (pp. 165–185). Baltimore: Paul H. Brookes Publishing Co.

Martin, J. E., Schneider, K. E., Rusch, F. R., & Geske, T. G. (1982). Training mentally retarded individuals for competitive employment: Benefits of transitional employment. *Exceptional Education Quarterly, 3,* 58–66.

Meyer-Voeltz, L., & Lynch, E. (1983). *Community integration strategies: A functional approach to programming.* St. Paul: Government Training Service.

Moon, S., Goodall, P., Barcus, M., & Brooke, V. (1985). *The supported work model of competitive employment for citizens with severe handicaps: A guide for job trainers.* Richmond: Rehabilitation Research and Training Center of Virginia Commonwealth University.

Naisbett, J. (1982). *Megatrends.* New York: Warner Books.

Noonan, M., Brown, F., Mulligan, M., & Rettig, M. (1982). Educability of severely handicapped persons: Both sides of the issue. *Journal of The Association for the Severely Handicapped.* 7(1), 3–12.

Norman, T. (1980). Telephone prospecting for greater success—A cassette/tape self study course developed with General Cassette Corporation. *Training/HRD, June,* 36.

Panyan, M. C., & Hall, R. V. (1978). Effects of serial versus concurrent task sequencing on acquisition, maintenance, and generalization. *Journal of Applied Behavior Analysis, 11,* 67–74.

Peters, T. J., & Waterman, R. H. (1982). *In search of excellence.* New York: Harper & Row.

Pomerantz, D. J., & Marholin, D. (1977). Vocational habilitation: Time for a change. In E. Sontag, N. Certo, & J. Smith (Eds.), *Educational programming for the severely and profoundly handicapped* (pp. 129–141). Reston, VA: Council for Exceptional Children.

Reichle, J., Williams, W., Vogelsberg, T., & O'Connor-Williams, F. (1980). Curricula for the severely handicapped: Components and evaluation criteria. In B. Wilcox & R. York (Eds.), *Quality education for the severely handicapped: The federal investment* (pp. 80–135). Washington, DC: United States Department of Education.

Revell, W. G., Kriloff, L. J., & Sarkee, M. (1980). Vocational evaluation. In P. Wehman & P. J. McLaughlin (Eds.), *Vocational curriculum for developmentally disabled persons.* Baltimore: University Park Press.

Rhodes, L., & Valenta, L. (1985). *Industry-based supported employment: Enclaves for persons considered severely handicapped.* Eugene, OR: Specialized Training Program.

Rusch, F. R. (1979). Toward the validation of social-vocational survival skills. *Mental Retardation, 17*(3), 143–145.

Rusch, F. R. (1983). Competitive vocational training. In M. Snell (Ed.), *Systematic instruction for the moderately and severely handicapped* (pp. 503–523). Columbus, OH: Charles E. Merrill.

Rusch, F. R. (Ed.). (1986). *Competitive employment issues and strategies.* Baltimore: Paul H. Brookes Publishing Co.

Rusch, F. R., & Mithaug, D. E. (1980). *Vocational training for mentally retarded adults: A behavioral analytic approach.* Champaign, IL: Research Press.

Rusch, F. R., Schutz, P. R., & Agran, M. (1982). Validating entry-level survival skills for service occupations: Implications for curriculum development. *Journal of The Association for the Severely Handicapped, 7,* 32–41.

Schatzki, M. (1981). *Negotiation: The art of getting what you want.* New York: New American Library.

Schneider, K. E., Martin, J. E., & Rusch, F. R. (1981, November). Costs versus benefits between sheltered and nonsheltered vocational programs: Are we sacrificing quality? *Counterpoint, 1,* 28.

Shafer, M. (1986). Utilizing co-workers as change agents. In F. Rusch (Ed.), *Competitive employment issues and strategies* (pp. 215–224). Baltimore: Paul H. Brookes Publishing Co.

Social Security Disability Benefits Reform Act of 1984. Report from the Committee on Ways and Means, March 14, 1984. Washington, DC: U.S. House of Representatives.

Sontag, E., Certo, N., & Button, J. E. (1979). On a distinction between the education of the severely and profoundly handicapped and a doctrine of limitations. *Exceptional Children, 45,* 604–616.

Specialized Training Program. (1985). *Perspectives on supported employment.* Eugene, OR: Author.

Stainback, W., & Stainback, S. (1983). A review of research on the educability of profoundly retarded persons. *Education and Training of the Mentally Retarded, 18*(2), 90–100.

Stern, F. M., & Zemke, R. (1980). *A guide to success for men and women in sales.* Englewood Cliffs, NJ: Prentice-Hall.

Stokes. F. T., Baer, D. M., & Jackson, R. L. (1974). Programming the generalization of a greeting response in four retarded children. *Journal of Applied Behavioral Analysis, 7,* 349–367.

Sweet, M., Shiraga, B., Ford, A., Nisbet, J., Graff, S., & Loomis, R. (1982). Vocational training: Are ecological strategies applicable for severely multihandicapped students? In L. Brown, J. Nisbet, A. Ford, M. Sweet, B. Shiraga, & L. Gruenewald (Eds.), *Educational programs for severely handicapped students, Vol. XII* (pp. 99–131). Madison, WI: Madison Metropolitan School District.

Tawney, J. T., & Smith, J. (1981). An analysis of the forum: Issues in education of the severely and profoundly retarded. *Exceptional Children, 48*(1), 5–17.

Taylor, F. W. (1895). A piece rate system. *Transactions of the American Society of Mechanical Engineers,* Paper No. 647.

Taylor, F. W. (1903). Shop management. *Transactions of the American Society of Mechanical Engineers,* Paper No. 1003.

United States Department of Labor. (1977). *Sheltered workshop study: A nationwide report on sheltered workshops and their employment of handicapped individuals (Vol. I).* Washington, DC: Author.

United States Department of Labor. (1979, March). *Study of clients in sheltered workshops (Vol. II)*. Washington, DC: Author.

Vogelsberg, R. T. (1986). Competitive employment in Vermont. In F. R. Rusch (Ed.), *Competitive employment issues and strategies* (pp. 35–49). Baltimore: Paul H. Brookes Publishing Co.

Walker, H. M., & Buckley, N. K. (1972). Programming generalization and maintenance of treatment effects across time and across settings. *Journal of Applied Behavioral Analysis, 5*, 209–224.

Wehman, P. (1981). *Competitive employment: New horizons for severely disabled individuals*. Baltimore: Paul H. Brookes Publishing Co.

Wehman, P., & Hill, J. W. (1983). Competitive employment for moderately and severely handicapped individuals. *Exceptional Children, 47*(5), 338–345.

Wehman, P., Hill, J. W., & Koehler, F. (1979). Placement of developmentally disabled individuals into competitive employment: Three case studies. *Education and Training of the Mentally Retarded, 14*, 269–276.

Wehman, P., & Kregel, J. (1984). *A supported work approach to competitive employment of individuals with moderate and severe handicaps*. Unpublished manuscript, Virginia Commonwealth University, Rehabilitation Research and Training Center, School of Education.

Wehman, P., Kregel, J., & Barcus, M. (1985). From school to work: A vocational transition model for handicapped students. *Exceptional Children, 52*, 25–38.

Wehman, P., & Moon, S. (1985). Critical values in employment programs for persons with developmental disabilities. In P. Wehman & J. Hill (Eds.), *Competitive employment for persons with mental retardation* (Vol. I, pp. 2–20). Richmond: Virginia Commonwealth University, Rehabilitation Research and Training Center.

Wehman, P., & Pentecost, J. H. (1983). Facilitating employment for moderately and severely handicapped youth. *Education and Treatment of Children, 6*(1) 69–80.

Whitehead, C. W. (1979). Sheltered workshops in the decade: Work and wages, or welfare? In G. T. Bellamy, G. O'Connor, & O. C. Karan (Eds.), *Vocational rehabilitation of severely handicapped persons* (pp. 71–84). Baltimore: University Park Press.

Will, M. (1984). Bridges from school to working life. *Programs for The Handicapped, 2*, 1–5.

Wolfe, J. (1974). *Disability is no handicap for DuPont*. Sacramento: California Governor's Committee for Employment of the Handicapped.

Wolfensberger, W. (1969). The origin and nature of our institutional models. In R. B. Kugel & W. Wolfensberger (Eds.), *Changing patterns in residential services for the mentally retarded* (pp. 59–71). Washington, DC: President's Committee on Mental Retardation.

Wolfensberger, W. (1972). *Principle of normalization in human services*. Toronto: National Institute on Mental Retardation.

Appendices

1. Employer Contact Sheet 182
2. Contact Listing and Card File 184
3. Suggested Letters of Introduction 185
4. Sample Informational Handout 189
5. Making Successful Contacts: Sample Telephone Calls 191
6. Questions and Objections Encountered During the Phone Call 193
7. Employer Information Sheet 195
8. Sample Follow-Up Letter 196
9. Summary of Expectations for Services Offered 197
10. Memos of Industrial Contact 199
11. Sample Employment Agreement 202
12. Employment Site Quality Consideration Checklist 204
13. Vocational Profile 206
14. Sample Completed Vocational Profile 212
15. Sample Job Posting 219
16. Job Analysis 221
17. Sample Completed Job Analysis 228
18. Suggested Letter Terminating Negotiations 236

APPENDIX 1

Employer Contact Sheet

Name of business	City	Date	Person making contact	Nature of business
Sterling Drugs	Gulfport	5/4	Ed	Laxatives/antacids
Ventrola Mfg.	Long Beach	5/5	Penny B.	Large airvents/fans
Pan Am, NASA	Bay St. Louis	5/5	Penny B.	Customer service area
Howard Ind.	Laurel	5/7	Ed	Electric transformers/motors
Dairy Fresh	Hattiesburg	5/10	Ed	Milk products
Milwaukee Electric Tool	Jackson	5/10	Harry M.	Electric tools
Swingster Corp.	Gulfport	5/11	Penny B.	Caps/clothing
Glass Container	Jackson	5/12	Harry M.	Glass containers
Inland Container	Jackson	5/12	Harry M.	Corrugated products
Interior Packaging	Pearl	5/14	Harry M.	Corrugated packaging
Pan Am—NSTL	Bay St. Louis	5/14	Penny B.	Subcontract for cafeteria/mail
Wendy's	Pascagoula	5/17	Penny B.	Fast foods
Murray Envelope	Hattiesburg	5/18	Mike C./ Kathy R.	Paper office supplies
NACO	Laurel	5/19	Kathy R.	Furniture mfg.
South Central Bell	Biloxi	5/21	Ed G.	Phone service
Ferson Optics	Ocean Springs	5/22	Ed G.	Precision optics
Standard Containers	Gulfport	5/25	Ed G.	Makes plastic/metal containers
Dresser Atlas Dresser	Laurel	5/27	Ed G.	Oil field hauling/loading
Drilco	Laurel	5/27	Ed G.	Oil field hauling/loading
Wendy's	Ocean Springs	5/29	Ed G.	Fast foods
M. H. Graham	Biloxi	5/29	Mike C.	Cookware mfg.

APPENDIX 1

(continued)

Method of contact		Job possibilities			Gave referral	Referral
Person	Telephone	Hot lead	Possible	No		
X	X		X		no	
X	X	X			yes	Fred Jones, Dairy Fresh
X	X	X			no	
X	X			X	no	
X	X		X		no	
X	X			X	no	
X	X			X	yes	Mary Kemp, South Central Bell
X	X		X		yes	Jim Smith, Lays Potato Chips
X	X			X	no	
X	X	X			yes	Jim Brown, Baker Box
X	X	X			yes	Morison's Cafeteria
X	X	X			yes	Ocean Springs Wendy's
X	X	X			no	
X	X			X	no	
X	X			X	no	
X	X		X		yes	Greg White, Alpha Optics
X	X	X			no	
X	X			X	no	
X	X		X		no	
X	X	X			yes	Mike Malone, Regional supervisor
X	X	X			no	

APPENDIX 2

Contact Listing and Card File

Company _____   Contacts:

Address _____   1. _____

       _____   Title_____

Type of work _____   2. _____

       _____   Title_____

Accessibility _____   3. _____

                                Title_____

- -

Follow-Up

Date	Action	Results

Letters: Intro _____   Follow-up _____   Brochure _____

Referred by _____   Company _____

Notes

_____

_____

_____

_____

_____

APPENDIX 3

Suggested Letters of Introduction

From a Traditional Agency

[your organization's letterhead]

[date]

Russell Parkerson, Division Manager
Murray Envelope Corp.
2020 Highway 11, North
Hattiesburg, MS 39401

Dear Mr. Parkerson:

You know, it seems that things are always changing. Just when we think that we've got "the" answer, a completely new set of issues comes up. At Southern Industries Workshop in Hattiesburg we have been providing the people we serve with sheltered employment services for over 10 years. Now we are finding out that it is possible to employ these people on regular jobs in our community.

Even though the economy has improved in our area, we realize that jobs are still hard to find in Forrest County. The people who work at Southern Industries can offer the flexibility often required during uncertain economic conditions. They are eager to work--a few hours per day, several days per week or even full-time. And, with the training and ongoing support services we are able to offer, at no charge, these workers can learn to perform quality work that meets your needs.

I am sure that you will be interested in hearing about how this project and local employers such as yourself can cooperate in training persons who are handicapped to be productive members of the labor force. Even if you currently have no job openings, I would appreciate the opportunity to meet with you. A brief meeting of about 25 minutes is all that we need to explain our project. I will be calling you in the next few days to see if we can set a time for an appointment.

Sincerely,

Penny Johnson

APPENDIX 3

(continued)

From an Alternative Agency

[your organization's letterhead]

[date]

Jane Maxwell, Manager
Apex Hotel Systems
191 Salina Street
Syracuse, NY 13200

Dear Ms. Maxwell:

How many times have you said to yourself, "No matter how hard we try to screen our applicants, we still have to train them how to do their jobs our way?" Community Options, a local agency that assists people with disabilities to find employment, agrees. We recognize that good employees are developed on the job, not in some other location. Since the people represented by our agency are eager to work, we have designed cost-free, on-the-job training procedures that can ensure that they will perform their jobs your way.

Community Options serves a broad range of people with disabilities in Syracuse. However, they share one common trait: They all want to work and need to work. Our approach carefully considers the needs of the employer and the skills of the applicant. We then negotiate with you to determine the best job for the applicant who is represented.

I would appreciate the opportunity to discuss this project with you, even if you have no openings at this time. It will require only 25 minutes of your time. I will be calling you in the next several days to see if we can set a time to meet.

Sincerely,

Teresa Callahan

APPENDIX 3

(continued)

Without a Referral

[your organization's letterhead]

[date]

[The name of the contact person
and the employer's address]

Dear _____:

Wouldn't it be refreshing if, when someone applied for work in your company, they said, "If I can't produce with the quality and consistency that you expect, then I shouldn't work here." The people we place and train feel just that way. It is our job to ensure that you are aware of this valuable source of workers.

This letter and brochure are sent to your company as an introduction to _____, Inc. We are a private corporation contracted by _____ to seek career and job opportunities for persons presently employed by work activity centers in our state. It is our purpose, through training, to provide these people with the skills necessary to meet the strict qualifications that business and industry require of their employees.

There is no cost to your company except in providing the wages and benefits to any person you might hire. Our company has been successful in other similar projects because we work closely with businesses in maintaining an atmosphere of cooperation and commitment to quality. We provide your new employee with the information and skills necessary to meet industrial standards.

I would appreciate the opportunity to explain our program in depth and will be calling you in the near future to see if we can get together to discuss this project.

Sincerely,

_____
Project Director

APPENDIX 3

(continued)

With a Referral

[your organization's letterhead]

[date]

[The name of the contact person
and the employer's address]

Dear _____:

I am writing concerning an issue of utmost importance to business:
the investment in the people. Our organization is a nationwide firm
contracting throughout the state to work with businesses on some common goals, those that focus on the investment in personnel and its impact on the economy.

Together with area businesses such as yours, we are developing approaches to employment, training, and production that I think you'll
find very interesting. Rob Jones at _____ Company in
_____ has been very pleased with our services. He would
be happy to give you information concerning the employees he hired
through our project.

I would like to meet with you briefly to describe this program in
greater detail and show you how your company might benefit. I will call
your office Friday to see when a meeting can be arranged.

Sincerely,

_____

Project Director

APPENDIX 4

Sample Informational Handout

**Fact Sheet Concerning the Community
Options Employment Development Project**

WHAT IS COMMUNITY OPTIONS?   Community Options is a local service agency in Syracuse that helps people with disabilities find employment. This project negotiates with area employers for a variety of community work experiences for the persons served by the agency. These work experiences include supported work jobs, part-time work, and full-time employment. Community Options provides recruitment, job-finding services, job analysis, on-the-job training, and ongoing support services to both the targeted employee and the participating employers.

The purpose of the agency is to offer people with disabilities the opportunity to gain work experience and skills in the best possible place—on actual jobs. These work experiences should offer each employee a better chance for lifelong employment in good jobs.

ARE WORK EXPERIENCES THE SAME THING AS REGULAR JOBS?   It depends on the individual *and* the needs of each employer. Our agency tries to match the skills of the people we represent with the needs of employers. We also closely observe potential job sites to determine if there are possible ways to restructure existing jobs to meet the needs of our applicants. We then negotiate with the employer to see if such an accommodation is feasible. Others may be able to perform their job responsibilities in much the same manner as any other employee. The bottom line is that the employer *always* is able to decide the extent of productivity and responsibilities for the employees they hire.

WHAT IS SUPPORTED WORK?   Some of the people we represent may require flexible work hours, reduced expectations for productivity, or subminimum wage pay in order to be successful employees. Supported work is a new concept of employment that allows all persons with disabilities to work in regular worksites. It is the responsibility of the agency to ensure that the employer and the targeted employee receive the assistance and support necessary for this to happen.

WHO ARE THE PEOPLE SERVED BY COMMUNITY OPTIONS?   All the participants of the project are adults from the Syracuse area who have been labeled "mentally retarded" or "developmentally disabled." Most applicants have attended high school, and many have had vocational experiences during school.

CAN THESE PEOPLE REALLY HANDLE A REGULAR JOB?   Some of the people we represent can perform a full-time job with the multiple responsibilities and the typical pressures present in any type of work. Others need the chance to be exposed to these pressures and responsibilities in order to learn how to deal with them.

When our applicants require more assistance or flexibility than other employees, our trainer is available to provide training, to perform a detailed job analysis, to design strategies by which the applicant can meet your needs, and to provide ongoing support—all at no charge to you.

(continued)

WHY DON'T THESE PEOPLE JUST GO TO SHELTERED WORKSHOPS?   The easiest way to answer this question is, "If people with disabilities are able to work successfully in the community, why should they go to a sheltered workshop?" Workshops were originally designed as places to prepare people for work. During the past 10 years, it has become increasingly evident that the *best* place for people with disabilities to learn to work is on real jobs, in the community.

Additionally, people are able to earn much more money on real jobs because workshops are rarely able to provide consistent, well-paid work. More importantly, people with disabilities can begin to feel that they are a part of the community if they can get a real job.

WHAT IS MY LIABILITY?   The liability for project employees paid by you is no different than for any other employee. If participants are in your company in a role other than as an employee, Community Options provides workmen's compensation coverage. You may also require the signing of release of liability forms, if necessary. However, the chance of having a problem with liability is quite low. National studies have shown that workers who are mentally retarded have no more accidents or injuries than other workers. Additionally, our training procedures can help ensure that the chances for accidents should actually be *less* than for your other workers.

WHY SHOULD I EMPLOY A PARTICIPANT OF THIS PROJECT?   There are many reasons why an employer might consider hiring an applicant from this project. The most important reason is that we believe that virtually every person we represent can be a productive employee, given proper training and support. Many employers feel that they are exemplary employees. We also let you know "up front" the conditions that we feel the employee can meet, and we strive earnestly to accomplish that goal.

In addition to their production, our applicants can offer your current employees a positive role model—that of an enthusiastic and motivated worker who is excited about coming to work.

A final reason for employing a participant of this project is that you will be providing an opportunity that can be offered *only* by employers such as yourself—a chance to work on a real job. Syracuse has long been a community that has offered opportunities to persons with disabilities. Your participation will continue that tradition.

APPENDIX 5

Making Successful Contacts: Sample Telephone Calls

Following Up Letter of Introduction: Sample 1

1. **Opening statement**

   "Hello, is this Mr. Jones? Good, this is (your name). I sent you a letter last week describing the employment development project through Community Options. We are a local agency that helps people who are disabled find jobs. We also provide cost-free training on the job. In my letter I asked for about 25 minutes of your time to discuss the services of the project with you. I wonder if we might be able to meet some time later this week?"

2. **Pause and wait for a response**

   "What kind of training do you use? This is a specialized business."

3. **Answer the response**

   [Answer the employer's response as briefly as possible and still cover all requested information]
   "Our job trainers are well-versed in general training procedures that are commonly used in the business world. They also take the time to observe the type of training that your company offers. The trainer then combines the general approaches, which have proven to be effective, with your specific style of training to train the employee we represent."

4. **Return to the purpose of the call**

   "At our meeting, I can show you some photographs of the training procedures we use and some of the jobs that we have performed. Remember, it won't take longer than 25 minutes."

5. **Be ready to set a firm meeting time**

   "How does Tuesday at 2:30 sound to you?"

Following Up Letter of Introduction: Sample 2

Hello, I'm _____ with _____. I'm calling to follow up the letter I sent you last week. As I mentioned in the letter, our firm specializes in employee development and offers a number of services to employers in the area.

I am sure you will find our service interesting and worthwhile.

Is there a convenient time during the next week to meet so I can describe our services in more detail?

I know you're busy, so I promise to be brief and to the point.

Would _____ at _____ o'clock be convenient?

APPENDIX 5

(continued)

Following Up Referral

Hello, _____. I'm _____ with _____.

I was talking with _____ the other day, and he suggested . . . I give you a call . . . (or) . . . that you might be interested in our service.

We specialize in employee development and offer a number of cost-free services to employers in this area.

I think you may be interested in what we are doing. We specialize in:
> —Recruiting and training employees for industry
> —This service also includes a customized job analyses of the positions we train.

[Referral] found it very interesting and thought you, also, might want to hear more about us.

I would like to meet with you and describe our services to you. I know you're busy so I promise I'll be brief and to the point.

Would Tuesday at 9:00 be convenient, or would Thursday at 2:00 be better?

Call from a Workshop

"I am _____ from Work Industries in _____.

I'm calling regarding the letter I sent you last week about our employee development program. We provide you with applicants and provide the employees you choose with a specialized training to meet your production requirements.

There is no cost to you for this service.

I would like to meet with you and explain our service further and describe its benefits to your company. I only need from 5 to 30 minutes of your time.

Could you meet with me at 1:00 Monday or Thursday of next week?"

APPENDIX 6

Questions and Objections Encountered During the Phone Call

You must be ready before you make the telephone call to answer questions and objections raised by the employer. It is helpful to write these down and practice them with other staff members.

Here are several questions or objections that you might have to handle. Remember, the purpose of the phone call is to get the appointment, not to win an argument! Try your best to keep it short.

1. Question: "Tell me all about your program."
   After a brief description, say,

   Answer: "Because it will only require a small amount of your time, I would like the opportunity to discuss this with you in person. I have several examples of our Job Analyses and some photographs of our training that I am sure you will find interesting.

   Note: If the employer insists, provide him or her with a brief outline of your program, but keep asking for an appointment. Possible response: "If you are like me, I don't like to buy anything over the phone; our services can be explained much better in person."

2. Question: "Are the people handicapped or retarded?"

   Answer: "All the applicants we represent are labeled "mentally retarded." However, because we represent employees who will perform to your quality standards, we find that this is not a very important factor."

   Note: Don't try to hide or obscure the fact that the prospective employees are considered to be mentally retarded. Rather, focus immediately on the fact that they should be expected to perform much like any other employee. Say, "We find that labels like 'retarded' often imply people who need sympathy and sheltering. The people we represent are ready and willing to go to work."

3. Objection: "We hire all our employees through Job Service."

   Answer: "We have a working agreement with Job Service. I'll be glad to send you a copy of the agreement. All of our applicants have made application with the local Job Service office in this area. I would like to explain how we can provide services to you by working with our program and Job Service."

   Note: It is very important that all applicants register with the local Job Service office. It is also important to develop a relationship with the staff at the local Job Service office.

(continued)

193

4. Objection: "We don't have any openings at this time," or "We've just laid off 25 employees."

   Answer: "We understand that many employers in this area are not hiring right now; however, we could use this time to discuss our services, perform a job analysis, and answer your questions, so that when the economy improves, we can be ready to offer you qualified employees."

   Note: Try to use layoffs to your advantage. They may offer you necessary lead time that may not be available during full production.

APPENDIX 7

Employer Information Sheet

Date of initial contact _____

Name of firm _____ Phone _____

Address _____

Location/site _____

Initial contact person _____ Position/title _____

_____ _____ _____
        Manager   Personnel manager   Supervisor

Description of targeted job(s) _____

_____

Typical work requirements: Hours/shifts _____

Special tools or uniforms required?   (Yes)   (No)

Union shop?   (Yes)   (No)   Name of union _____

Union contact _____ Dues _____

Wages and benefits _____ _____
                            Start   Top salary expected

Fringe Benefits?   (Yes)   (No)   _____ _____
                                      Medical plan   Insurance company

Paid Holidays?   (Yes)   (No)   Overtime pay _____

Turnover rate _____ Absenteeism rate _____

Written production rate?   (Yes)   (No)   _____

Is worksite accessible?   (Yes)   (No)   _____

Availability to public transportation: _____

– –

Contact person to facilitate employment _____ Phone _____

Date(s) for job analysis _____
Date(s) for interview _____
Date(s) for employment _____

Participants hired:

Name	Agency	Date hired	Job

1.

APPENDIX 8

Sample Follow-Up Letter
(after tour)

[your organization's letterhead]

[date]

[The name of the contact person
and the employer's address]

Dear _____:

    I enjoyed the opportunity to meet with you last week and the tour of your plant. I was impressed with the size of your plant, the sophisticated design of the work stations, and the integration of all production elements. These items lead to a high-quality product.

    Regarding employment opportunities for project participants, I will contact you in November to see if the improvement in the economic climate and subsequent increased production will lead to our making a placement in your plant.

    Thank you for the opportunity of meeting with you, and I hope that we will be able to work together in the next few months.

Sincerely,

_____

Coordinator of Job Development

APPENDIX 9

Summary of Expectations for Services Offered

I. The Employer is expected to
   a. Hire an employee at minimum wage or the wage paid to all new employees, whichever is higher, with the same benefits as similar company employees unless subminimum wages have been negotiated and approved.
   b. Provide the agency Employment Trainer with the following resources necessary to perform the Job Analysis and training of the employee(s):
      1. An orientation to the plant as given to any new employee, and training on the job to be filled
      2. Time to learn and analyze the job before employment begins
      3. Access to the equipment, machines, materials, and time required for the job during the Job Analysis
      4. Assistance of an identified supervisor or co-worker to answer questions during Job Analysis and Training
      5. Use of new and rejected materials to be used for training
      6. Written production rate(s) or expectations for the job to be filled
      7. Written approval of the procedural methods outlined in the job analysis as meeting your specifications and requirements
      8. Approval of a comprehensive job description for the targeted employee that includes the extent of responsibilities, the rate of pay, the initial hours and days of work, and a schedule of work routines to be compiled by the job trainer.
   c. Participate in the interview process by interviewing the applicant(s) and making the final approval for the position.
   d. Provide the new employee hired through the project with a probation period for at least as long as is offered to other employees; during this time, it is understood that you may summarily dismiss the employee for violations of company standards or for other just cause. A notice of the problem should be sent to the job trainer. We will attempt to resolve the problem to your satisfaction. We may also recommend termination of the employee during probation and recommend that another person be hired for the vacant position.
   e. Provide the job trainer with the employee's attendance and payroll information on a monthly basis during training.
   f. Designate a liaison person who will work with us during the term of this agreement.
   g. Notify the agency if the employee is experiencing difficulty on the job that the employer cannot handle and that may cost the employee his or her job.
   h. Notify the agency if the employee is terminated for any reason, unless specifically requested otherwise by the employee or his/her family.
II. The Agency agrees to
   a. Recruit, evaluate, and recommend applicants to the employer whom we feel would be successful in the agreed-upon position.
   b. Train the employee(s) on the job until the agreed-upon standards have been met.

(continued)

197

c. Develop a written Job Analysis of targeted jobs and provide the employer with a copy of such upon successful completion of the training period.

d. Provide ongoing support and or follow-up to the employee necessary for the continued success of the employee for as long as necessary.

e. Provide assistance in processing paperwork concerning reimbursements, sub-minimum wage certificates, and other governmental forms.

f. Provide supervisors and co-workers with assistance in training the employee to perform new tasks.

g. Perform the following additional services (to be negotiated):

APPENDIX 10

Memos of Industrial Contact

Initial Presentation

SUBJECT: Initial presentation at _____ Inc., Atlanta, GA.

I talked with Mr. Bob Johnson, personnel manager, about job possibilities at the _____ plant. He has no openings at this time as the company has a policy to hire students to work during the summer. He did say that the company also has a policy to hire a 10% ratio of handicapped workers under an affirmative action plan. Mr. Johnson feels that the handicapped workers hired under the affirmative action plan must perform their jobs as competently as other employees. I assured him that we agreed with that philosophy.

The types of jobs that are performed at this plant include machine operators, milk processors, freezer workers, packers and shippers, quality control, maintenance, and warehousemen. Because Mr. Johnson had not received my introductory letter or brochure of June 2, I will send him a brochure and the _____ Corporation reference letter. I will also contact James Miller, trainer, for a tour and quality analysis.

Mr. Johnson agreed that I should call every 2 weeks to check on openings. I feel as their employment situation improves, we should get a placement there.

_____
Job Development Specialist

APPENDIX 10

(continued)

Follow-Up Memo: Sample 1

FROM: (Your organization's representative)

SUBJECT: Follow-Up Visit to _____ Company.

DATE: July 8, 1986

Ed Brown and I met with Fred Jones, Personnel Director of _____, and two other managers-quality assurance and production. We reviewed our previous contacts during May and June and updated them on the status and goals of the project.

I showed a slide presentation of the Austin Project and explained the way in which a trainee might be placed into a company. All three men were supportive of employment, and Mr. Jones said that his plant was willing to work with us in placing a participant in a job at the plant.

Mr. Jones gave Ed and me a tour and targeted several positions that we might be able to have access to. These were in the wire manufacture section. The various machines in this area manufactured the cords used on appliances.

We told Mr. Jones that Kathy Rutherford would contact him for applications and also for a tour. He agreed and said that he felt a placement would be available in early August.

_____

Project Director

APPENDIX 10

(continued)

Follow-Up Memo: Sample 2

TO: (Your target company's representative)

FROM: Kathy Robinson

SUBJECT: Tour of _____ Company.

DATE: July 13, 1986

I met Fred Jones, Personnel Director at _____. He escorted me on a tour of the Cord Set Department and pointed out the operations they were interested in having us train:

- MOSLO (Machine operation)--molds plugs to cords
- Insulating--sleeving
- Crimping--female cylinder to exposed wire
- Dip soldering--exposed wire

Mr. Jones also pointed out the hanking operation--I'm not certain it is one of the operations he wants us to train.

The plant runs three shifts. When a day shift position is available, it is offered to second and third shift personnel first. Mr. Jones said people very seldom leave those shifts because they pay more. We may have to take another shift.

Starting pay is minimum wage and up, and the plant has standard production quotas for each position. I mentioned that we will need a memo or some documentation of their standards. They have also established training periods (2 to 6 weeks, depending on the operation) and keep production records both during the training period and afterward.

For employee evaluation, they have a "reduced point" system. Mr. Jones gave a brief explanation. For each employee a daily attendance record is kept--points are charged for lateness and absence. Two warnings are given before a termination.

I gave Mr. Jones a summary of expectations and told him I would contact Ronnie Smith, cord supervisor, on Wednesday, to schedule a time to begin the job analysis.

APPENDIX 11

Sample Employment Agreement

[Forms such as this may be required by federally funded employment programs; in that case, the requirement for signing this form needs to be negotiated during job development.]

This is an Agreement made between _____ (the Employer) and _____ (your organization) for the purpose of identifying the responsibilities regarding the training and employment of specific personnel.

1. The Employer agrees to:

    1.1 Hire _____ Employee(s) at the wage of _____ with the same benefits as similar company employees (including, but not limited to, workman's compensation or adequate medical and accident insurance) in the following positions:

    _____
    _____
    _____

    1.2 Provide (your organization's) Training Specialist with the following resources necessary for the job analysis and training of the Employee(s):

    _____
    _____
    _____

    1.3 Provide the Employee(s) with a probation period of _____ from the date of hire. During this time, it is understood that the Employer may summarily dismiss the Employee for gross violations of company standards, or for just cause and a _____ notice to (your organization). During this time, (Your organization) will attempt to resolve the problem to the Employer's satisfaction. (Your organization) may also recommend termination of the Employee during probation and recommend that other persons be hired for the vacant position.

    1.4 Participate in the employee selection process by interviewing all applicants and making the final selection for the agreed-upon position.

    1.5 Designate _____ as the liaison person during the term of this Agreement.

    1.6 Provide (your organization) with the Employee(s)' attendance and payroll information on a monthly basis for a period of _____.

    1.7 The Employer agrees to hire on _____.

2. (Your organization) agrees to:

    2.1 Recruit, evaluate, and recommend applicants to the Employer for the agreed-upon positions.

    2.2 Train the Employee(s) chosen by the employer until the established standard of the Employer have been met.

    2.3 Develop a written Job Analysis of targeted jobs and provide the Employer with a copy of such upon successful completion of the training period.

    2.4 Arrange for any assistance or follow-up necessary for the continued success of the Employee(s).

(continued)

3. Termination of this Agreement:

    3.1   This agreement shall continue until one of the following events occurs:

        3.1.1   Upon completion of the goals of this Agreement, by mutual agreement of both parties.

        3.1.2   After a 30-day written notice by one part to another.

4. Authority:

    4.1   Each party declares that it is authorized to proceed with this Agreement.

5. Signatures:

(Your organization's rep.):   By: _____

                                      Date: _____

                                      By: _____

                                      Date: _____

(Employer's representative):   By: _____

                                      Date: _____

                                      By: _____

                                      Date: _____

APPENDIX 12

Employment Site Quality Consideration Checklist

Company _____ Contact _____

Issue	Above average	Acceptable	Not acceptable
1. **Interactions available with nondisabled co-workers***			
2. **Wages:**			
a. regular			
b. subminimum allowable			
3. **Benefits:**			
a. workman's compensation			
b. health insurance			
c. vacation, sick days, etc.			
d. comfortable			
4. **Working conditions:**			
a. safe*			
b. friendly			
c. accessible			
d. comfortable			
5. **Long-term employment:**			
a. nonseasonal			
b. stable, growing industry			
6. **Enhancing features:**			
a. increasing responsibilities			
b. raises			
c. upward mobility			
d. status			
7. **Work expectations:**			
a. clearly defined			
b. stable			
c. flexible			
8. **Internal controls**			
9. **In-house training and support**			
10. **Transportation availability**			
11. **Marketable experience is gained**			
12. **Entry-level positions available**			

*If these items are marked as not acceptable, the site should not be used.

_____

(continued)

204

Issue	Above average	Acceptable	Not acceptable
13. **Employer agrees to "expectations"***			
14. **Company viewed favorably:**			
a. by employees			
b. by community			
15. **Employer open to innovation**			
16. **Proximity to community resources**			
17. **Co-workers:**			
a. turnover rate			
b. potential for support			

Filled out by _____ Inclusive dates _____

*If these items are marked as not acceptable, the site should not be used.

APPENDIX 13

Vocational Profile

Date(s) of profile _____

Compiled by _____

Part One: Basic Data

I. Identification Information

A. Name _____

B. Date of birth _____

C. Social Security # _____

D. Address _____

_____

E . Phone _____

F . Marital status: Single _____   Married _____

G. Current occupation/status:

II. Residential/Domestic Information

A. Family (parent/guardian, spouse, children, siblings):

B. Extended family:

C. Names, ages, and relationships of persons living in the same home/residence:
1.   Age: Relation:
2.   Age: Relation:
3.   Age: Relation:
4.   Age: Relation:
5.   Age: Relation:

(If more than five, place on back of form)

D. Residential history:

E. Family support available:

F. Description of typical routines (attach on separate sheet if necessary):

G. Friends and social group(s):

H. Description of neighborhood:

I. Location of neighborhood in community:

J. Services near home:

K. General types of employment near home:

L. Transportation availability:

III. **Educational Information**
   A. History and general performance (from school records, interview data, observations):

B.   Vocational programming/performance:

C.   Community functioning programming/performance:

D.   Recreation/leisure programming/performance:

IV. **Work Experience Information**
A.   Informal work performed at home:

B.   Formal chores at home:

C.   Informal jobs performed for others:

D.   Sheltered employment:

E.   Paid work:

V.   **Summary of Present Level of Performance**
A.   Domestic skills:

B. Community functioning skills:

C. Recreation/leisure skills:

D. Academic skills (Reading, Math, Time, Money):

E. Motor/mobility skills:

F. Sensory skills:

G. Communication skills:

H. Social interaction skills:

I . Physical/health-related skills and information:

J . Vocational skills:

VI. Learning and Performance Characteristics

VII. Preferences
A. Type of work the applicant wants to do:

B. Type of work the parent/guardian feels is appropriate:

C. What the applicant enjoys doing at home:

D. Observations of the kinds of work applicant likes to do best:

E. Observations of social situations applicant likes best:

VIII. Connections
A. Potential employers in family:

B. Potential employers among friends:

C. Potential employment sites in neighborhood:

D. Business/employer contacts for leads through applicant, family, friends:

IX. Flexibility/Accommodations That May Be Required in Workplace

    A.   Habits, routines, idiosyncrasies, etc.:

    B.   Physical/health restrictions:

    C.   Behavioral challenges:

Part Two: Description of "Ideal" Employment Situation

(This is a composite, narrative description based on input by applicant, parents/guardians, service agency staff, and data from profile.)

APPENDIX 14

Sample Completed Vocational Profile

Date(s) of profile _____

Part One: Basic Data   Compiled by _____

I.   Identification Information

A. Name <u>Carl Richards (Pseudonym)</u>

B. Date of birth <u>February 16, 1965</u>

C. Social Security # <u>987-64-5432</u>

D. Address <u>123 South Main Street</u>

<u>Our Town, NY 12345</u>

E. Phone <u>(101) 555-1234</u>

F. Marital status: Single <u>X</u>   Married _____

G. Current occupation/status: Carl has recently graduated from high school. He is currently unemployed. His parents want him to work--not so much for the money--but to spend his days as most people do. They do not want him to enter a sheltered workshop. At this time, he is sitting at home watching a lot of television.

II.   Residential/Domestic Information

A. Family (parent/guardian, spouse, children, siblings):   Carl lives at home with his parents, Sam and Marian Richards, and his sister Ann. He has another sister, Debbie, who attends college out of state.

B. Extended family: Carl's extended family includes an uncle, William Carelli, who is a city council member in Our Town; an aunt, Mary Richards, who is a professor at the City University; and a cousin, Randy Carelli, who owns a clothing shop.

C. Names, ages, and relationships of persons living in the same home/residence:

1.	Sam Richards	Age:	56	Relation:	Father
2.	Marian Richards	Age:	55	Relation:	Mother
3.	Ann Richards	Age:	18	Relation:	Sister
4.		Age:		Relation:	
5.		Age:		Relation:	

(If more than five, place on back of form)

D. Residential history: Carl has always lived with his family in the same house in Our Town, New York. Until recently, both his sisters, his parents, and his grandmother lived in the house. His grandmother died last year, and his older sister has gone away to college. Carl's younger sister, Ann, plans to leave for college in September.

E. Family support available: Carl's parents are very supportive of Carl working in a regular work setting. They initiated a search for agencies that could help Carl find and learn a job. They offer assurance that they will assist with transportation and also with encouragement once Carl has been employed.

F. Description of typical routines (attach on separate sheet if necessary): (See attached sheet)

G. Friends and social group(s): Carl is very close to his parents and his sisters. He does not maintain frequent contact with fellow students from his Special Education high school class. His parents have plans to enroll him in a course offered by the local community college called "College for Living." They hope that he will meet more friends at this program.

H. Description of neighborhood: Carl lives in an older, well-maintained neighborhood in Our Town. He has known his neighbors for many years. There is a small commercial area three blocks from his home. There are sidewalks and street lights along the streets in the area. There is one major traffic light and crossing two blocks from his house. The neighborhood is considered to be safe for walking, day and night.

I. Location of neighborhood in community: The neighborhood is on the north side of town, in a primarily residential area. Within a 10-block radius, there are a large number of service-related businesses. These are mostly small, owner-operated businesses that specialize in retail sales and food service.

J. Services near home: There is a city bus stop one block from Carl's home. A small commercial area is nearby--three blocks away. Carl's dentist and doctor are in that business district. A branch library is five blocks away, and a small park is in easy walking distance.

K. General types of employment near home: Elementary school, library, three restaurants, hardware store, corner deli, four small retail outlets, city work in the local park, five professional offices

L. Transportation availability: The city bus runs approximately every 20 to 25 minutes to and from downtown. Carl's mother does not work and she has a car. She has expressed willingness to provide initial transportation for Carl if he gets a job within a couple of miles of home.

Profile Attachment

II. F. Description of typical routines:

7:00 A.M.
9:00 A.M.

1. Wakes up independently at approximately 7:00 A.M. with the aid of an alarm clock that he turned on the previous night
2. Showers and dresses himself independently (3 mornings per week Carl's mother assists him to shave himself using an electric razor; also if special dress is required, Carl's mother selects his clothing for him.)
3. Eats breakfast that his mother has prepared
4. Takes out the trash from the bathroom, kitchen, and bedrooms to the large garbage cans
5. Picks up his clothing in his bedroom and in the bathroom and places in hamper
6. Sits outside on porch and watches neighbors and others walk and drive by; speaks to some of the neighbors (He does this only in warm weather; in winter, go to 9:00 A.M.)

9:00 A.M.
12:00 noon

Watches television

12:00
1:00 P.M.

Sets table for lunch as per request by mother; eats lunch.

1:00
3:00 P.M.

Accompanies his mother on any of several of her daily afternoon trips (shopping, visiting, errands, etc.)

3:00
5:00 P.M.

Watches television

5:00
6:00 P.M.

Begins to help mother prepare for dinner by setting table, washing hands, etc.

6:00
7:00 P.M.

Eats dinner with mother and father and occasionally, his sister; helps clean up after dinner

7:00
9:45 P.M.

Often accompanies his sister as she babysits in the neighborhood; plays with the children and watches television

9:45
10:00 P.M.

Returns home and prepares for bed

10:00 P.M.

Goes to bed after setting alarm to "on"

III. Educational Information

A. History and general performance (from school records, interview data, observations): Carl attended a special segregated elementary school during his early school years. He was placed in a self-contained special education class for students labeled "mentally retarded" in junior high and high school. Carl was diagnosed by a psychologist when he was 9 as being "severely mentally retarded." His records indicate that he did well in his classroom experiences on the typical nonfunctional tasks offered in his program. His IEPs continued to reflect nonfunctional goals until late in his high school experience. Carl's high school teacher felt that he was capable of "learning all sorts of things--if he just applied himself." Carl consistently made "As" and "Bs" on his report cards throughout his schooling. Carl's parents thought that he could have learned much more than he did. (Carl's IEP indicated that he recognizes most letters of the alphabet, can print his name, can match items up to 10, can identify numbers up to 10, and recognizes basic colors.)

214

B. Vocational programming/performance: Carl received no community-based vocational programming during school. He was required to perform classroom-based chores, and occasionally he was asked to deliver messages to the principal's office.

C. Community functioning programming/performance: Carl's school program included weekly community outings. The outings were in locations near to the school. Carl was able to order food independently from three different fast-food restaurants. He needed assistance in paying for the purchases. Carl is able to walk to nearby community sites, for which he has received training, without assistance, such as the library and the local deli. Carl has mastered street-crossing skills on familiar streets, but continued to need assistance on novel streets.

D. Recreation/leisure programming/performance: Carl was introduced to bowling through weekly school activities. He now enjoys going bowling whenever he can; however, he tires of playing after about 20 minutes, according to his teacher. Carl's mother reports that he is initially uncomfortable in new settings, especially if there are large crowds-- like at ballgames and concerts. Carl's IEP indicates that he learned to play table games that were available in the classroom, and he enjoyed playing computer games.

IV. Work Experience Information

A. Informal work performed at home: Carl empties the trash cans, helps set the table, and likes to return dishes, glasses, etc. to the kitchen after meals. Carl's mother stated that she attempted to teach Carl to make his bed, but he never did too well. Carl enjoys raking leaves in the Fall and he helps his Dad shovel snow in the winter.

B. Formal chores at home: Carl is expected to keep his clothes picked up in his bedroom. He also is responsible for sweeping the front porch and taking the trash cans to the street on pickup day and returning them to the back of the house when emptied.

C. Informal jobs performed for others: Carl occasionally accompanies his younger sister when she babysits. He enjoys entertaining young children, and his sister says that he is very good at doing it. Carl likes to "help out" at his cousin's clothing store. His cousin allows him to unload stock after hours and to clean up on occasion. His cousin seems reluctant to allow Carl to work part-time during regular hours.

D. Sheltered employment: None.

E. Paid work: Except for his allowance of $5.00 per week, Carl has not performed work for pay.

V. Summary of Present Level of Performance

A. Domestic skills: Carl dresses himself without assistance, and he cares for all of his hygiene needs. His mother indicates, however, that he often leaves the door open to the bathroom while toileting and bathing and that he must be reminded to close the door. Carl has not been required to help with cooking, but he does set the table when asked to. Carl is responsible for keeping his things picked up in his room, but his mother actually cleans and makes the bed. Carl has run the vacuum cleaner, but he is not asked to do so regularly.

B. Community functioning skills: Carl recognizes most of his nearby neighbors, and he stops and chats with them if he passes by their house. He accompanies his parents to most shopping trips, but he does not actually participate in making purchases unless they are specifically for him. Carl enjoys going out to eat--especially at McDonald's. He places his own order and takes his food. His parents pay for the food. He can locate a vacant table. Carl knows the route to nearby services, such as the library, the park, and the local deli. He is allowed to walk unaccompanied to these places, and he seems to enjoy the freedom to go unassisted.

C. Recreation/leisure skills: Carl's favorite activity is watching television. He watches adventure programs and cartoons. He also enjoys bowling and walking through shopping malls. He can walk to the branch library to browse through magazines. He does this about once every 1 or 2 weeks. Carl is especially comfortable in small group, informal situations when he can talk to others. Carl is able to participate in organized games, such as volleyball and softball, but he doesn't seem to enjoy these types of activities.

D. Academic skills (Reading, Math, Time, Money): Carl can print his first name. He is aware that giving money to a cashier is expected after making a purchase, but he doesn't know how to count money. Carl can read the numbers on a digital clock/watch, and he relates time to daily routines. Carl has difficulty reading commonly used words. His mother reports that he often enters the wrong restroom in a public place. She also reports that Carl can learn specific words for specific sites if the teaching is consistent.

E. Motor/mobility skills: Carl can walk, and he has use of both arms, hands, and all his fingers. His gait is marked with minor coordination difficulties. Carl can run without falling. He is uncertain on slippery surfaces--like icy walks--and holds onto railings or to others.

F. Sensory skills: Carl can hear, and he has functional vision. He is nearsighted, and he has to wear glasses to get around effectively.

G. Communication skills: Carl can speak in complete sentences. He converses easily with people he knows well. His speech is rapid and occasionally difficult to understand. He will usually slow down if he is asked to repeat what he has said. Asking questions is the typical manner in which Carl interacts with others. Carl follows directions consisting of three to four words. However, he will respond with "OK" even if he doesn't understand the instructions, according to his high school teacher. After asking a question to another person, Carl will often walk away to do another activity, without listening to the response.

H. Social interaction skills: Carl enjoys asking questions of people. He is not particularly shy in one-to-one situations. He will often walk up to a person he doesn't know and ask them a question like, "What are you doing?" Most people like being around Carl. His attitude is usually cheery and upbeat. Most of his interactions with others are enthusiastic but brief.

I. Physical/health-related skills and information: Carl's health is generally excellent. He is seldom sick, and he is not currently under a doctor's care. He does have allergies, and he takes allergy medication when necessary.

J. Vocational skills: Vocational programming was not included in Carl's high school IEPs. For this reason most of his vocational skills are home-related and are described in an earlier section of this profile.

VI. **Learning and Performance Characteristics:** Carl has difficulty transferring information from one setting to another. He learns very well from a variety of instructional cues. Verbal cues can easily turn into conversation with Carl, as he enjoys conversation with others. His parents feel that he can quickly learn to perform tasks that are repeatedly performed. Carl seems to have difficulty attending to natural cues. Trainers must consistently point out the features of tasks and the environment. Carl responds well to adaptations. He learned to tell the correct time for a class to be over by using a digital watch and a small card with the correct time printed on it.

VII. **Preferences**
   A. Type of work the applicant wants to do: Carl has stated that he wants to work at McDonald's restaurant in his neighborhood. He also said that he would work in any kind of restaurant. When asked about other kinds of work, he said that nothing else interested him.
   B. Type of work the parent/guardian feels is appropriate: Carl's parents also feel that restaurant work would be best for him. They also said they would support work in an office setting. They particularly did not want him to work around dangerous machinery.
   C. What the applicant enjoys doing at home: Watching TV, especially football games and cartoons. He also enjoys helping his mother around the kitchen. He enjoys taking rides in the family car with his parents or his sister.
   D. Observations of the kinds of work applicant likes to do best: Carl has had few experiences on which to judge this consideration. He enjoys any kind of work that allows him to talk to others while working.
   E. Observations of social situations applicant likes best: Carl seems to enjoy being with a small, stable group of people. He likes it when he gets to know individuals so he can ask them questions.

VIII. **Connections**
   A. Potential employers in family: Carl has an uncle who is a city council member and a cousin who owns a clothing store. Carl's father works at a local manufacturing plant that produces industrial air conditioners.
   B. Potential employers among friends: Steve Smith, a family friend, runs a local Pizza Hut restaurant. Carl's mother has a friend, Sherry Aiken, who runs a small bakery. The next-door neighbors are retired. There are some possibilities among other neighbors for employment leads.
   C. Potential employment sites in neighborhood: The small commercial district has several restaurants and other retail outlets. The library is within walking distance.
   D. Business/employer contacts for leads through applicant, family, friends: Carl's father knows the supervisor at the plant who is in a personnel manager's organization. Carl's mother attends a bridge club with area businesswomen. A member of the bridge club owns a photo store. Carl's parents belong to the following organizations: Knights of Columbus, Our Town Garden Club, VFW, Association for Retarded Citizens.

IX. **Flexibility/Accommodations Which May be Required in Workplace**
   A. Habits, routines, idiosyncrasies, etc.: Carl talks to himself frequently. He also goes to the bathroom often when he is in a stressful activity.
   B. Physical/health restrictions: Carl dislikes being outside in very cold weather. He also has vision problems when he forgets his glasses.
   C. Behavioral challenges: He occasionally gets on people's nerves when he constantly asks questions.

Part Two: Description of "Ideal" Employment Situation
(This is a composite, narrative description based on input by applicant, parents/guardians, service agency staff, and data from profile.)

Based on this information, it seems to make sense to try to find Carl a job in a restaurant that has a low turnover rate. This may exclude most fast-food outlets. Carl needs the consistency of both co-workers and supervisors. The local Pizza Hut is a possibility as the manager is a friend of the family.

Possible jobs in a restaurant might include dishwashing, bussing tables, assisting in food preparation, and general clean up.

The worksite needs to be on a city bus line. Carl's parents are certain that he can learn to ride a bus to and from work.

Carl is not an extremely fast worker. Therefore, he would probably require an initial job with flexible wage payment. There is no reason that he could not eventually work up to minimum wage, but he will likely require sub-minimum work at first.

The same consideration holds for his work hours. A job with flexible hours should be sought. If the hours could be increased gradually from about 2 or 3 hours per day toward full-time, it would be better than a fixed-time job. This is felt to be necessary because Carl has had no work experience.

A job coach will probably be required to be with Carl full-time during the initial period of training. Carl can easily learn from others, and the trainer should be able to fade over a reasonable period of time.

APPENDIX 15

Sample Job Posting

Job title: Buffing Machine Operator

Location: M. H. Gilmore Corp., Bruceton, MS

Date of posting: September 14, 1986

SUMMARY

Worker will operate machinery used to buff and polish stainless steel cookware. Gilmore Corp. manufactures high-quality cookware and coffee pots for Salad Master, Amway, and other retail suppliers. This work is done in a standing position, inside, in a well-ventilated, heated building.

KNOWLEDGE AND ABILITY REQUIRED

Workers must have the willingness to work on repetitive machine operations for an 8-hour shift. Workers must have the ability to lift up to 25 pounds. Use of both hands. Sufficient vision necessary to operate machinery and to determine if sufficient polish or buffing compound is applied to cookware.

EDUCATION AND EXPERIENCE

Prior experience is not required. Willingness to participate in and complete on-the-job training is required. Degree of education is not a factor in selection.

TRAINING AND ASSISTANCE RECEIVED

Tasks are completed under the close direction of a trainer. Assignments are well-defined, and specific operational procedures are established by written task analyses prior to training. Additional close supervision is provided by Gilmore Corp. supervisors on an ongoing basis. Applicants will be assisted during the interview as necessary by project trainers.

GENERAL JOB RESPONSIBILITIES

Willingness to work day shift (7:00 A.M. to 3:30 P.M., 5 days a week). Worker must be responsible for getting to work on time and for being at work every day. Worker is expected to clock in and out on a time clock. Employees in the buffing department will be expected to operate several different buffing and polishing machines in the course of their work responsibilities. Workers must also move finished products from the buffing area to other machine areas in the plant.

ADDITIONAL JOB REQUIREMENTS

Applicants must be able to get to and from interview.

You must also be willing to participate in training-based assessment at interview. Bring a resume to the interview.

If you are unable to keep your interview appointment, you will not be considered for this job. You must have a plan to get to and from work. We will ask.

(continued)

ADDITIONAL INFORMATION

There will be a 30-day and 60-day salary performance review and a 90-day probationary period. There are specific production quotas for buffing machine operator. However, the rate of pay is not directly tied to rate of production.

Persons interested in making an application, please contact:

[your name and contact address would go here]

Please call during the following times only: (You may call collect only if *absolutely* necessary.)

October 19 (Monday)	8:00 A.M. to 5:00 P.M.
October 20 (Tuesday)	8:00 A.M. to 5:00 P.M.

Important Note: The interview for this job will be on Wednesday, October 28. The starting date will be Thursday, October 29, or as soon thereafter as is possible. You must plan to attend the interview on October 28 and, if chosen for employment, be ready to work immediately.

Starting salary: $4.65 per hour. 40 hours per week. Raises possible after 30 and 60 days based on evaluation by supervisors.

Benefits: Insurance—Company pays Blue Cross/Blue Shield medical benefits after 90-day probationary period.

Holidays—They have 5 paid holidays.

Required overtime work should not be expected.

Note: *Do not,* under any circumstance, contact M. H. Gilmore Corp.

APPENDIX 16

Job Analysis

Company _____   Phone no. _____

Address _____   Contact person _____

_____   Title _____

Job title _____

Employee _____   Phone no. _____

(See profile for personal information.)

Core work routines: Episodic work routines:
(Identified by employer)   (Identified by employer)

_____   _____

_____   _____

_____   _____

_____   _____

_____   _____

_____   _____

Job-related routines: Accommodations required:
(Identified during job analysis)   (Based on information in profile)

_____   _____

_____   _____

_____   _____

_____   _____

_____   _____

Job summary:

Job trainer _____

Job Requirements as Typically Performed

(Check only critical items; fully describe the extent of the demand and outline possible adaptations/accommodations if felt to be problematic for targeted employee.)

Physical demands:
____ Lifting
____ Standing
____ Continuous movement
____ Rapid movement
____ Walking
____ Climbing
____ Stooping
____ Crawling

Sensory/communication demands:
____ Vision
____ Hearing
____ Speaking
____ Judgment

Academic demands:
____ Reading
____ Writing
____ Math

GENERAL STRENGTH/ENDURANCE REQUIREMENTS:

PACE OF WORK:

POTENTIALLY DANGEROUS COMPONENTS OF JOB:

CRITICALLY IMPORTANT COMPONENTS OF JOB:

ESTABLISHED LEARNING CURVE OR PROBATIONARY PERIOD FOR JOB:

Worksite Considerations

SPECIAL CLOTHING, UNIFORMS, SAFETY EQUIPMENT REQUIRED:

TOOLS TO BE USED:

EQUIPMENT TO BE OPERATED:

MATERIALS TO BE HANDLED:

SPECIAL TERMS USED AT WORKSITE:

DESCRIPTION OF ENVIRONMENTAL CONDITIONS OF WORKSITE:

Training Considerations

POSITION OF TRAINER IN RELATION TO EMPLOYEE (initially and during fading):

ROLE OF TRAINER AT WORKSITE (list site-specific requirements):

AVAILABILITY OF CO-WORKERS/SUPERVISORS AS TRAINERS:

DESCRIPTION OF TRAINING AVAILABLE FROM EMPLOYER:

POTENTIAL FOR USE OF ADAPTATIONS, MODIFICATIONS IN WORKSITE:

WILLINGNESS OF CO-WORKERS/SUPERVISORS TO PROVIDE SUPPORT AND ASSISTANCE:

"Culture" of the Worksite

EMPLOYER'S CONCERN FOR QUALITY:

EMPLOYER'S CONCERN FOR PRODUCTIVITY:

FLEXIBILITY/RIGIDITY OBSERVED:

EMPLOYEE SOCIAL GROUPS AND NON-WORK ACTIVITIES:

LEADERS AND POTENTIAL ALLIES AMONG CO-WORKERS AND SUPERVISORS:

Job Description

SCHEDULE:

Number of days of work per week _____

Days: _____   Hours _____- _____
      _____   Hours _____- _____
      _____   Hours _____- _____
      _____   Hours _____- _____
      _____   Hours _____- _____

SEQUENTIAL CHRONOLOGY OF TYPICAL WORKDAY (include all routines):

Type of Routine _____
          (Core, episodic, job-related)

ROUTINE _____
HOW OFTEN PERFORMED:

CONTENT STEPS/SKILLS	DECISION (see Decision-Making Sequence for Training, attached)	INFORMING STRATEGIES (including instructional and natural cues and adaptations)

Decision-Making Sequence for Training

1. **PROVIDE NO DIRECT INTERVENTION; FACILITATE THE ROUTINE TO OC-CUR USING ONLY THE NATURAL CUES FOUND IN THE WORKPLACE.**

   This decision allows the learner to acquire the skills of a task/routine merely by regular participation. This is the same manner most people acquire information about routines.

2. **PROVIDE SYSTEMATIC TRAINING.**

   a. Train the step each time it occurs in the natural sequence.

   b. Break the step into smaller, more teachable steps. Then teach as in step a.

   c. When the step occurs in the natural sequence, halt the sequence, teach the step using a number of massed trials, then continue the sequence.

   d. Pull the step out of the natural sequence and teach it in massed trials until criterion. Then plug it back into the natural sequence.

3. **MODIFY THE NATURAL METHOD.**

   Change the natural method typically used to perform the task to a method that better matches the needs of the learner.

4. **PROVIDE AN ADAPTATION.**

   Add an assisting device or other aid to the method that will assist the learner to perform the task.

5. **ARRANGE FOR PARTIAL ASSISTANCE FROM CO-WORKERS.**

   Provide ongoing assistance on targeted steps of the task that will enable the worker to participate in the routine, if it is found that strategies 1, 2, 3, or 4 did not facilitate successful performance. The assistance can initially come from the trainer, but eventually must be provided by someone in the work environment.

APPENDIX 17

Sample Completed Job Analysis

Company <u>ABC Electric</u>   Phone no. <u>(555) 876-4321</u>

Address <u>1111 Highway 49</u>   Contact person <u>Brian Jones</u>

      <u>Hattiesburg, MS 39401</u>   Title <u>Personnel Manager</u>

Job title <u>Hanker Machine Operator and Supplier</u>

Employee <u>John Fasthands</u>   Phone no. <u>(555) 876-1234</u>

(See profile for personal information.)

Core work routines: (Identified by employer)	Episodic work routines: (Identified by employer)
Hanker machine operation	Moving supplies from warehouse to floor
Loading supply bins for operators	Disposing empty boxes
	Cleaning work area
	Marking production data
	Assisting supply manager--moving
	materials

Job-related routines: (Identified during job analysis)	Accommodations required: (Based on information in profile)
Clocking in	Wrapping fingers with protective tape
Getting to work area	(assistance from co-worker)
Finding restrooms, lunch, and break	Use manual rather than electric
area	floor jack
Using vending machines	The supervisor must tell John when to
Using employee lockers	operate the machine

Job summary:

    The primary responsibilities of this job are to check on the supply bins of
workers in the hanking area of the plant and to keep the bins full. A secondary
responsibility is to operate an idle hanking machine once all bins are full.
The hanking machine automatically coils electric cord of various sizes so that
a twist tie can be placed on to secure the hank. The area supervisor is responsible for telling John when to operate the machine, which machine to operate,
and when to do supply work. John must also move supplies of cord from the warehouse to the work floor as instructed by his supervisor.

Job trainer <u>Kathleen Rutherford</u>

Job Requirements as Typically Performed

(Check only critical items; fully describe the extent of the demand and outline possible adaptations/accommodations if felt to be problematic for targeted employee)

Physical demands:
X___ Lifting
X___ Standing
____ Continuous movement
____ Rapid movement
X___ Walking
____ Climbing
X___ Stooping
____ Crawling

Sensory/communication demands:
X___ Vision
____ Hearing
____ Speaking
____ Judgment

Academic demands:
____ Reading
____ Writing
____ Math

GENERAL STRENGTH/ENDURANCE REQUIREMENTS: John must be able to lift boxes of cord that weigh up to 40 pounds. The trainer can adjust the weight initially to allow for strength to build. Operation of the hanker machine is tiring on hands and fingers after about 1 hour of operation. Because John will not have to operate the machine initially for over approximately 45 minutes at a time, this should not present a problem. Workers must stand when not operating a machine.

PACE OF WORK: The pace of the job is constant but not hectic. Evenly paced actions, even at a relatively slow speed, should be sufficient for production. The operation of the hanker machine is a "fill-in" job and does not carry full production requirements.

POTENTIALLY DANGEROUS COMPONENTS OF JOB: The hanking arm of the machine spins at a high rate of speed. If the arm is touched while spinning, a sharp blow could occur. The resulting injury could be painful but not serious. The machine is designed to shut off automatically at any unusual resistance. Careful training should reduce the likelihood of any injury on this process.

CRITICALLY IMPORTANT COMPONENTS OF JOB: The bins of the hankers must be filled with sufficient cord to keep the machines going. This is a relatively easy job, but it is critical. Operators lose time if they have to get up to fill their bins.

ESTABLISHED LEARNING CURVE OR PROBATIONARY PERIOD FOR JOB: John will begin working one-half days (4 hours) at 50% of minimum wage. The employer will review his productivity after 4 months to determine if wages and/or hours should be increased. The trainer must ensure that the operator's bins are filled during this period.

Worksite Considerations

SPECIAL CLOTHING, UNIFORMS, SAFETY EQUIPMENT REQUIRED: Regular factory-type clothing is appropriate. Closed-toed shoes are required. Cotton gloves are worn during supply jobs. A special cloth tape is wrapped around the fingers during hanking to protect the fingers from sharp wire ends. The supply supervisor has agreed to assist John in doing the wrap. (Assistance is required for all employees.)

TOOLS TO BE USED: A small "mold release" tool is used to remove wires that get stuck in the hanker arm.

EQUIPMENT TO BE OPERATED: Hanker machine, manual floor jack, tie-wrap dispenser.

MATERIALS TO BE HANDLED: Supply goods from the warehouse to the production floor. Individual cords during hanker machine operation. Tie wraps to bind the hanks of cord.

SPECIAL TERMS USED AT WORKSITE:
Hank: a bound electric cord
6's: 6-foot cord
8's: 8-foot cord
Bare wire: wire without a plug molded on
Plugged: wire with a plug molded on

DESCRIPTION OF ENVIRONMENTAL CONDITIONS OF WORKSITE: The hanking area is in the cordset department, which is in a large open area of the plant. The plant itself is very large (80,000+ square feet) consisting of four large rooms. The plant is air conditioned and well heated. There is a constant background noise from all the machinery. The hanking area is marked by the large supply and finished-goods boxes.

Training Considerations

POSITION OF TRAINER IN RELATION TO EMPLOYEE (initially and during fading): The trainer will be able to stand near John during both the supply operations and the machine operations. The work area is open, and there is plenty of space around all machines, both for close supervision and for fading. While training the hanker machine, the trainer can sit to John's left to observe and to give information.

ROLE OF TRAINER AT WORKSITE (list site-specific requirements):
1. The trainer is expected to teach the hanker machine operation.
2. The trainer is expected to assist the supply supervisor to train the supply job and to fill in as necessary to keep the supply bins filled.
3. The trainer is expected to complete a Job Analysis and present it to the contact person within 4 weeks of the starting date.
4. The trainer is expected to facilitate the acquisition of all routines of the job.

AVAILABILITY OF CO-WORKERS/SUPERVISORS AS TRAINERS: The supply supervisor seems particularly willing to provide training to John as long as the trainer is willing to ensure that the bins are full. The warehouse personnel have agreed to assist John in finding and loading supply boxes and to locate his way back to the hanking area. The machine operators in the hanking area are excited about John's starting work because they met him during his tour.

DESCRIPTION OF TRAINING AVAILABLE FROM EMPLOYER: Most jobs are learned from co-workers who have been assigned by the area supervisor. The quality of training varies with the co-worker assigned. Each job has, more or less, a "standard" procedure that is not written down. The supervisor is responsible for showing the correct way to operate a machine or process. Production data, rather than acquisition data, are stressed.

POTENTIAL FOR USE OF ADAPTATIONS, MODIFICATIONS IN WORKSITE: The supply supervisor has already developed an adaptation to cue John when a box needs to be filled. He will place a red tape approximately 6" from the bottom of each supply bin in the hanking area. When John can see the red tape, it is time to fill the bin. The supervisor has also agreed to be responsible for notifying John when it is time to start and stop machine operation.

WILLINGNESS OF CO-WORKERS/SUPERVISORS TO PROVIDE SUPPORT AND ASSISTANCE: Most co-workers who are not on production quotas seem to be willing to assist John in any way possible. Machine operators cannot be counted on to provide much assistance. The attitude of the supervisors is excellent. They are well-paid, and there is little turnover.

"Culture" of the Worksite

EMPLOYER'S CONCERN FOR QUALITY: The employer has a high regard for quality work. This affects John most particularly during the hanking-machine operation. The hanks of cord must be neat and consistent. However, the machine ensures a quality hank when done correctly. The tie wrap must be tightly wound around the hank.

EMPLOYER'S CONCERN FOR PRODUCTIVITY: High productivity is the watchword of this factory. However, the job for which John is hired can easily be done without a frantic pace. The main production concern is to keep the supply bins full for the operators. This job would easily be within John's capabilities.

FLEXIBILITY/RIGIDITY OBSERVED: There is a definite factory "protocol" about the way the employees of this plant go about their jobs. However, this does not seem to be mandated by the employer. The plant is large enough that any small problems that may occur with John would not cause him undue harm. The willingness of the supervisors to assist John indicates a rather high level of flexibility to depart from typical routines.

EMPLOYEE SOCIAL GROUPS AND NON-WORK ACTIVITIES: The plant sponsors several bowling leagues and softball teams for the employees. Each production area seems to have its own informal social group. The employees who live in the immediate Hattiesburg area go out after work--especially on Thursday and Friday nights, according to Ben, the supply supervisor. The best chance to develop relationships seems to center around car pools. There have been several employees who have offered to take John into their car pool--for the regular charge of $10 per week.

LEADERS AND POTENTIAL ALLIES AMONG CO-WORKERS AND SUPERVISORS:
   Ben Brown, supervisor of the supply area
   Mary Bennet, supervisor of the warehouse
   Fred Tifton, lead operator on the hanking machines

Job Description

SCHEDULE:

Number of days of work per week <u>5</u>

Days: <u>Monday</u>   Hours <u>12:00</u> - <u>4:00</u>

       <u>Tuesday</u>   Hours <u>"</u> - <u>"</u>

       <u>Wednesday</u>   Hours <u>"</u> - <u>"</u>

       <u>Thursday</u>   Hours <u>8:00</u> - <u>12:00</u>

       <u>Friday</u>   Hours <u>"</u> - <u>"</u>

SEQUENTIAL CHRONOLOGY OF TYPICAL WORKDAY (include all routines):

11:45   Arrive at work and report to employees' locker area; store belongings.
12:00   Clock in.
12:05   Report to supervisor and begin work.
12:10   Check bins of hanker operators.
12:20   Locate supply boxes and fill supply bins, as needed.
12:45   Go to warehouse with floor jack, request four boxes of wire (as per note from supervisor), load boxes onto floor jack, and return to hanker area.
1:15   Fill all supply bins to top.
1:30   Begin operation of hanker machine.
2:15-   Stop machine operation; refill bins.
2:30
2:45   Check with supervisor for supply request, go to warehouse, request four boxes, load boxes, and return to hanker area.
3:00   Take a break in break area
3:15   Resume work, refill bins with cords.
3:30   Resume hanker machine operation.
3:55   Shut off machine, clean work area.
4:00   Clock out.
4:05   Collect belongings from locker and wait for ride.

Type of Routine <u>CORE WORK ROUTINE</u>
           (Core, episodic, job-related)

ROUTINE <u>Hanker Machine Operation</u>

HOW OFTEN PERFORMED: Initially, for 30-minute to 60-minute periods, two to three times per 4-hour shift. Expected productivity: 80 to 120 hanks per hour (100% productivity = 240 hanks per hour).

CONTENT STEPS/SKILLS	DECISION (see Decision-Making Sequence for Training, attached)	INFORMING STRATEGIES (including instructional and natural cues and adaptations)
1. Turn machine to "on" position with switch under front arm.	2(a)	Gesture to red switch.
2. Select one cord from supply bin with plug end with LH.	2(a)	Verbal cue and/or gesture to indicate "1" cord.

(continued)

232

CONTENT STEPS/SKILLS	DECISION (see Decision-Making Sequence for Training, attached)	INFORMING STRATEGIES (including instructional and natural cues and adaptations)
3. Grasp cord at plug end with LH.	3	Initially, hang 5-10 cords over edge of supply bin. Point out features of plug.
4. Grasp cord with RH approximately 6" from LH.	2(a)	Point out features of cord.
5. Seat plug end into left load bar with LH.	2(a)	Initially, use physical assist to show correct seating method.
6. Position cord under right load bar with RH.	2(a)	It is vital that the trainer assists the correct procedure for quality hank.
7. Hold loose end of wire lightly with RH--place LH on lap.	5-2(a)	Initially, perform step for operator until step 8 is learned. Make sure LH is in lap.
8. Press foot pedal with either foot until bars stop revolving.	2(a)	Verbal plus physical assist at first--may have to assist with foot of trainer.
9. Grasp hanked cord between load bars with RH and pull until removed from bars.	2(a)	
10. Regrasp hank with LH, over plug, release RH, hold tightly with LH.	2(a)	Remind operator to "hold tight."
11. Grasp tie writ with RH and pull until it releases from dispenser.	3-2(a)	Initially, have ties loose on table, introduce dispenser once steps 10 and 12 are learned.
12. Bend wire with thumb of RH in middle.	2(a)	

CONTENT STEPS/SKILLS	DECISION (see Decision-Making Sequence for Training, attached)	INFORMING STRATEGIES (including instructional and natural cues and adaptations)
13. Place bended tie around center of hank and squeeze.	2(a)	Place tie close to LH for natural cue.
14. Hold tie in place with LH index finger.	2(a)	
15. Overlap ends of tie around hank.	2(a)	Point out even ends.
16. Grasp tie ends with RH and twist strongly once.	2(a)	Use gesture to model movement.
17. Repeat Step 16 until tight.		
18. Visually inspect the hank for quality.	4	Place a quality hank on table for inspection sample. Point out features of "correctness."
19. Toss cord into finished goods box if it passes inspection. a. Redo if too loose or uneven.	2(a)	
20. Begin with Step 1.		

Decision-Making Sequence for Training

1. **PROVIDE NO DIRECT INTERVENTION; FACILITATE THE ROUTINE TO OC-CUR USING ONLY THE NATURAL CUES FOUND IN THE WORKPLACE.**

   This decision allows the learner to acquire the skills of a task/routine merely by regular participation. This is the same manner most people acquire information about routines.

2. **PROVIDE SYSTEMATIC TRAINING.**

   a. Train the step each time it occurs in the natural sequence.

   b. Break the step into smaller, more teachable steps. Then teach as in step a.

   c. When the step occurs in the natural sequence, halt the sequence, teach the step using a number of massed trials, then continue the sequence.

   d. Pull the step out of the natural sequence and teach it in massed trials until criterion. Then plug it back into the natural sequence.

3. **MODIFY THE NATURAL METHOD.**

   Change the natural method typically used to perform the task to a method that better matches the needs of the learner.

4. **PROVIDE AN ADAPTATION.**

   Add an assisting device or other aid to the method that will assist the learner to perform the task.

5. **ARRANGE FOR PARTIAL ASSISTANCE FROM CO-WORKERS.**

   Provide ongoing assistance on targeted steps of the task that will enable the worker to participate in the routine, if it is found that strategies 1, 2, 3, or 4 did not facilitate successful performance. The assistance can initially come from the trainer, but eventually must be provided by someone in the work environment.

APPENDIX 18

Suggested Letter Terminating Negotiations

[your organization's letterhead]

[date]

[The name of the contact person and the employer's address]

Dear Mr. Jones:

Kathleen and I discussed at length the meeting that she had with you and John Johnson. There were several points that she felt weren't clear among the three of you when the meeting was over. First, we sincerely appreciate the opportunity to work in the injection mold area for purposes of determining whether or not we could perform the training. John and the operators were most helpful, as has been the rule at your plant.

The problem was that we felt, because of the changing nature of the job, that special training procedures were necessary. I understand that your data show that this job is easier to learn than the hanking position. However, for the people we represent, the changing nature of the job presents as much or more of a problem as the speed required for hanking. We feel we can train the job, but in order to assure that you would have a competent employee, extra time is considered necessary.

We feel that due to the amount of time we have remaining in the project--until January 1--that further training would not be advisable. We would not want to leave you and the employee in an incomplete training situation.

I want you and all the people at the _____ Company to know how much we appreciate the opportunities that you made available to us this year. Please be aware, however, that this excellent source of employees exists in the _____ Activity Center and at _____ State School through Joe Ferguson.

Thanks again.

Sincerely,

_____
Project Director

236

Index

Accommodations to the worksite culture, 124,
    128–130
  evaluation of, 141
  see also Core work routines; Episodic work
    routines; Job-related routines
Advancement, 14
Advisory boards (business), 42
Agreements, *see* Employment, agreements;
    Media
Applicant number, 35–36
  see also Multiple applicants; Single
    applicants
Applicant selection, *see* Employee selection
Artificial approximations, 19–20
Assessment of new employee, *see* Evaluation,
    of new employee

Benefits, 99–100
Brochures, *see* Media
Business advisory boards, 42
Business cards, *see* Media
Business consultant model, 37–40, 164
  see also Employee representation model;
    Representational strategies

Call list, 50–51, 57–58, 184
Categorical decision-making models, 17–18
Competitive employment, 11, 35
Consulting interview, 92–93
Contact Listing and Card File, 184
Core work routines, 121, 124–125
  evaluation of, 139–140
  see also Accommodations to the worksite
    culture; Episodic work routines; Job-
    related routines
Cost effectiveness, 3, 6
Co-worker interactions, *see* Interactions with
    nondisabled co-workers
Criterion in training, 145
Criterion-referenced training activities, 20–21
Cues in training
  instructional, 142–143
  natural, 143–144
Cycle constancy in training, 145

Data collection
  for production rate, 158–159
  in training, 148–149
Developmental Disabilities Act of 1984, 27
Direct representation, 36–37

Ecologically referenced training systems,
    20–21
Educability, 18
Employability, 17–18, 21
Employee-employer matches, 112, 115–117
Employee profiles, *see* Vocational profiles
Employee representation model, 37–40,
    164–165
  see also Business consultant model;
    Representational strategies
Employee selection, 111–112, 117–122
Employer account strategy, *see* Business
    consultant model
Employer Contact Sheet, 182–183
Employer-directed materials, *see* Media
Employer Information Sheet, 195
Employers
  contact of, 57–78, 92–93, 185–188,
    191–194
  follow-up meetings and negotiations with,
    79–92, 236
  initial meetings and negotiations with,
    67–79, 82
  list of, 49–51, 184
Employment, 7, 9–11
  agreements, 80–81, 91, 106, 197–198,
    202–203
  long-term, 100–102
  models, 163–165
  opportunities (community), 48–55
  services, 9, 25–29, 33–45, 47–55
  skills, prerequisite, 19–20
  training, 170–172, 174–175
    environment for, 172–174
  values hierarchy, 13–14
Employment Site Quality Consideration
    Checklist, 202–203
Episodic work routines, 124, 126–127
  evaluation of, 140

Episodic work routines—*continued*
  see also Accommodations to the worksite
    culture; Core work routines; Job-related
    routines
Evaluation
  of new employee, 138–141
  during production rate training, 160

Fading in training, 144–145, 159
Follow-up services, 163–170
Formats in training, 146
Forms, *see* Media

Hole cards, 81–82

Inherent selling points, 81
Instructional power in training, 144
Integrated employment, 3, 6–7, 9–12, 14, 23,
    28–29, 34–35, 170–175
Interactions with nondisabled co-workers,
    10–11, 97, 107–108, 123–124, 150–151
Interview of applicant, 117–118, 120–121

Job analysis, 123–135, 221–235
Job coach role, 43–45
Job development, 33–45, 47–55, 58–78
Job posting, 119–120, 219–220
Job-related routines, 124, 127–128
  evaluation of, 140
  see also Accommodations to the worksite
    culture; Core work routines; Episodic
    work routines
Job satisfaction, 167–168
Job targeting, 90–91
Judgment in training, 148

Letters of introduction, 59–60, 187–190

Making Successful Contacts: Sample Telephone
    Calls, 191–192
Matching, *see* Employee-employer matches
Materials, *see* Media
Meaningful work, 11
Media, 59–61, 71–72, 182–190, 195–198,
    202–236
Meetings with employers
  follow-up, 79–92
  initial, 67–79, 82, 201–203
Memos of Industrial Contact, 199–201
Multiple applicants, 35–36, 117–118
  see also Applicant number; Single applicants

Natural proportion principle, 11–12
Negotiations with employers

follow-up, 79–92, 236
  initial, 74–78
Norm-referenced vocational evaluations, 20–21

Objections from employer, 66, 85–90,
    193–194
Outcomes of services, 23–25, 29

Pace and speed in training, 147–148
Presentation materials, *see* Media
Production rate, increase in, 155–161
Production versus placement, 6
Profiles, *see* Vocational profiles
Program philosophy, 3–6
Progressive status quoism, 25, 29

Quality Consideration Checklist, 95–97, 112,
    204–205
  see also Quality considerations
Quality considerations, 95–108
  see also Quality Consideration Checklist
Quality in training, 146–147
Quality indicators, *see* Quality considerations
Quality of life, 15–16
Questions and Objections Encountered During
    the Phone Call, 193–194

Recruitment of applicant, 117–120
Referrals, 36–37, 53, 71
Representational strategies, 35–37
  see also Business consultant model;
    Employee representation model

Safety, *see* Working conditions
Sample Completed Job Analysis, 228–235
Sample Completed Vocational Profile, 212–218
Sample Employment Agreement, 202–203
Sample Follow-Up Letter, 196
Sample Informational Handout, 189–190
Sample Job Posting, 219–220
Sheltered workshops, 3–6, 9–14, 23, 28
Single applicants, 35–36, 117–118
  see also Applicant number; Multiple
    applicants
Staffing the employment agency, 43–45
Stalls, *see* Objections from employer
Status-enhancing jobs, 14–15
Structures of services, 23–25, 29
Suggested Letter Terminating Negotiations, 236
Suggested Letters of Introduction, 185–188
Summary of expectations, *see* Employment,
    agreements
Summary of Expectations for Services Offered,
    197–198

Supplemental Security Income, 13
Supported employment, 11, 25–28, 35, 165
Sweeteners, 81

Telephoning employers, 61–66, 191–194
Termination of employee, 165–170
Termination of negotiation, 238
Tour of company, 83–84
Training of new employee, 137–154
Transitional employment, 25–27, 37–40

Vocational evaluation, 17–21
Vocational Profile, 206–211, 212–218
    see also Vocational profiles
Vocational profiles, 38, 41–42, 112–115
    see also Vocational Profile
Vocational training, 9, 24–25, 29

Wages, 12–14, 98–99
Work activity center, 11
Worker's role, 8–9
Working conditions, 100, 102–108